A Walk Through
ETERNITY

Bill W. Belter

WestBow
PRESS
A DIVISION OF THOMAS NELSON

WestBow Press books may be ordered through booksellers or by contacting:

WestBow Press
A Division of Thomas Nelson
1663 Liberty Drive
Bloomington, IN 47403
www.westbowpress.com
1-(866) 928-1240

ISBN: 978-1-4497-1669-1 (e)
ISBN: 978-1-4497-1668-4 (sc)

Library of Congress Control Number: 2011928748

Printed in the United States of America

WestBow Press rev. date: 5/13/2011

Contents

Introduction and Purpose of this Book

"He has made everything beautiful in its time. Also He has put eternity in their hearts, except that no one can find out the work that God does from beginning to end" (Ecclesiastes 3:11, NKJV).

Generally speaking, people want peace and joy in their lives, and they desire to love and be loved. *God has written eternity into our hearts.* We all understand in our souls that there is life after death.

I was born in 1954 and was raised in Warren, Ohio. I graduated from Cornell University in 1976 with a degree in Industrial and Labor Relations.

On the third Sunday of June in 1986 at about 4:00 a.m., I became a born-again Christian. For the previous six months, I had been studying various religions. I was surprised to find that most religions had a lot to say about Jesus Christ, and all of those religions seemed to have a different Jesus. I studied and investigated, and I came to believe that the Jesus that was prophesied in the Old Testament of the Bible was fulfilled in Jesus of Nazareth. God changed my life. I used to be afraid of dying. I knew if God really created everything, I was in big trouble.

After salvation and over the past seventeen years, I have worked hard for the cause of Christ. After coming to the Lord, I have read hundreds of books, listened to thousands of audio tapes, and watched hundreds of video tapes. I have worked in a church nursery, taught Sunday school, headed a singles ministry, worked in a radio ministry, and helped clean churches. I have conducted teen Bible studies, been active in Wycliffe Bible Associates, and was also active in the pro-life movement.

For four and one half years, I was a bi-vocational pastor of a satellite church of Houston's First Baptist Church. We baptized thirty-two people in these four and one half years and were part of leading about one hundred people to the Lord. This church was located in an apartment complex. At all times, I have been in full-time employment in the paper merchant industry.

My desire is to enable the new believer in Christ to come up to speed quickly concerning the Word of God—the Bible. I want to condense major facts, Bible verses, and Biblical knowledge and wisdom in this book.

For an unbeliever, my desire is for you to come to the point—as I did in 1986—to understand that it takes more faith to believe in evolution than it does to believe in the God of the Bible. One purpose of this book is to prove that mankind is created in the image of God. God has written eternity in our hearts and given all men light to believe the gospel of Jesus Christ.

This book is written in order to study and explain the truths that affect your life here on earth and in eternity.

1. Salvation—how you can know you will spend eternity with God in heaven after your death.
2. God's purpose for mankind, why evil exists, and a discussion about our bodies, souls, and spirits.
3. The case for creationism and design and order in the universe.
4. An overview of the Old Testament from 4000 BC to the birth of Christ. I will focus on types and shadows of Jesus Christ, the feasts of the Lord, truths of the Jewish Temple, and prophecies of the first coming of Jesus Christ. World empires and chronologies are also included.
5. An overview of the New Testament from 3 BC to the present with chronologies.
6. Signs of the second Coming of Jesus Christ, the future millennium, and eternity.
7. A summary.

I will attempt to summarize and describe heaven and eternity. I will also put into chronological order events that have occurred in the time, matter, space, and universe in which we now live. I believe it takes more faith to believe in atheism than it does to believe God. The purpose of creation is for God to show His attributes—that would be impossible in any other plan—and to show His manifold wisdom to all in heaven and in the earth.

There are logical reasons for pain and suffering. Evil, rebellion, and death will be allowed by God to exist for only a short period of time (six thousand to seven thousand years). Sin and rebellion will collapse under their own weight and by the Word of God. The increase of the government of God will be from everlasting to everlasting, with created beings with a free will being in the perfect will of God forever.

Basically, the purpose of this book is to answer four questions:

1. How did we get here?
2. Why are we here?
3. Where are we going?
4. Why does evil exist?

All of these questions and more will be examined.

Answers to the above four questions:

1. God created mankind abruptly. He created Adam and Eve, and thus all people are ultimately related to each other.
2. To love God with all our heart, mind, strength, and soul and to love our neighbors as ourselves. We are further exhorted to love our neighbors as God loves us.
3. After death, we have eternal life with God, or we will be eternally separated from God. God calls us to choose life.

4. Any being created with a free will such as mankind, angels, and archangels have the free will option of being in God's perfect will, acceptable will, good will, or to be in rebellion to God. When a being that has a free will chooses rebellion to God, evil, pain, and suffering will exist.

A Salvation Message

How to be Saved from Your Sins and Spend Eternity in Heaven

Jesus, speaking of Himself, said, "I am the Way, the Truth and the Life, no man cometh unto the Father but by me" (John 14:6).

Jesus is the truth, and the truth is that everyone needs to be saved or rescued from the consequences of sin. Salvation is having your personal relationship with God the Father restored by accepting what Jesus Christ accomplished for you on the cross so that all of your sins are forever forgiven and there is no longer anything standing in the way of that relationship any longer. Salvation is also being saved from eternal punishment and shame. Salvation for you means the difference between spending eternity in heaven with God and spending eternity separated from God. Waiting until you are on your deathbed is not the time to try to determine what the truth is.

Evangelism Explosion is an outstanding program that teaches people how to lead others to a saving relationship with the Lord Jesus Christ. Their Bible tract asks two insightful questions:

1. If you were to die today, do you know for sure that you would go to heaven, or is that something you would say that you are still working on?
2. If you were to die today and stand before God and He were to say, "Why should I let you into My heaven?" what would you say?[1]

If you don't know where your soul will go after death, read on to learn how you can know for sure how to inherit eternal life. If you ever have the opportunity, I strongly suggest taking the Evangelism Explosion course.

The reason God would let you into His heaven will be explained in this book. However, should you desire to accept Jesus Christ as Lord and Savior immediately, you may in the next few minutes. If not now, at any time while reading this book or at any time that God is calling you, you may call upon the Lord Jesus Christ to be saved.

To be saved, it helps to understand these truths:

1. Know that you are a sinner.
2. Know who Jesus Christ is and what He did for you.
3. Know that the nature of God is that God is love and God is just.
4. Salvation is by the grace of God through faith not of your own works.

---

1 Evangelism Explosion International, P.O. Box 23820, Ft. Lauderdale, FL 33307

"It is God's desire that none should perish and all have eternal life" (I Peter 3:9).

God's desire is for all people to be saved.

"For all have sinned, and come short of the glory of God" (Romans 3:23).

Everyone is a sinner.

"For the wages of sin is death; but the gift of God is eternal life through Jesus Christ our Lord" (Romans 6:23).

The consequence of sin is death and eternal separation from God. However, God has a plan for our redemption.

"For I delivered unto you first of all that which I also received, how that Christ died for our sins according to the scriptures; And that he was buried, and that he rose again the third day according to the scriptures: And that he was seen of Cephas, then of the twelve: After that he was seen of above five hundred brethren at once; of whom the greater part remain unto this present, but some are fallen asleep" (I Corinthians 15:3–6).

Over five hundred people saw Jesus after His resurrection. This resurrection displays the creative power of God and gives us hope for a meaningful life after death.

"For God so loved the world, that he gave his only begotten Son, what whosoever believeth on him should not perish, but have everlasting life. For God sent not his Son into the world to condemn the world; but that the world through him might be saved. He that believeth on him is not condemned: but he that believeth not is condemned already, because he hath not believed in the name of the only begotten Son of God" (John 3:16–18).

Believe in Jesus, and you will have everlasting life.

Jesus, speaking in the first person, stated, "Behold, I stand at the door, and knock: if any man hear my voice, and open the door, I will come in to him, and will sup with him, and he with me" (Revelation 3:20).

We have to open the door of our soul (heart) to God's Holy Spirit.

"For by grace are ye saved through faith; and that not of yourselves: it is the gift of God: Not of works, lest any man should boast" (Ephesians 2:8–9).

We are saved by the grace of God through our faith; we must believe God.

"The thief cometh not, but for to steal, and to kill, and to destroy: I am come that they might have life, and that they might have it more abundantly" (John 10:10).

Jesus said the above verse about Himself; He wants to give us an abundant life.

"Jesus answered and said unto him, 'Verily, verily, I say unto thee, Except a man be born again, he cannot see the kingdom of God'" (John 3:3).

A person is born again when they receive the Holy Spirit of God.

"That if thou shalt confess with thy mouth the Lord Jesus, and shalt believe in thine heart that God hath raised him from the dead, thou shalt be saved. For with the heart man believeth unto righteousness; and with the mouth confession is made unto salvation" (Romans 10:9–10).

We must believe in our hearts and verbally confess our sins to the Lord Jesus to be saved.

"For whosoever shall call upon the name of the Lord shall be saved" (Romans 10:13).

"But as many as received Him, to them He gave the power to become sons of God, even to them who believe on his name" (John 1:12).

Whoever calls on the Lord will be save,d and God calls the believer in Christ a son of God.

"A new heart also will I give you, and a new spirit will I put within you: and I will take away the stony heart out of your flesh, and I will give you a heart of flesh. And I will put my spirit within you, and cause you to talk in my statutes, and ye shall keep my judgments, and do them" (Ezekiel 36:26–27).

At the time of salvation, God puts His Holy Spirit within you. That is what is meant by being born of the spirit or being born again.

"Therefore if any man be in Christ, he is a new creature: old things are passed away; behold, all things are become new" (II Corinthians 5:17).

When a person gets saved, he is able to start his life over again.

To be saved, you must come to the point that you are broken and convicted of your sins. The Holy Spirit of God will be moving in your life, and you must have the faith to believe in the finished work of Jesus Christ on the cross.

The following is a sample salvation prayer. However, you can pray a prayer of salvation however the Lord leads you.

A Sample Salvation Prayer

My Heavenly Father, I am a sinner.
I believe Jesus Christ was God in the flesh and lived a sinless life.
I believe Jesus was crucified, buried, and raised from the dead on the third day.
I make the Lord Jesus Christ the Lord of my life.
I ask for your Holy Spirit to be put into me and that I will be born again.
I turn from my sins and accept the free gift of eternal life.

Thank you for saving my soul.
In Jesus' name, Amen.

1. Has the Holy Spirit of God revealed to you that Jesus Christ was God in the flesh and was crucified and raised from the dead on the third day?
2. If you died today, do you know for sure you would go to heaven?
3. Do you believe that God has the power to speak the universe into existence?
4. Is the Bible alive to you and understandable, and not just another book?
5. Do you believe the Bible?
6. Does the Holy Spirit of God direct your soul?
7. Can you pray to God, and do you obey the voice of God?
8. Can you praise God in a church service?
9. Has anyone made fun of you or rejected you because you are a Christian?
10. Was there a time in your life when you were able to get away with sin easily; is this no longer the case?
11. Do you know the date or general time you became a Christian?
12. Was there ever a time you started to get new friends because you were a Christian?
13. Have you told others about Jesus Christ?
14. Do you go to a Bible-believing church?

"For there are three that bear witness in heaven, the Father, the Word, and the Holy Ghost: and these three are one. And there are three that bear witness in the earth, the Spirit and the Water, and the Blood: and these three agree in one" (I John 5:7–8).

Bear Witness In Heaven	=	Father	Word=Jesus Christ	Holy Ghost = Holy Spirit
Bear Witness In the Earth	=	Water	Blood	**Spirit**
Believer on Earth	=	Body	Soul	**Spirit**

The same Holy Spirit that bears witness on the earth is in the believer on the earth and is the same Holy Spirit that lives in heaven.

God's Purpose for Mankind

Jesus told us what must be the major purpose of our lives: "Jesus said unto him, 'Thou shalt love the Lord thy God with all thy heart, and with all thy soul, and with all thy mind. This is the first and great commandment. And the second is like unto it, Thou shalt love thy neighbour as thyself. On these two commandments hang all the law and the prophets'" (Matthew 22:37–40).

In this chapter, I will discuss the purpose that God has for His created beings, who have a free will and/or are created in His image. I will investigate the spirit world and the soul, and I will discuss our bodies. I will also discuss heaven, hell, and many other interesting subjects. All of us make life more complicated than it needs to be; all we need to do is love God with all our heart, mind, soul, and strength and love our neighbors as Jesus loved us. This is one of the many exciting purposes we have in life.

Why People Do Not Believe God

Before we tackle these issues, we need to discuss why many people have a problem believing in God or believing God. I believe there are seven main reasons people do not believe God:

1. *People do not physically see God with their eyes while they are on earth.*

   "No man hath seen God at any time; the only begotten Son, which is in the bosom of the Father, he hath declared him" (John 1:18).

   "If a man say, 'I love God,' and hateth his brother, he is a liar: for he that loveth not his brother whom he hath seen, how can he love God whom he hath not seen?" (I John 4:20)

   "Whom having not seen, ye love; in whom, though now ye see him not, yet believing, ye rejoice with joy unspeakable and full of glory: Receiving the end of your faith, even the salvation of your souls" (I Peter 1:8–9).

   "Even the Spirit of truth; whom the world cannot receive, because it seeth him not, neither knoweth him: but ye know him; for he dwelleth with you, and shall be in you" (John 14:17).

The Bible tells us that the way we can show that we love God—who we cannot see with our eyes—is to love our fellow man who we can see with our eyes. This is one of the most important points in this book. When I was a young child in church, I wanted God to prove Himself by moving an object on a wall in the church sanctuary. God did not do this, because if He had, I would have just raised the bar and asked for more proof. However, ultimately one of our main purposes on earth is to show love to God—who we do not see—by doing acts of kindness to our fellow man who we can see. These actions bring judgment against the principalities and powers of hell itself.

2. Mankind comes into existence through the process of procreation through a mother and father. You are conceived as one cell at conception, and approximately 280 days later, you are born. Your first memories are not of seeing God but are probably of seeing your parents.

The Bible tells us that God put us into a situation for our time on earth in which we do not physically see God with our eyes. If we were abruptly created in heaven—as, let's say, an angel—then our first memories would be that of seeing God, the creator of the universe. Think back on your first memories. My first memories were not about God; I just wanted to play and daydream. As one grows up, it is time to think about eternity. On your deathbed, you will not wish you swore one more time or stole more things. My desire is to be a blessing to others until my last breath.

3. We have a sinful nature because of Adam. The flesh takes possession of the mind. We are guided by affections, lusts, and covetousness until the time of our salvation.

   "For if by one man's offence death reigned by one; much more they which receive abundance of grace and of the gift of righteousness shall reign in life by one, Jesus Christ" (Romans 5:17).

The "one man's offence" in this verse is referring to Adam in the Garden of Eden. Through Adam and Eve, we have a sinful nature.

"Enter ye in at the strait gate: for wide is the gate, and broad is the way, that leadeth to destruction, and many there be which go in threat: Because strait is the gate, and narrow is the way, which leadeth unto life, and few there be that find it" (Matthew 7:13–14).

4. God's desire is that all would be saved, but in foreknowledge, His design was that few would be saved. When you become a Christian, you go against the grain and flow of the world. In God's foreknowledge, He knew that most people would reject His grace. However, in spite of this fact, He loved His creation so much that He chose to allow it to unfold with all of its pain and suffering, keeping His eternal purposes in mind. These eternal purposes are described in the remainder of this book. God is always just and fair and never acts arbitrarily.

5. In biblical Christianity, the doctrine of hell makes Christianity unpopular. However, the question we should be asking is what the truth is, regardless of whether the truth is pleasant or not.

6. There are some Bible stories that may seem fictitious. Particularly troublesome to people can be the first nine chapters in the Book of Genesis. There are logical answers to all objections to the Bible, and we will deal with some of them in this book.

7. People decide to not believe God or to stop believing God because they get mad at Him. Charles Darwin and Ted Turner each lost a close loved one, and I believe they use this as an excuse to fight against God. People getting mad at God is the reason for hundreds of millions of violent deaths and despair in the last six thousand years.

God's Purpose for Mankind as it Relates to Eternity

"Unto me, who am less than the least of all saints, is this grace given, that I should preach among the Gentiles the unsearchable riches of Christ; And to make all men see what is the fellowship of the mystery, which from the beginning of the world hath been hid in God, who created all things by Jesus Christ: To the intent that now unto the principalities and powers in heavenly places might be known by the church the manifold wisdom of God, According to the eternal purpose which he purposed in Christ Jesus our Lord: In whom we have boldness and access with confidence by the faith of him. Wherefore I desire that ye faint not at my tribulations for you, which is your glory" (Ephesians 3:8–13).

A main purpose of mankind is to show the manifold wisdom of God to all creatures that were created in the image of God and/or with a free will in eternity past. God does this through the church, and the head of the church is the person of Jesus Christ.

Because of the lessons we can learn on this earth as well as the lessons that seraphim, cherubim, archangels, and angels can learn by watching and ministering to mankind, there is a great eternal purpose for the pain and suffering we go through while on this earth.

God showed His wisdom by entering a fallen world as a man to deal with events in eternity past for the purpose of establishing a perfect, eternal future. God directs seraphim, cherubim, archangels, angels, and the saints to fight against fallen demons, which helps us to trust God and to stop the cycle of rebellion against God in eternity forever.

Our Bodies, Souls, and Spirits

Jesus Christ was 100 percent God and 100 percent man when He walked on the earth.

"And the very God of peace sanctify you wholly; and I pray God your whole spirit and soul and body be preserved blameless unto the coming of our Lord Jesus Christ" (I Thessalonians 5:23).

Mankind is made up of body, soul, and spirit. In this chapter, I will discuss the proof of the existence of the soul and spirit of God and the existence of your soul.

The only way for evil to have never occurred is for God to have never created any beings in His image or to have never created intelligent beings with a soul that had a free will to love or rebel against their creator. First, let us examine the Spirit of God.

"And the earth was without form, and void; and darkness was upon the face of the deep. And the Spirit of God moved upon the face of the waters" (Genesis 1:2).

God created the laws of nature, but He is not subject to these laws. God's Holy Spirit did all the creation work at the direction of God the Father and God the Word—Jesus Christ.

"Then shall the dust return to the earth as it was: and the spirit shall return unto God who gave it" (Ecclesiastes 12:7).

Our bodies will decay in the grave after death. Our spirit returns to God. Our soul is not mentioned here. While you are on the earth, the battle is for your eternal soul.

"But the hour cometh, and now is, when the true worshippers shall worship the Father in spirit and in truth: for the Father seeketh such to worship him. God is a Spirit: and they that worship him must worship him in spirit and in truth" (John 4:23–24).

This verse tells us that God is Spirit. God does not have a body. God can give Himself a body, to be made known to created beings; however, God is spirit in essence.

Prior to anything being created, only God existed. From the Bible, it is clear that history did not first start with the creation of the earth and our universe. First, in eternity past, God developed the perfect plan. This perfect plan included imperfect beings such as you and me.

"But with the precious blood of Christ, as of a lamb without blemish and without spot: Who verily was foreordained before the foundation of the world, but was manifest in these last times for you" (I Peter 1:19–20).

"And all that dwell upon the earth shall worship him [Lucifer and/or the Antichrist], whose names are not written in the book of life of the Lamb [Jesus Christ] slain from the foundation of the world" (Revelation 13:8).

In reality, these verses could be the first major event concerning you and me in all eternity. These verses tell us that Jesus Christ was crucified in the mind of God for our rebellion and sin prior to the creation of anything.

God has a soul, and thus God has a mind, will, and emotions. God has stated that He is love, He is eternal, and He is spirit—but He also thinks logically. You were in the mind of God prior to God creating the world, and thus, your spirit was in the mind of God before the creation; however, you did not become a living soul until you took a breath.

Jesus made the following two statements about Himself:

"And saith until them, My Soul is exceeding sorrowful unto death: tarry ye here, and watch" (Mark 14:34).

"Now is my soul troubled; and what shall I say? Father, save me from this hour: but for this cause came I unto this hour" (John 12:27).

Jesus was God in the flesh; therefore, God has an eternal soul.

"'And it shall come to pass in the last days,' saith God, 'I will pour out of my Spirit upon all flesh: and your sons and your daughters shall prophesy, and your young men shall see visions, and your old men shall dream dreams'" (Acts 2:17).

In the Old Testament, God's Spirit resided in various temples that God told His people to build to Him. God's Spirit also came upon His prophets and workers so they could do specific acts for God's purposes. I used to believe the church was a physical location. After I was saved, I was told that persons who have been saved from their sins have God's Holy Spirit dwelling in their bodies. In the New Testament, the Holy Spirit of God resides in the believer.

"But if the Spirit of him that raised up Jesus from the dead dwell in you, he that raised up Christ from the dead shall also quicken your mortal bodies by his Spirit that dwelleth in you" (Romans 8:11).

This verse tells us that the same Holy Spirit which raised Jesus from the dead lives in those who are saved. This means a saved person has unbelievable power at hand. If you are a believer in Christ, I beg you to believe this verse.

"For ye are bought with a price: therefore glorify God in your body, and in your spirit, which are God's" (I Corinthians 6:20).

This verse tells us that the body and the spirit belong to God. Again, the battle is for your soul, which is your mind, will, and emotions.

"For the flesh lusteth against the Spirit, and the Spirit against the flesh: and these are contrary the one to the other: so that ye cannot do the things that he would. But if ye be led of the Spirit, ye are not under the law. Now the works of the flesh are manifest, which are these; Adultery, fornication, uncleanness, lasciviousness, Idolatry, witchcraft, hatred, variance, emulations, wrath, strife, seditions, heresies, Envyings, murders, drunkenness, revellings, and such like: of the which I tell you before, as I have also told you in time past, that they which do such things shall not inherit the kingdom of God. But the fruit of the Spirit is love, joy, peace, longsuffering, gentleness, goodness, faith, Meekness, temperance: against such there is no law. And they that are Christ's have crucified the flesh with the affections and lusts. If we live in the Spirit, let us also walk in the Spirit. Let us not be desirous of vain glory, provoking one another, envying one another" (Galatians 5:17–26).

"And the LORD God formed man of the dust of the ground, and breathed into his nostrils the breath of life; and man became a living soul" (Genesis 2:7).

"Hear, O Israel: The LORD our God is one LORD: And thou shalt love the LORD thy God with all thine heart, and with all thy soul, and with all thy might" (Deuteronomy 6:4–5).

Your heart and your strength are in your soul. Your heart is what you truly believe. Again, the battle is for your soul. If you are saved, the flesh, body, and the old nature in you wants to sin and fights God's Spirit in you for your soul. Your soul belongs to you. Your soul—you—will either yield to your flesh, Adamic nature, or will yield to God's Holy Spirit.

"The law of the LORD is perfect, converting the soul: the testimony of the LORD is sure, making wise the simple" (Psalm 19:7).

The law of God shows us that we are sinners. What is converted is our soul. We are to yield ourselves and obey God's Holy Spirit.

"He restoreth my soul: he leadeth me in the paths of righteousness for his name's sake. Yea, though I walk through the valley of the shadow of death, I will fear no evil: for thou art with me; thy rod and thy staff they comfort me" (Psalm 23:3–4).

God will heal your hurts when you allow Him to do so. Also, death is a shadow; it is not real. Your soul will continue to live for eternity after your body dies.

Jesus said in Matthew 10:28, "And fear not them which kill the body, but are not able to kill the soul: but rather fear him which is able to destroy both soul and body in hell." This verse tells us not to fear man but to only fear God, who has the power to send our souls to hell. Heaven and hell will be described in greater detail later in this chapter.

"Now the just shall live by faith: but if any man draw back, my soul shall have no pleasure in him" (Hebrews 10:38).

God has a soul; therefore, He has a mind, will, and emotions. You are created in the image of God. The reason you are emotional is because God is emotional. God loves you with a deep and abiding love. The only way you can love God is to love His Son, who is God in the flesh—Jesus Christ.

"Then they that gladly received his word were baptized: and the same day there were added unto them about three thousand souls" (Acts 4:21).

It is your soul which is added to the Kingdom of Heaven at salvation.

"Whom having not seen, ye love; in whom, though now ye see him not, yet believing, ye rejoice with joy unspeakable and full of glory: Receiving the end of your faith, even the salvation of your souls" (I Peter 1:8–9).

It is your soul that is saved.

"And I saw thrones, and they sat upon them, and judgment was given unto them: and I saw the souls of them that were beheaded for the witness of Jesus, and for the word of God, and which had not worshipped the beast, neither his image, neither had received his mark upon their foreheads, or in their hands; and they lived and reigned with Christ a thousand years" (Revelation 20:4).

The Apostle John saw souls in heaven. Your soul has a visible form but is awaiting an eternal resurrected body.

Our Five Senses are in Our Souls

Souls can be seen in heaven. *Your soul contains your five senses: sight, hearing, touch, taste, and smell.*

Jesus spoke these words in Luke 16:19–24: "There was a certain rich man, which was clothed in purple and fine linen, and fared sumptuously every day: And there was a certain beggar named Lazarus, which was laid at his gate, full of sores, And desiring to be fed with the crumbs which fell from the rich man's table: moreover the dogs came and licked his sores. And it came to pass, that the beggar died, and was carried by the angels into Abraham's bosom: the rich man also died, and was buried; And in hell he lift up his eyes, being in torments, and seeth Abraham afar off, and Lazarus in his bosom. And he cried and said, Father Abraham, have mercy on me, and send Lazarus, that he may dip the tip of his finger in water, and cool my tongue: for I am tormented in this flame."

These verses show us we have our senses in either heaven or hell. The rich man in hell and Lazarus in heaven could touch, taste, see, hear, and smell. At this time, they had a soul body, not a resurrected body. We do not receive our resurrected bodies until the second coming of Jesus Christ.

A Study of the Fallen Cherub, Lucifer

We will continue our study by investigating the person the Bible refers to as Lucifer. Before Satan's fall, his name was Lucifer, which means "light-bearer." After the fall, Lucifer was also called by the names of Satan, devil, serpent, dragon, accuser, adversary, deceiver, enemy, and prince of this world.

"How art thou fallen from heaven, O Lucifer, son of the morning! how art thou cut down to the ground, which didst weaken the nations! For thou hast said in thine heart, I will ascend into heaven, I will exalt my throne above the stars of God: I will sit also upon the mount of the congregation, in the sides of the north: I will ascend above the heights of the clouds; I will be like the most High. Yet thou shalt be brought down to hell, to the sides of the pit. They that see thee shall narrowly look upon thee, and consider thee, saying, Is this the man that made the earth to tremble, that did shake kingdoms; That made the world as a wilderness, and destroyed the cities thereof; that opened not the house of his prisoners?" (Isaiah 14:12–17)

This chapter describes the fall of Lucifer. In these verses, Lucifer says the words "I will" five times. Go back and reread them. Lucifer is full of himself—this is pride. Lucifer wanted to be equal the Most High. However, the weight of his own pride will bring him to the lowest depths.

Our Battle is with Fallen Demons and with Satan

"Now there was a day when the sons of God came to present themselves before the LORD, and Satan came also among them. And the LORD said unto Satan, Whence comest thou? Then Satan answered the LORD, and said, From going to and fro in the earth, and from walking up and down in it. And the LORD said unto Satan, Hast thou considered my servant Job, that there is none like him in the earth, a perfect and an upright man, one that feareth God, and escheweth evil? Then Satan answered the LORD, and said, "Doth Job fear God for nought? Hast not thou made an hedge about him, and about his house, and about all that he hath on every side? thou hast blessed the work of his hands, and his substance is increased in the land. But put forth thine hand now, and touch all that he hath, and he will curse thee to thy face." And the LORD said unto Satan, "Behold, all that he hath is in thy power; only upon himself put not forth thine hand." So Satan went forth from the presence of the LORD" (Job 1:6–12).

The book of Job has forty-two chapters. All of the events in the book of Job revolve around a conversation between God and Satan. God asks Satan what he is doing. Satan answers sarcastically, "Walking up and down the earth."

God asked Satan, "What do you think of Job?" and God stated that Job feared God. Satan accused Job of only following God because all was going well in Job's life. God basically turned Job over to Satan with the exception that Satan would not be allowed to kill Job.

I believe that Job 1:6–12 gives us great insight into the battles we face on earth. Satan only has the power that God gives him. *Our battle on earth is with Satan and his demons, not with other human beings.*

There are eternal reasons why events happen to us. First and foremost, we—like Job—are being tested here on the earth, and we are also learning lessons for eternal purposes. The faith of Job was tested, and he passed the test.

> God's government is one of persuasion and not force. God will force no one to love Him. The seeds of rebellion have been planted in eternity past, and God devised a plan before eternity past to put down rebellion.[2]

This plan included Jesus being crucified before the foundation of the world. God designed that the outcome for those who would stay loyal and believe in the Lord Jesus Christ is that they would be born of the spirit and live eternally with God

It is not just that those who would believe God and His Word would spend eternity with God, but that they would also enjoy eternity and know the deep love that God has for His creation.

God's foreknowledge of the rebellion of those created beings with a free will and/or those created in the image of God does not mean that God has ever moved to Plan B. God has a perfect, acceptable, or good plan for our lives. Beyond these three levels, mankind can also choose rebellion. However, the purpose of Christianity was ordained by God to have one person in the Godhead—that person being Jesus Christ—to enter into a fallen creation, to never sin, and to show that fallen creation in the heavens and on the earth the attributes of God that could never have been revealed under any other plan. Jesus Christ has shown His love to the creation by His birth, the way He lived His life, His crucifixion, His burial, and His physical resurrection.

---

2   Harold J. Chadwick. *And We Shall Judge Angels*, 188.

"For we wrestle not against flesh and blood, but against principalities, against powers, against the rulers of the darkness of this world, against spiritual wickedness in high places" (Ephesians 6:12).

Our battle is with our flesh and with demons, not fellow mankind. I have to remind myself of this fact frequently. Remembering this fact will lead you to pray for those who are unkind to you.

The Requirements for Rebellion and Sin and for Reconciliation

"At the mouth of two witnesses, or three witnesses, shall he that is worthy of death be put to death; but at the mouth of one witness he shall not be put to death" (Deuteronomy 17:6).

"One witness shall not rise up against a man for any iniquity, or for any sin, in any sin that he sinneth: at the mouth of two witnesses, or at the mouth of three witnesses, shall the matter be established" (Deuteronomy 19:15).

"But if he will not hear thee, then take with thee one or two more, that in the mouth of two or three witnesses every word may be established. And if he shall neglect to hear them, tell it unto the church: but if he neglect to hear the church, let him be unto thee as a heathen man and a publican. Verily I say unto you, Whatsoever ye shall bind on earth shall be bound in heaven: and whatsoever ye shall loose on earth shall be loosed in heaven. Again I say unto you, That if two of you shall agree on earth as touching any thing that they shall ask, it shall be done for them of my Father which is in heaven. For where two or three are gathered together in my name, there am I in the midst of them" (Matthew 18:16–20).

For evil to be established, there needed to be at least two beings—one to plan a rebellion, and another to listen and agree to rebel against God. When you hear people gossiping, the best thing to do is quietly walk away and mind your own business.

"And, having made peace through the blood of his cross, by him to reconcile all things unto himself; by him, I say, whether they be things in earth, or things in heaven" (Colossians 1:20).

God is currently reconciling things on earth, and is also reconciling things in heaven and in eternity.

"So the last shall be first, and the first last: for many be called, but few chosen" (Matthew 20:16).

> There is a relationship of events in heaven and on the earth. There was a rebellion in heaven and on the earth Adam and Eve listened to and believed Satan and disobeyed God. Lucifer caused rebellion in heaven as well as on the earth.[3]
>
> Lucifer brought down a multitude of angels with him from the heavenlies. With their own free will, angels listened to and believed lies from Lucifer. Adam and Eve listened to and believed lies on the earth. Lucifer's rebellion was the seed for rebellion of a multitude of angels and mankind. This parallels wars on the earth. The seeds of WWII came from WWI. One result of WWII was Israel was formed as a nation in 1948.

---

3   Harold J. Chadwick. *And We Shall Judge Angels*, 209.

The seeds of WWII will bring about further [world wars] followed by Armageddon. Armageddon is a physical, literal location within Israel's borders.[4]

Consider if God had destroyed Lucifer immediately after a hint of rebellion. All created beings in heaven which stayed loyal to God would be walking on pins and needles. They would wonder could we be next. However God devised a plan wherein Lucifer and his fallen angels would also fall under the weight of their own sin. They are and will humiliate themselves.[5]

Lucifer and fallen angels are strong, intelligent, and powerful and have lived throughout history. This compares to mankind which was created innocent, weak, and relatively unintelligent, and because of the fall of mankind, we have a sin nature as well as bodies that will die and decay.[6]

Satan was defeated at the Cross by the resurrection of Jesus Christ. However, Satan was also brought down by his own pride, greed, lust for power, and arrogance. God has used mankind to show the nature of God through the person of Jesus Christ, who was God in the flesh. God shows that His nature is love. Lucifer also shows his nature being one as a liar, murderer—but most of all, Lucifer wants you to fear him more than you love God.[7]

If everything were perfect, there would never have been Adam and Eve or Noah, Abraham, Moses, David, the Apostle Paul, and Peter, and Jesus would not have had to come into the creation to save mankind. Had Jesus not entered into the creation, we would not totally understand that God is patient, humble, and forgiving—but most of all, He could not have been a living example. Jesus was a servant on the earth and thus is a living example for saints today to follow.

If everything would have been perfect in eternity past, there would not have been free will, and therefore, there would not have been any purpose to the creation. It is impossible to mock God, and God would not have created archangels, angels, and mankind without a purpose. God is sovereign, and mankind has a free will. God harmonizes these truths. God is not limited to the time, space, and matter of the universe in which we live.

We have a free will, but not an unlimited free will. We only have the choices God gives us. We can choose to be dependent on God or independent of God. We can choose to obey or disobey God. We can choose to have faith in God and believe His Word or live in unbelief. We can choose evil or we can choose good. We can choose to display love, joy, peace, longsuffering, gentleness, goodness, faith, meekness, and temperance, or we can choose drunkenness, lying, and fornication. We can choose to love God and our neighbor or to hate God and our neighbor. We can choose heaven or hell, but we cannot choose heaven or hell or somewhere else. Have you chosen life or death? This will be answered by what you do with the person of Jesus Christ.

---

4   Harold J. Chadwick. *And We Shall Judge Angels*, 188.

5   Gary Stearman. *Prophecy in the News*, 11.

6   Harold J. Chadwick. *And We Shall Judge Angels*, 186.

7   Gary Stearman. *Prophecy in the News*, 13.

God does not simply judge. God judges righteously. God proves to all people that we are sinners. There will be no excuses on judgment day for our sin or unbelief while we were on this earth in this age.

"By faith Noah, being warned of God of things not seen as yet, moved with fear, prepared an ark to the saving of his house; by the which he condemned the world, and became heir of the righteousness which is by faith" (Hebrews 11:7).

Noah believed God, and it was counted as righteousness. Believing God and having faith in God are the same. Noah was faithful, and his faith comes against those who did not believe his warnings.

"And thou, Capernaum, which are exalted unto heaven, shalt be brought down to hell: for if the mighty works, which have been done in thee, had been done in Sodom, it would have remained until this day. But I say unto you, That is shall be more tolerable for the land of Sodom in the day of judgment, than for thee" (Matthew 11:23–24).

Had Sodom seen the miracles that Jesus performed in Capernaum, the residents in Sodom would have believed, and the city would still exist to this day.

"The men of Nineveh shall rise in judgment with this generation, and shall condemn it: because they repented at the preaching of Jonas; and, behold, a greater than Jonas is here" (Matthew 12:41).

Nineveh comes in judgment against the world because they believed the prophet Jonah. Most people in the world do not believe in the second coming of Jesus Christ. At the great white throne, judgment for those who believe God will rise up in judgment against those who did not place their faith in God but instead relied on their own dead works. Those who would have believed God if they had heard the good news of God will rise up in judgment against those who heard and understood or had the opportunity to believe the Bible but chose not to believe.

> There are members of mankind who are saved and remain faithful to God and obey God's Holy Spirit who do not even know that they are being tested. Many true Christians don't think much about eternal purposes and still do the will of God the Father. These people come in judgment against those who do not believe the gospel, which is the Good News of Jesus Christ.[8]

> We have not been put on this earth to compete with other people for higher positions in heaven. We are not to compete with others for nicer abodes or mansions in heaven or to get better assignment or favors.[9]

---

8   Harold J. Chadwick. *And We Shall Judge Angels*, 232.
9   Harold J. Chadwick. *And We Shall Judge Angels*, 162.

We are to be like Jesus Christ while He was on the earth. We are to be servants to others. We are to forgive others and show patience. We must believe that God exists and rewards those who follow Him. We are in training on this earth to always choose by faith God's way of grace.

"But God, who is rich in mercy, for his great love wherewith he loved us, Even when we were dead in sins, hath quickened us together with Christ, (by grace ye are saved;) And hath raised us up together, and made us sit together in heavenly places in Christ Jesus: That in the ages to come he might shew the exceeding riches of his grace in his kindness toward us through Christ Jesus" (Ephesians 2:4–7).

God says that because we love Him, trust Him, and believe Him, in ages to come, He will give us exceeding riches of His grace, kindness, and glory in eternity. *Everything is about eternity.*

"And you, being dead in your sins and the uncircumcision of your flesh, hath he quickened together with him, having forgiven you all trespasses; Blotting out the handwriting of ordinances that was against us, which was contrary to us, and took it out of the way, nailing it to his cross; And having spoiled principalities and powers, he made a shew of them openly, triumphing over them in it" (Colossians 2:13–15).

The resurrection of Jesus Christ was, in essence, God mocking Satan. If you are saved, the powers of hell cannot keep your soul in the grave.

"Even the mystery which hath been hid from ages and from generations, but now is made manifest to his saints: To whom God would make known what is the riches of the glory of this mystery among the Gentiles; which is Christ in you, the hope of glory" (Colossians 1:26–27).

The church age is a mystery. God's eternal purpose to include Gentiles to be saved was a fact hidden to the Old Testament church. Hell and the lake of fire are reserved for creatures with a free will and/or who created in God's image and have rebelled against God. Hell and the lake of fire exist so all can see that rebellion to God is futile and that there are consequences for one's actions.

Heaven and a Believer's Resurrected Body

Heaven, on the other hand, shows that God's way is the best way. Having faith and believing God brings blessings, honor, glory, and riches—more than our minds can imagine.

"And as it is appointed unto men once to die, but after this the judgment" (Hebrews 9:27).

Reincarnation is not the truth. We get the opportunity to love or rebel against God only within the lifetime in which we are currently living.

"For our conversation is in heaven; from whence also we look for the Saviour, the Lord Jesus Christ: Who shall change our vile body, that it may be fashioned like unto his glorious body, according to the working whereby he is able even to subdue all things unto himself" (Philippians 3:20–21).

This verse tells us our bodies will be like Jesus' resurrected body. Jesus' resurrected body is a flesh and bone body; blood was not mentioned.

"Now this I say, brethren, that flesh and blood cannot inherit the kingdom of God; neither doth corruption inherit incorruption. Behold, I shew you a mystery; We shall not all sleep, but we shall all be changed, In a moment, in the twinkling of an eye, at the last trump: for the trumpet shall sound, and the dead shall be raised incorruptible, and we shall be changed. For this corruptible must put on incorruption, and this mortal must put on immortality" (I Corinthians 15:50–53).

"But I would not have you to be ignorant, brethren, concerning them which are asleep, that ye sorrow not, even as others which have no hope. For if we believe that Jesus died and rose again, even so them also which sleep in Jesus will God bring with him. For this we say until you by the word of the Lord, that we which are alive and remain unto the coming of the Lord shall not prevent them which are asleep. For the Lord himself shall descend from heaven with a shout, with the voice of the archangel, and with the trump of God: and the dead in Christ shall rise first: Then we which are alive and remain shall be caught up together with them in the clouds, to meet the Lord in the air: and so shall we ever be with the Lord. Wherefore comfort one another with these words" (I Thessalonians 4:13–18).

These two verses say that if you are in Christ at the time of the second coming and are still alive, you will be among those who will escape physical death. When sleep is mentioned in the New Testament, it concerns saints who have died, not sinners who have died without Christ.

"And he said unto them, Why are ye troubled? and why do thoughts arise in your hearts? Behold my hands and my feet, that it is I myself: handle me, and see; for a spirit hath not flesh and bones, as ye see me have" (Luke 24:38–39).

Jesus spoke this to his disciples after God resurrected Him from the dead. *Jesus stated that His body was one of flesh and bones. He did not mention blood.*

"For no man ever yet hated his own flesh; but nourisheth and cherisheth it, even as the Lord the church: For we are members of his body, of his flesh, and of his bones" (Ephesians 5:29–30).

Jesus' resurrected body is a body of flesh and bone. The apostle Paul restated this fact.

"But of the times and the seasons, brethren, ye have no need that I write unto you. For yourselves know perfectly that the day of the Lord so cometh as a thief in the night. For when they shall say, Peace and safety; then sudden destruction cometh upon them, as travail upon a woman with child; and they shall not escape. But ye, brethren, are not in darkness, that that day should overtake you as a thief. Ye are all the children of light, and the children of the day: we are not of the night, nor of darkness. Therefore let us not sleep, as do others; but let us watch and be sober. For they that sleep sleep in the night; and they that be drunken are drunken in the night. But let us, who are of the day, be sober, putting on the breastplate of faith and love; and for an helmet, the hope of salvation. For God hath not appointed us to wrath, but to obtain salvation by our Lord Jesus Christ, Who died for us, that, whether we wake or sleep, we should live together with him. Wherefore comfort yourselves together, and edify one another, even as also ye do" (I Thessalonians 5:1–11).

"And I saw another sign in heaven, great and marvelous, seven angels having the seven last plagues; for in them is filled up the wrath of God. And I saw as it were a sea of glass mingled with fire: and them that had gotten the victory over the beast, and over his image, and over his mark, and over the number of his name, stand on the sea of glass, having the harps of God. And they sing the song of Moses the servant of God, and the song of the Lamb, saying, Great and marvelous rare thy works, Lord God Almighty; just and true are thy ways, thou King of saints. Who shall not fear thee, O Lord, and glorify thy name? for thou only art holy: for all nations shall come and worship before thee; for thy judgments are made manifest" (Revelation 15:1–4).

I believe the sea of glass is the judgment seat of Christ. Are you ready for the judgment seat of Christ? Someday all believers will stand on the sea of glass in Heaven. Another purpose of this book is to help you get ready for this day.

Description of Heaven: I will give brief descriptions of heaven and hell in the following pages.

"And there came unto me one of the seven angels which had the seven vials full of the seven last plagues, and talked with me, saying, Come hither, I will shew thee the bride, the Lamb's wife. And he carried me away in the spirit to a great and high mountain, and shewed me that great city, the holy Jerusalem, descending out of heaven from God, Having the glory of God: and her light was like unto a stone most precious, even like a jasper stone, clear as crystal" (Revelation 21:9–11).

In various places in the Bible, heaven is called a city, a kingdom, and a country. Heaven is the home of God.

"But as it is written, Eye hath not seen, nor ear heard, neither have entered into the heart of man, the things which God hath prepared for them that love him" (I Corinthians 2:9).

While on this earth, the mind of mankind cannot grasp the beauties and wonders of heaven.

The Judgment Seat of Christ

"For we must all appear before the judgment seat of Christ; that every one may receive the things done in his body, according to that he hath done, whether it be good or bad" (II Corinthians 5:10).

"I charge thee therefore before God, and the Lord Jesus Christ, who shall judge the quick and the dead at his appearing and his kingdom" (II Timothy 4:1).

"For other foundation can no man lay than that is laid, which is Jesus Christ. Now if any man build upon this foundation gold, silver, precious stones, wood, hay, stubble; Every man's work shall be made manifest: for the day shall declare it, because it shall be revealed by fire; and the fire shall try every man's work of what sort it is. If any man's work abide which he hath built thereupon, he shall receive a reward. If any man's work shall be burned, he shall suffer loss: but he himself shall be saved; yet so as by fire. Know ye not that ye are the temple of God, and that the Spirit of God dwelleth in you?" (I Corinthians 3:11–16).

"Know ye not that they which run a race run all, but one receiveth the prize? So run, that ye may obtain" (I Corinthians 9:24).

These verses deal with judgment day. Eventually everyone dies and meets God to be judged. Now is the time to prepare for death. If you are found in Christ at your death or at the second coming of Jesus Christ, you will spend eternity in heaven.

If you do not believe the gospel (the good news of the death, burial, and resurrection of Jesus), you spend eternity in the lake of fire. If you are a believer, you will be judged for your deeds, works, words, intercessions in prayer, and giving. Other rewards deal with running the race until the end, being a soul-winner, loving God by being an overcomer, loving the appearing of Jesus at the second coming, and for a pastor, rewards for having led and protected their congregation. We are to treat people well while in our bodies. Our works must abide in Christ, and we must have sound doctrine.

Our rewards will be like gold, silver, and precious metals—or if our works are dead, they will be burned up like wood, hay, and stubble. You may think you just want to get into heaven, but the reality is that once you are before God, you will want to hear from Jesus, "Good and faithful servant, enter into my rest."

"And I saw a great white throne, and him that sat on it, from whose face the earth and the heaven fled away; and there was found no place for them. And I saw the dead, small and great, stand before God; and the books were opened: and another book was opened, which is the book of life: and the dead were judged out of those things which were written in the books, according to their works. And the sea gave up the dead which were in it; and death and hell delivered up the dead which were in them: and they were judged every man according to their works. And death and hell were cast into the lake of fire. This is the second death. And whosoever was not found written in the book of life was cast into the lake of fire" (Revelation 20:11–15).

Eternal Damnation

In the state of eternal damnation, the soul first goes to hell, and at the second resurrection, the soul is thrown into the lake of fire. The battle is for your soul. The soul contains your five senses, which include touch, smell, sight, hearing, and taste. Your soul is also the home of your mind, will, emotions, and heart. Your heart is what you truly believe.

In hell and in the lake of fire, your senses will experience extreme heat, horrible smells, darkness, groans, screams and curses, and extreme hunger and thirst. Hell is a bottomless pit, and all this will last forever.

Emotions will include fear, anger, and hatred, but most of all, shame and hopelessness. The shame will come from believing lies—and in some cases, the knowledge that you helped lead others to destruction. Hopelessness will be replaced with even more hopelessness. Any questions you have about eternity past will never be answered. In hell, when you get used to one level of misery, it will get worse and worse. Every curse of God will stoke the fires of hell even hotter.

Those saved and in Christ will have bodies like Jesus' resurrected body. That body will be a body of flesh and bones that contains no blood but will contain your spirit and soul.

There will be no sicknesses, disease, or death, as nothing dies in heaven. You will never be tired, and you will always be at perfect rest. Transportation will be miraculous; your body will not be subject to gravity and will be able to travel through the universe at will. You will be ageless, sexless, and not of any observable race. By ageless, I mean you won't be young, middle-aged, or old; you will not have an observable age. Your body will not be male or female. There will be no jealousy, strife, or worry.

We will take part in power-releasing, praise, and worship of Almighty God. Emotions will be joyful, loving, and peaceful. We will be filled with happiness and rest—but mostly, we will be aware of the perfect love of God. I look forward to no phones, no watches, and no stock problems at work.

Everything in heaven works harmoniously. Pure motives will drive all thoughts, intentions, and actions. Heaven is more real than earth. Jesus will be everywhere you go. A saint will occupy one space at a time in heaven. However, God transcends time, matter, and space. Just because Jesus is with you doesn't mean that Jesus can't be with me or with someone else at the same time.

You will have no temptation to sin, but you will still have a free will. There will be more colors than you can imagine, and there will be no shadows. You will never be hot or cold. There will be plenteous vegetation and diversity of animals.

Again, heaven is more real than earth. My desire is to hear these words from God at the resurrection: "Well done, good and faithful servant." Heaven won't be boring, and joy will be elevated from one level to a higher level of glory and honor continuously throughout all eternity. The increase of God's government will be everlasting.

Summary of God's Purpose for Mankind

1. Mankind is created in God's image, and we are to love and fear God, imitate God in our lives, and read His Word daily.
2. People don't believe in God because they don't see Him with their natural eyes. One must overcome this fact and believe God by faith to be saved.
3. We are to love God will all of our mind, heart, soul, and strength. We are to love our neighbor as ourselves.
4. God is showing His wisdom to principalities and powers in heavenly places through the person of Jesus Christ and through His church.
5. God is in total control of time (past, present, and future).
6. When dealing with free-will creatures, God does not operate the universe solely by force, but also by persuasion.
7. God is always on His plan A.
8. Our five senses are in our soul, and our souls are eternal. Our senses are sight, hearing, taste, touch, and smell.

9. Present events will prevent further rebellions of free-will created beings in eternity.
10. Sin will fall under its own weight.
11. One of our purposes is to humiliate and mock free-will creatures who rebel against God.
12. God judges righteously.
13. There will be no excuses for anyone on judgment day.
14. We are *not* on this earth to compete with others for higher positions in eternity.
15. We are on this earth to learn to live by faith.
16. Earth is a boot camp for eternity.
17. The benefits of believing God always bring great joy and riches beyond our imagination.
18. The judgment of God against those created, free-will beings who rebel against God are more terrible than can be imagined—and they are eternal.
19. If everything had been perfect throughout all eternity, then there would have been no purpose for the Creation.
20. Let the Holy Spirit reveal to you what your purpose is on this earth. This is the most asked question by people about their own lives. You can have a personal relationship with Jesus Christ and find out these answers by asking God in prayer. If you are broken over your own sin and desire a personal relationship with God, go back to the salvation message at the beginning of this book or just pray your own prayer.

The Case for Creationism, Design, and Order in the Universe

"It is the glory of God to conceal a thing: but the honour of kings to search out a matter" (Proverbs 25:2).

God conceals truths. It is up to us to search out the truth. Those people who truly search out the truth are called kings by God.

"But if from thence thou shalt seek the LORD thy God, thou shalt find him, if thou seek him with all thy heart and with all thy soul" (Deuteronomy 4:29).

I encourage you to seek out the truth that comes from the God of the Bible. If you seek for the true and living God, you will find Him.

"Remember this, and shew yourselves men: bring it again to mind, O ye transgressors. Remember the former things of old: for I am God, and there is none else; I am God, and there is none like me. Declaring the end from the beginning, and from ancient times the things that are not yet done, saying. My counsel shall stand, and I will do all my pleasure" (Isaiah 46:8–10).

This is God speaking in the first person. God states at the beginning of time everything that will occur throughout all time. God will perform all that He purposes to do. God created time, and He lives in time, which is past, present, and future equally.

The Bible is full of thousands of prophecies that have been fulfilled or are in the process of coming to pass. No other belief system has prophecies which show that God not only knows the future but can bring to pass all that He declares He will do.

The First Sentence in the Bible

"In the beginning God created the heaven and the earth" (Genesis 1:1).

This sentence explains how the universe came into existence.

God = God
Beginning = Time

Heaven = Space
Earth = Matter

The first verse in the Bible is a scientific and an historical statement. In other words, God created time, space, and matter.

"Through faith we understand that the worlds were framed by the word of God, so that things which are seen were not made of things which do appear" (Hebrews 11:3).

This verse tells us that God made everything from nothing. God spoke the universe into existence.

"And the earth was without form, and void; and darkness was upon the face of the deep. And the Spirit of God moved upon the face of the waters. And God said, 'Let there be light' and there was light" (Genesis 1:2–3).

God spoke the elements into existence. God said, "Let there be light," and there was light. There is a spiritual truth—not just an historical truth—in the first verses in the Bible. There is a battle between light and darkness. When a person receives Christ, he becomes a son of light and moves out of the realm of spiritual darkness.

The Creation Points to a Creator; Therefore, There is No Excuse Not to Believe God

"For the wrath of God is revealed from heaven against all ungodliness and unrighteousness of men, who hold the truth in unrighteousness; Because that which may be known of God is manifest in them; for God hath shewed it unto them. For the invisible things of him from the creation of the world are clearly seen, being understood by the things that are made, even his eternal power and Godhead; so that they are without excuse: Because that, when they knew God, they glorified him not as God, neither were thankful; but became vain in their imaginations, and their foolish heart was darkened. Professing themselves to be wise, they became fools, And changed the glory of the uncorruptible God into an image made like to corruptible man, and to birds, and fourfooted beasts, and creeping things. Wherefore God also gave them up to uncleanness through the lusts of their own hearts, to dishonour their own bodies between themselves: Who changed the truth of God into a lie, and worshipped and served the creature more than the Creator, who is blessed for ever. Amen" (Romans 1:18–25).

> The Bible tells us that by observing the creation we do understand that we are created beings, that someone separate from the creation creased us. The character of the creation reveals the character of the maker. These verses show us that we have no excuse for not understanding this fact.[10]

God clearly reveals to us in our souls that we were created. The creation also shows mankind God's eternal power, and even the Godhead. The Godhead consists of God the Father, God the Word (who is Jesus Christ), and God the Holy Spirit. God the Father did the planning; God the Word, Jesus Christ, spoke the world into existence; and God the Holy Spirit did the work. The physical universe is a trinity.

---

10   John D. Morris. *The Young Earth*, 16.

In the beginning, God created heaven and the earth. This represents time, matter, and space. God spoke time, matter, and space into existence.

Trinities in the Universe

The physical universe has many trinities. The creation is made up of these trinities:

The Creation	=	Time	Matter	Space
Time	=	Past	Present	Future
Space	=	Length	Breadth	Height
Matter	=	Solid	Liquid	Gas
Substance	=	Energy	Motion	Phenomenon
Substance	=	Space	Motion or Matter	Time
Water	=	Liquid	Gas	Solid

Space exists in length, breadth, and height, and is in one space. Time is in the past, present, and future in one time.[11] These trinities did not happen by accident. Each of the three, space, matter, and time, then necessitates the other two.[12]

These truths just mentioned point to the trinity of the Godhead.

"And God said, 'Let us make man in our image, after our likeness: and let them have dominion over the fish of the sea, and over the fowl of the air, and over the cattle, and over all the earth, and over every creeping thing that creepeth upon the earth'" (Genesis 1:26).

God said He made man after His image and likeness. God said, "Let us make man after our likeness." We are not God, but made in His image.

"Hear, O Israel: the Lord our God is one Lord" (Deuteronomy 6:4).

One God	=	God the Father	God the Word, Jesus Christ	God the Holy Spirit
God	=	Omniscient—knows everything	Omnipotent—has all power	Omnipresent—is everywhere
Mankind—not God, but in His image	=	Spirit	Body	Soul
The Soul of mankind—His heart	=	Mind	Will	Emotions

"For of Him and through Him and unto Him are all things" (Colossians 1:17).

---

11   Nathan R. Wood. *The Trinity in the Universe*, 21.
12   Nathan R. Wood. *The Trinity in the Universe*, 138.

This verse above is a scientific statement.

> The physical universe becomes, then, a vast circuit from the mind of God to the mind of God, and this vast circuit is in the absolute likeness of the Three in One. Space, or the outspreading of power, is the source, like the Father in the Three in One; Motion or matter is the visible, active embodiment, like the Son in the Three in One. Time is from space, through matter, as the Spirit is from the Father through the Son in the Three in One. And as the Spirit is the return of the Godhead again into the life of God, so time is the return of the physical universe into the life of God.[13]

"Who is the image of the invisible God, the firstborn of every creature: For by him were all things created, that are in heaven, and that are in earth, visible and invisible, whether they be thrones, or dominions, or principalities, or powers: all things were created by him, and for him: And he is before all things, and by him all things consist. And he is the head of the body, the church: who is the beginning, the firstborn from the dead; that in all things he might have the preeminence" (Colossians 1:15–18).

> This verse is speaking of Jesus Christ. What we have just found to be true of triune space is true also of the other triunities which compose the universe. In space, one dimension generates the second. The two dimensions generate the third. The three dimensions generate the reality, the existence of space.[14]

All Living Things Bring Forth Only their Own Kind

God created all things which are visible as well as those things that are invisible. The invisible would include: atoms, electrons, muons, and sub-atomic substances. There are things smaller than these, because they truly are invisible. God also created seraphim, cherubim, archangels, and angels, which are not visible to us now but will be in eternity.

"And the earth brought forth grass, and herb yielding seed after his kind, and the tree yielding fruit, whose seed was in itself, after his kind: and God saw that it was good" (Genesis 1:12).

"And God created great whales, and every living creature that moveth, which the waters brought forth abundantly, after their kind, and very winged fowl after his kind: and God saw that it was good" (Genesis 1:21).

"And God said, 'Let the earth bring forth the living creature after his kind, cattle, and creeping thing, and beat of the earth after his kind,' and it was so. And God made the beast of the earth after his kind, the cattle after their kind, and every thing that creepeth upon the earth after his kind: and God saw that it was good. And God said, 'Let us make man in our image, after our likeness: and let them have dominion over the fish of the sea, and over the fowl of the air, and over the cattle, and over all the earth, and over every creeping thing that creepeth upon the earth.' So God created man in his own image, in the image of God created he him; male and female created he them" (Genesis 1:24–27).

---

13 Nathan R. Wood. *The Trinity in the Universe*, 145.
14 Nathan R. Wood. *The Trinity in the Universe*, 168–169.

We see here over and over again that animals and plants come from their own kind and did not evolve. However, man—male and female—were created in God's image. We are not God, but we represent His image and attributes.

> This universe contains personal beings, who think, who love, who hate, who hope, who fear, who choose, who determine. The cause of such beings, of a universe which contains such beings, must be at least as personal as they. The equation of the universe is clear. A vast, rational, personal cause of the universe—God.[15]

"In the beginning was the Word, and the Word was with God, and the Word was God. The same was in the beginning with God. All things were made by him; and without him was not any thing made that was made. In him was life; and the life was the light of men. And the light shineth in darkness; and the darkness comprehended it not. There was a man sent from God, whose name was John. The same came for a witness, to bear witness of the Light, that all men through him might believe. He was not that Light, but was sent to bear witness of that Light. That was the true Light, which lighteth every man that cometh into the world. He was in the world, and the world was made by him, and the world knew him not. He came unto his own, and his own received him not. But as many as received him, to them gave he power to become the sons of God, even to them that believe on his name: Which were born, not of blood, nor of the will of the flesh, nor of the will of man, but of God. And the Word was made flesh, and dwelt among us, (and we beheld his glory, the glory as of the only begotten of the Father), full of grace and truth. John bare witness of him, and cried, saying, 'This was he of whom I spake, He that cometh after me is preferred before me: And of his fulness have all we received, and grace for grace. For the law was given by Moses, but grace and truth came by Jesus Christ. No man hath seen God at any time; the only begotten Son, which is in the bosom of the Father, he hath declared him'" (John 1:1–18).

The apostle John—under the guidance of the Holy Spirit—writes to us that *Jesus is the Word of God.* By Jesus, who was God in the flesh, all things were created. God has existed eternally—now and forever. God did not come from anywhere. He had nowhere to come from. God just is.

Intelligent, Purposeful Design is the Only Possible Explanation for the Universe

Another proof of design and order is the common shoe. The existence of this shoe can only be explained in one of the following four ways:

1. It is an illusion—in other words, the shoe does not exist (nonsense).
2. The shoe has existed eternally (nonsense).
3. The shoe created itself (nonsense).
4. The shoe was made by something more complex than the shoe itself.

The correct answer is number four. Just as something greater than the shoe made the shoe, God—who is greater than us—made you and me.

---

15   Nathan R. Wood. *The Trinity in the Universe*, 23.

All of us have walked through a park. As you walk through a park, you look at hundreds if not thousands of plants and animals of all sizes. If you were to come across a metal folding chair, the first thought you would have is that someone would have put it there—not that it got there by accident. However, the pure, atheistic evolutionist would tell you that everything except the chair got there by accident. The truth is, someone (God) who is above mankind created you and me in His image. In a like fashion, someone created the chair that is not as complex as mankind.

The Miracle of Life, the Simple Cell, and the Complexity of Life

"The fool hath said in his heart, 'There is no God.' They are corrupt, they have done abominable works, there is none that doeth good" (Psalm 14:1).

"The fool hath said in his heart, 'There is no God.' Corrupt are they, and have done abominable iniquity: there is none that doeth good" (Psalm 53:1).

Again, Christians have long pointed out that the works of creation are proof of design and thus a designer, who is God. A person is a fool if they choose not to believe God.

Investigating the molecular level of life, scientists have discovered a very complex design and function that is beyond our imagination. King David of Israel stated three thousand years ago: "I will praise thee; for I am fearfully and wonderfully made: marvelous are thy works" (Psalm 139:14).

Each person at the moment of conception begins life as a single blood cell. These cells could not know what to do to construct a body composed of trillions of individual cells of different kinds and different functions without an intelligent designer, known as God.

> It is estimated that there are over six billion people in the world, if it were possible to reduce every individual to the original blueprint from which he or she originated, a container the size of an aspirin tablet could store the blueprints for the entire world's population. Once again, we are staggered when we consider the awesome complexity of life. It becomes absurd when we consider evolution accepts that the origin and complexity of life came about my random accidental processes. Such a claim is a contradiction to sound logical thinking.[16]

> A simple cell consists of microfilaments, chromosones, nucleus, nucicoll, residual body, transfer pores, ribosones, transportation channels, mitochondria, cell membrane, pinocytosis vesiches, digestive vacuole, microvilli, Cilla oars, microtubules.[17]

Do you have the faith to believe this simple cell came together by chance?

> There is no way that chemicals could put together intelligent thoughts in a language that contains the instructions for constructing and operating even a single cell, much

---

16   Caryl Matrisciana and Roger Oakland. *The Evolution Conspiracy*, 89.
17   M. Bowden. *Science verses Evolution*, 111.

less the trillions of cells in the human body! The fact that DNA is designed to replicate itself precisely and only fails to do so through destructive error eliminates even theistic evolution.

For all of its complexity, the brain no more originates or understands what it is doing than does DNA. The brain does not originate thoughts. If it did, we would have to do whatever our brains decided. On the contrary, we (the real persons inside) do the thinking and deciding, and our brains take these nonphysical thoughts and translate them into physical actions through a connection between the spirit and body that science can't fathom.

Science cannot escape the fact that man himself, like his creator, must be a nonmaterial being in order to originate the thoughts processed by the brain. But man did not originate thought itself. He did not create himself nor give himself the capacity to think. The Bible says that God, who is a spirit, created man "in His own image" (Genesis 1:27), that man is a "living soul" (Genesis 2:7), i.e., a nonphysical being made like unto his Creator, capable of thinking thoughts and making decisions. This ability makes him morally responsible to God. To escape that responsibility is the sole reason for atheism.[18]

Note that evolution, if it ever occurred, did so in the unobserved past, and each supposed stage only occurred once. No one ever saw the origin of life from non-living chemicals. No one has ever seen any type of organism give rise to a completely different type (macroevolution). No one has ever claimed to have seen meaningful evolutionary changes take place. The minor variations (micro-evolution) in plant and animal groups (e.g., DDT resistance in insects, shift in dominant color of peppered moths, etc.) which do occur in the present are not evolutionary changes. In fact, since creation allows for adaptation and variation within created kinds, small changes are perfectly compatible with creation theory as well, and certainly not the proof of evolution. Major changes (macro-evolution) have never been scientifically observed, and thus the theory of evolutionary descent from a common ancestor has not been and could never be proven scientifically. How could you ever run a test to see if it happened in the past? Or how could you ever prove that it didn't happen in the past? Evolution is a belief system some scientists hold about the past, and they use this view of history to interpret the evidence in the present.[19]

The inability of biologists to discover precisely how a cell operates and reproduces itself is one of the major stumbling blocks of evolution. Many of the workers in this field admit that they are a long way from understanding the phenomenally complex interactions within the cell. The molecule to cell transition is a jump of fantastic dimensions which lies beyond the range of testable hypothesis. In this area all is

18   David Hunt. *The Berean Call.*
19   John D. Morris. *The Young Earth*, 18.

conjecture. The available facts do not provide a basis for postulating that cells arose on this planet.[20]

Again, the idea that a living cell should be capable of reproducing itself without a designer (most call Him God), is impossible.

> If human beings, on the other hand, are simply the end-products of a long process of evolution from the primordial nothingness (as taught today in most secular schools and information media), then "let us eat and drink; for tomorrow we die" (I Corinthians 15:23). There are now many thousands of scientists who have become creationists, and this includes scientists in every field and every nation. Polls show that half of the people in the United States now believe in special creation.[21]

We have all heard at various times evolutionists say that the creation once existed in a mass about the size of a softball. These evolutionists would further state that about 18 billion years ago, this mass expanded in a matter of a few seconds in what is called the the Big Bang into the universe in which we now live.

After the stars and planets formed on their own, life came from non-life. I have read and heard over the years that living organisms came into existence with one or all of the following explanations:

1. Meteorites carried the building blocks of life from other galaxies.
2. Life began spontaneously from the oceans or swamps.
3. Lightening strikes brought forth life.
4. Volcanoes caused natural forces to bring forth life.
5. A tar pit is the location for the origin of life.

In defining life, I am defining it as anything that has a DNA chain capable of reproducing itself. From non-life to life, evolutionists believe through the process of natural selection—survival of the fittest—mankind evolved from amoebas to fish to mammal creatures.

"Not my might, nor by power, but by my spirit, saith the LORD of hosts" (Zechariah 4:6).

The Bible says that all living creatures—whether they be in God's image, mammals, birds, or plants—came into existence by God speaking them into existence and not through the process of survival of the fittest.

The Impossibility of the Jump from Non-life to Life

Again, the jump from non-life to life is beyond science. The jump from non-life to life involves the accidental appearance of the elements which appear on a periodical chart such as gold, silver, etc. Life appearing from non-life could only occur if random atoms became amino acids, then switched to protein molecules to complex proteins and finally a DNA chain capable of reproducing itself by accident

---

20   D. E. Green and R. F. Goldberger. *Molecular Insights into the Living Process*, 407
21   John D. Morris. *The Young Earth*, 4.

without God. The jump to DNA, cells, and amoebas is a jump performed by God very easily. This is impossible with men.

Sweeping Claims of Evolutionists

Over the past 100 years, many skeletal remains have been used to promote the idea we evolved from the ape family. Nebraska man was found to be a constructed tooth of a pig. Piltdown man was a deliberate hoax, the jawbone was from an ape. The teeth were filed down and colored to deceive the public. Peking man was a big ape. The scientist who discovered the so-called Java man admitted later in his life it was probably a giant gibbon.[22]

I believe the way many evolutionists work their theories is convoluted. Many evolutionary theories involve the following thought processes and consequences:

1. Develop a theory—any theory.
2. Make a sweeping claim for reliability of that theory.
3. Numerous discrepancies and valid objections will arise.
4. A new layer of rationalizations and new theories come forward to attempt to explain away problems.
5. More sweeping claims are made.
6. More objections are raised to these sweeping claims.[23]

In all cases, there will never be an answer to how living plants and animals came from non-living elements. Theories about the age of the earth are most sweeping. If the age of the earth is of interest to you, I suggest you read the book *The Mythology of Modern Dating Methods* by John Woodmorappe.

Sweeping Claims Concerning Whales

Evolution cannot give us answers as it relates to hundreds of unique types of animals. Whales are mammals because they suckle their young. The evolution of whales was discussed in a December, 1976 *National Geographic* magazine. This issue of *National Geographic* stated, "the whales ascendancy to sovereign size apparently began 60 million years ago when hairy, four-legged mammals, in search of food or sanctuary, ventured into water. As eons passed, changes slowly occurred: hind legs disappeared, front legs changed into flippers, hair gave way to a thick, smooth blanket of blubber, nostrils moved to the top of the head, the tail broadened into flukes and in the buoyant water world the body became enormous."[24]

Once again the imagination is stretched beyond the breaking point in order to support the theory of evolution. One cannot but have a degree of admiration for the indomitable faith of the evolutionist in his theory in the face of so much opposing evidence![25]

---

22 Duane T. Gish. *The Bible League, Brainwashed.*
23 John Woodmorappe. *The Mythology of Modern Dating Methods*, 28.
24 *National Geographic*, December, 1976.
25 Malcolm Bowden. *Science versus Evolution*, 74.

The *Houston Chronicle* ran a story concerning whales being related to hippos. The *Chronicle* stated that new fossil discoveries add weight to the conclusion that whales are related to land-based plant-eaters such as cows and hippopotamuses rather than to an extinct group of carnivores, two groups of researchers report. Scientists have known that whales evolved from four-legged land animals millions of years ago. However, which branch of the animal kingdom whales split from has been a matter of debate.[26]

The article goes on to say that someone saw a hippo eating gazelles that came too close to the water. Since some killer whales eat fish and other mammals, these scientists now believe that whales could have come from hippos, not cows. This is just a sweeping claim with no science behind it.

Sweeping Claims about Pond Scum and Us

The *Houston Chronicle* ran another story titled "Pond Scum and Us." The *Chronicle* stated that "single-cell organism that swam in the earth's primordial soup hundreds of millions of years ago is an evolutionary sibling of humans and all other animals, according to research published by scientists at the University of Wisconsin in Madison. While the finding advances the knowledge of human evolution, the idea that people and pond scum are related is bound to draw criticism from creationists and other religious groups that abhor the thought of such genetic connections between people and other species."[27]

This is just another sweeping claim with no science behind it. Basically what many evolutionists are saying is that there are many similarities in the genetic makeup of humans and animals. Creationists like myself believe that just because dogs and mankind have two eyes, that does not mean that we are related; it does mean that we have the same creator. The difference between mankind and animals is that mankind is created in the image of God and animals are not.

Sweeping Claims of Life Coming from Meteorites

The *Houston Chronicle* science writer, Eric Berger, wrote an article in 2002 titled "Scientists discover sugar in meteorites." In the article, he stated, "Scientists have discovered sugar in meteorites that fell to Earth from outer space, filling a hole in the theory that such space rocks may have spurred the development of life by delivering the necessary chemical building blocks."[28]

The article went on to say all of this started about 4.5 billion years ago. The article did acknowledge that many questions about the chemistry of life's origins remain. However, the simple answer is that God spoke them into existence.

---

26   Dominguez, Alex. "Fossil discovery not a big fish story." *Houston Chronicle,* September 20, 2001.
27   John Fauber. "Pond Scum and Us." *Houston Chronicle,* December 20, 2001.
28   Eric Berger. "Sugar in Meteorites." *Houston Chronicle,* Spring, 2002.

The Gap Theory

Many creationists believe in the Gap Theory. The Gap Theory states that the earth has existed for millions or billions of years but that God abruptly placed Adam and Eve on the earth in the recent past, approximately six thousand years ago. Creationists who believe in the Gap Theory use Genesis 1:1–2 for their argument. They believe that God created the universe billions or millions of years ago. They further believe that Genesis 1:2 describes a rebellion and/or destruction of pre-mankind beings. After this event, they believe God restored and replenished the earth and abruptly created Adam and Eve approximately six thousand years ago.

I believe old and young earth creationists are considered orthodox as long as they believe Adam and Eve were real people created in the image of God and are not related to the animal kingdom. I don't believe in the Gap Theory because Adam and Eve brought death into the time, matter, space, and universe in which we live.

"In the beginning God created the heaven and the earth. And the earth was without form, and void; and darkness was upon the face of the deep. And the Spirit of God moved upon the face of the waters" (Genesis 1:1–2).

Earth's Magnetic Field and the Diffusion of Helium from Rocks

The earth's magnetic field has been steadily decreasing. Records have been kept since 1835 on the earth's magnetic field. At the rate it is decreasing, life could not have existed just 10,000 years ago on the earth. The earth would have generated so much heat life on earth would have been impossible.[29]

With no magnetic field, the earth would experience continuous high winds. Some scientists speculate that living cells would be hindered from dividing if there was no magnetic field in the earth.

Helium is accumulating in the atmosphere so quickly that all the helium in the earth's atmosphere would have accumulated in no more than 2,000,000 years, not the billions of years evolutionists state.[30]

The results of laboratory measurements of helium diffusion as a function of temperature in biotites (containing helium from uranium decay in zircons) from two different rocks have been reported. The measurements confirm the RATE prediction that diffusion in biotite is rapid. Helium formed from the decay of uranium millions of years ago should have diffused through the granites in the earth's crust and be present in today's atmosphere. Yet, the atmosphere contains less than 1/2000th of the amount it should have if the earth is 4.6 billion years old. Much of the helium is still found in granites

29   Malcolm Bowden. *True Science Agrees with the Bible*, 201–202.
30   John D. Morris. *The Young Earth*, 83.

of the crust. The diffusion rate appears to agree closely with a young earth and recent accelerated decay.[31]

At the rate helium is being diffused into the atmosphere, if the earth was billions of years old, we would be speaking with very high, squeaky voices (like when you inhale helium from a helium balloon).

I believe the rapid decrease of the earth's magnetic field and the quick diffusion of helium from rocks into the atmosphere point to a young earth. Just because these and other documented truths are not in your local newspapers does not mean they are not the truth. A lot of people and publishers have staked their reputations on evolution.

Evolutionary thought is in great distress. Creationists who are well trained will always win a debate against an evolutionist. If you are a Christian, you can gain sufficient expertise to defend the faith easily. I encourage you to take the time, turn off your TV, and determine what the truth is and why you believe what you believe. Remember, if evolution is not the truth, there should be no evidence of it. There is no evidence supporting evolution.

Mutations

There is no evidence that mutations in cells lead to evolution to higher life. Mutations almost always are harmful to an organism. When organisms mutate, they generally lose information, not gain complexity or purpose.[32]

The First and Second Laws of Thermodynamics

The first law of thermodynamics states that matter cannot be created or destroyed. If matter cannot be created, how did matter come into existence? The answer is that God spoke matter into existence. Science has no explanation for the creation of matter.

The second law of thermodynamics states that things go from order to disorder. This would make evolution impossible.

Continental Erosion

The continents are eroding at a rate in which all land mass should have already have eroded into the oceans by now if the earth was just 14 millions years old.[33]

The Fossil Record and No Evidence of Plant Evolution

Extensive searches throughout the world have not uncovered any evidence that one type of animal ever changed into another type of animal. That frogs came from fishes,

---

31   "Acts & Facts." *Institute of Creation Research,* October, 2001.
32   Lee Spetner. *Not By Chance,* 159–160.
33   Malcolm Bowden. *True Science Agrees with the Bible,* 222.

that reptiles changed to birds or that man descended from apelike creatures, there is no fossil record to support this theory. No "intermediary fossils," that is "fossils in the middle stages" of development between fish and bird, or mammal and man, have ever been discovered to prove that such a theory is more than merely speculation. Charles Darwin himself said that the fossil record was "perhaps the most obvious and serious objection" to his theory.[34]

If the theory of evolution is correct then one would expect to see much reference to the evolution of plants in the various books. Yet when they are consulted, the very small amount of space devoted to the evolution of plant life is very noticeable.[35]

The Impossibility of Simple Cell Creatures Splitting into Distinctively Male and Female Animals

Evolutionists have no answers to the jump from non-life to life or to the jump from single-cell creatures to mammals and other animals which are male and female. The question has never been answered as to how a single-cell creature is transformed into a creature which is distinctively male and female. For male and female genitals to appear by chance is ludicrous. For males and females to find each other, they would need senses such as sight, smell, touch, and hearing. For distinctive male and female species to arise with their needed senses and appendages such as arms and legs is impossible. This topic seldom makes it into the evolution/creation debate, but for me, it is an important point.

Anthropocentricy

Anthropocentricy is defined as man being the final aim of the universe. An example of the anthropocentric view of life is that if the earth were 10 percent smaller, there would be no life on earth. There are literally thousands of examples like this that point to a creator God interested in His creation and having a specific purpose for mankind on this earth.

> A slower or faster rotation of the earth would eliminate life on earth. A smaller or larger earth would eliminate life on earth. A larger or smaller moon would eliminate life on earth. A thinner or thicker crust on the earth would eliminate life on earth. A lesser or greater ratio of oxygen to nitrogen would eliminate life on earth.[36]

In study it is apparent that the earth and our universe were made for mankind. I believe the earth was created as a battlefield to deal with issues that took place in eternity (past and future). This was explained more fully in the last chapter.

Quotations from Scientists

Sir Francis Bacon said, "A little science estranges man from God, but a lot of science brings him back."[37]

---

34   Caryl Matrisciana and Roger Oakland. *The Evolution Conspiracy*, 99.
35   Malcolm Bowden. *Science versus Evolution*, 16.
36   Sigmund Browner. *The Unramdon Universe*, 67.
37   Sigmund Browner. *The Unramdon Universe*, 39.

Astronomer Fred Hoyle said, "An explosion in a junk yard does not lead to a sundry bit of metal being assembled into a useful working machine."[38]

No one would believe that a tornado hitting a junkyard would create a jet plane. You are much more complicated than a jet plane, and you are not reading this book by chance.

Biblical Statements of Science in the Bible

"He stretcheth out the north over the empty place, and hangeth the earth upon nothing" (Job 26:7).

The earth is suspended in space and hangs on nothing.

"It is he that sitteth upon the circle of the earth, and the inhabitants thereof are as grasshoppers; that stretcheth out the heavens as a curtain, and spreadeth them out as a tent to dwell in" (Isaiah 40:22).

The Bible describes the earth as a circle. Isaiah knew this in 650 BC. For thousands of years, people knew the earth was round. From the mathematical calculations of the builders of the great pyramids four thousand to five thousand years ago, people knew the earth was round. The prophet Isaiah, under the inspiration of the Holy Spirit, knew the earth was round. Man lost this knowledge during the dark ages (AD 300–1500) because the Bible was taken out of the hands of the common man.

"And the seventy returned again with joy, saying, Lord, even the devils are subject unto us through thy name. And he said unto them, I beheld Satan as lightning fall from heaven. Behold, I give unto you power to tread on serpents and scorpions, and over all the power of the enemy: and nothing shall by any means hurt you. Notwithstanding in this rejoice not, that the spirits are subject unto you; but rather rejoice, because your names are written in heaven" (Luke 10:17–20).

The Bible describes many things that move faster than the speed of light.

"He telleth the number of the stars; he calleth them all by their names" (Psalm 147:4).

"Through faith we understand that the worlds were framed by the word of God, so that things which are seen were not made of things which do appear" (Hebrews 11:3).

God made everything from nothing.

"Praise him, ye heavens of heavens, and ye waters that be above the heavens" (Psalm 148:4).

"Thus saith the LORD; If heaven above can be measured, and the foundations of the earth searched out beneath, I will also cast off all the seed of Israel for all that they have done, saith the LORD" (Jeremiah 31:37).

---

38   Sigmund Browner. *The Unramdon Universe*, 53.

There is, I believe, a water canopy around the universe; however, the universe is big, and it is expanding—thus it cannot be measured by man. Eternity dwells within God, but not in a pantheistic or occult way.

Summary

Because of the overwhelming problems which evolutionists have, many so-called scientists are moving to new-aged thinking. Qualities normally given to God are now given to the creation. It is becoming clear that the theory of evolution is a hoax.[39]

Evolution not only robs God of His Glory in creating life, it also destroys God's purpose of death and God's plan to overcome it through the resurrection of Jesus Christ. The Bible says in Romans 6:23, "For the wages of sin is death; but the gift of God is eternal life through Jesus Christ our Lord."[40]

The evolutionist paradigm (or worldview, if preferred) is steadily disintegrating. Not only is it Biblically indefensible for Christians, but also its scientific foundations have been almost fatally eroded. No real organic evolution has ever been observed during the period of human history and no true evolutionary transitional forms have ever been found among the billions of fossils from the past. The evidence of design is overwhelming in even the simplest living organism: the laws of probability and thermodynamics seem to make macro-evolution not only non-existent but also not possible. The evidence of creative design seems (to us, at least) to be overwhelming.[41]

We would suggest that the evidence set out above is brought to the attention of school teachers and university lecturers in order to "put the record straight." This should help to counterbalance the evolutionary propaganda to which pupils are incessantly and insidiously subjected to without realizing it every time the words "millions of years" are casually dropped into TV programs and elsewhere in the mass media.[42]

It has been well documented by several writers that true science (i.e., the discovery of laws governing the universe) could only arise in such a culture which acknowledged that the universe was created and sustained by a God who was ultimately rational and all-powerful, and who would insure that the laws which nature obeyed were constantly in operation.[43]

To support this statement, I would suggest reading the book *Men of Science, Men of God* by Dr. Henry Morris. The vast majority of the founders of the modern science were Christians. Sir Isaac Newton wrote more about the Bible than of science. I have read his commentary on the books of Daniel and

---

39 John D. Morris. *The Young Earth*, 121.

40 Caryl Matrisciana & Roger Oakland. *The Evolution Conspiracy*, 116.

41 John Woodmorappe. *The Mythology of Modern Dating*, v.

42 Malcolm Bowden. *True Science Agrees with the Bible*, 227.

43 Malcolm Bowden. *Evolution Fraud*, 7.

Revelation. He believed in the literal bodily resurrection of Jesus Christ and wrote extensively on the literal second coming of Christ.

> To put it simply, the question is; has every living organism arrived by a series of chance combinations of chemicals or was it all designed and created by an omnipotent God? How we answer this question can have a fundamental effect upon our concept of God and consequently upon the way in which we conduct our lives.[44]

1. God spoke the universe into existence.
2. The creation itself shows there is a creator; therefore, we have no excuse for not believing God.
3. There are a multitude of trinities in the universe that point us to the trinity in the Bible—that being the trinity of God the Father; God the Word, Jesus Christ; and God the Holy Spirit. These are one God in three distinct persons.
4. Everything created brings forth only its own kind.
5. The immense complexity of the universe points to a creator.
6. Evolutionists make sweeping, unscientific claims with no evidence. There is not one shred of evidence supporting the theory of evolution.
7. The purpose of evolution is to do away with being responsible to a creator God.
8. The earth's decreasing magnetic field and the accumulation of helium in the atmosphere point to a young earth.
9. The first law of thermodynamics, which states that matter cannot be created or destroyed, points to a creator.
10. The second law of thermodynamics points towards ever-increasing disorder in the universe which points to an abrupt, purposeful beginning of the universe.
11. The fossil record does not point to any transitional forms in animals or plants.
12. It's okay to believe in evolution, but don't blame God for it. Theistic evolution points to a mean, spirited god who has no purpose for the creation and a creation with no end to pain and suffering.

Let me repeat—the purpose of evolution is to do away with being responsible to a personal, creator God.

At one time, I allowed evolutionary thinking keep me away from believing the Bible. I did not want to hurt other people's faith by asking questions I thought they might not be able to answer. The last thought I had before I got saved back in June, 1986 was that it takes as much or more faith to believe in evolution that it does to believe in the Bible. I believed the prophecies in the Bible, but God had to tear down my faith in evolution for me to become a Christian. God's healing hand began a quick work on my body and soul the day I believed on the Lord Jesus Christ.

The reason so much evil is occurring in the USA (murder, adultery, theft, lying) is because over 50 percent of US citizens believe in evolution. The foundation of all major news networks, most colleges, the public school systems, and many churches is the belief in evolution.

---

44   Malcolm Bowden. *Science versus Evolution, 227.*

Public schools point their guns at a foundation of Christianity (i.e., Adam and Eve were abruptly created by God and were real people). The public schools teach that we evolved from monkeys, blast away at the foundations of Christianity, and mock the genealogies listed in the Bible.

I believe that in all reality, the public school systems teach that contrary to our Declaration of Independence, mankind was not in fact created by God with inalienable rights, and that we are not created in the image of God. Rather, we are taught that our existence can be explained by mindless chance. Prior to salvation, my battle cry was this: "When I am dead, I am dead all over like my dog Red Rover."

The church in the USA would be wise to point its guns at the teaching of evolution. Most of our nation's ills would evaporate if 70 percent or more of the citizens of America were creationists.

An Overview of the Old Testament—4000–3 BC

Christianity was foreordained by God in eternity before the foundation of the world to be the vessel in which God would work out His plan, and through which He would fulfill His eternal purpose in Christ![45]

God designed a plan wherein He would be worshipped, loved, and obeyed by a group of beings with a free will and/or created in His image. The possible and/or probable chronological order of God's creation history through previous ages would be mirrored by our own age.

"The thing that hath been, it is that which shall be; and that which is done is that which shall be done: and there is no new thing under the sun" (Ecclesiastes 1:9).

This verse tells us that history repeats itself.

The Creation of Heaven, Seraphim, and Cherubim

Because of the fact that history repeats itself, I believe the first creation event God spoke into existence was that heaven was made as a dwelling place for seraphim, cherubim, archangels, and angels. God—who is Spirit—would then allow Himself to be manifest (to be seen) by those whom He created. Seraphim, cherubim, archangels, angels, and mankind are created beings with a free will and are in essence spirit beings. This is in contrast to beasts of the field which have souls but not spirits.

"Above it stood the seraphim: each one had six wings; with twain he covered his face, and with twin he covered his feet, and with twain he did fly. And one cried unto another, and said, Holly, holy, holy, is the LORD of hosts: the whole earth is full of his glory" (Isaiah 6:2–3).

"And before the throne there was a sea of glass like unto crystal: and in the midst of the throne, and round about the throne, were four beasts full of eyes before and behind. And the first beast was like a lion, and the second beast like a calf, and the third beast had a face as a man, and the fourth beast was like a flying eagle. And the four beasts had each of them six wings about him; and they were full of eyes within: and they rest not day and night, saying, Holy, holy, holy, Lord God Almighty, which was, and is, and is to come. And when those beasts give glory and honour and thanks to him that sat on the throne, who liveth for ever and ever" (Revelation 4:6–9).

---

45   Harold J. Chadwick. *And We Shall Judge Angels*, 66.

In the book of Isaiah, the seraphim seem to have the same description as the four beasts in heaven mentioned in the book of Revelation surrounding the throne of God. These both had six wings and are in very close proximity to God. Seraphim receive greater and greater revelations from God, moment by moment.

"Whithersoever the spirit was to go, they went, thither was their spirit to go; and the wheels were lifted up over against them: for the spirit of the living creature was in the wheels. When those went, these went; and when those stood, these stood; and when those were lifted up from the earth, the wheels were lifted up over against them: for the spirit of the living creature was in the wheels. And the likeness of the firmament upon the heads of the living creature was as the colour of the terrible crystal, stretched forth over their heads above" (Ezekiel 1:20–22).

"And the sound of the cherubim's wings was heard even to the outer court, as the voice of the Almighty God when he speaketh …. When they stood, these stood; and when they were lifted up, these lifted up themselves also: for the spirit of the living creature was in them …. This is the living creature that I saw under the God of Israel by the river of Chebar; and I knew that they were the cherubims" (Ezekiel 10:5, 17, 20).

The cherubim and the living creatures mentioned in the Book of Ezekiel seem to describe the same order.

There are only three beings outside of mankind given a name in the Bible. These names are the names of the archangel Michael and the angel Gabriel. The third heavenly being was Lucifer, who was called a covering cherub in Ezekiel 28.

Michael

"Yet Michael the archangel, when contending with the devil he disputed about the body of Moses, durst not bring against him a railing accusation, but said, 'The Lord rebuke thee'" (Jude 1:9).

"And there was war in heaven: Michael and his angels fought against the dragon; and the dragon fought and his angels" (Revelation 12:7).

Created beings with a free will are literally in a struggle with free-will beings who sinned against God in eternity.

Lucifer, the Anointed Cherub; the Archangel Michael; Gabriel, an Angel; and Angels

"Thou hast been in Eden the garden of God; every precious stone was thy covering, the sardius, topaz, and the diamond, the beryl, the onyx, and the jasper, the sapphire, the emerald, and the carbuncle, and gold: the workmanship of thy tabrets and of thy pipes was prepared in thee in the day that thou wast created. Thou art the anointed cherub that covereth; and I have set thee so: thou wast upon the holy mountain of God; thou hast walked up and down in the midst of the stones of fire. Thou wast perfect in thy ways from the day that thou wast created, till iniquity was found in thee. By the multitude of thy merchandise they have filled the midst of thee with violence, and thou hast sinned: therefore I will cast thee as profane out of the mountain of God: and I will destroy thee, O covering cherub, from the midst of the stones of fire. Thine heart was lifted up because of thy beauty, thou hast corrupted thy wisdom by reason of thy brightness: I will cast thee to the ground, I will lay thee before kings, that they may behold thee. Thou hast defiled thy sanctuaries by the multitude of thine iniquities, by the iniquity of thy traffick; therefore will I bring forth a fire from the midst of thee, it shall devour thee, and I will bring thee to ashes upon the earth in the sight of all them that behold thee. All they that know thee among the people shall be astonished at thee; thou shalt be a terror, and never shalt thou be any more" (Ezekiel 28:13–19).

Lucifer started the rebellion in heaven as well as masterminding the rebellion on the earth in the persons of Adam and Eve. In the Bible, this Michael is listed as an archangel. The archangel Michael also fights against demonic powers in Daniel 10. Michael also leads in the battle to permanently banish Lucifer and his demons from heaven.

Gabriel

"And I heard a man's voice between the banks of Ulai, which called, and said, 'Gabriel, make this man to understand the vision'" (Daniel 8:16).

And the angel answering said unto him, 'I am Gabriel, that stand in the presence of God; and am sent to speak unto thee, and to shew thee these glad tidings' … And in the sixth month the angel Gabriel was sent from God unto a city of Galilee, named Nazareth" (Luke 1:19, 26).

The angel Gabriel is given assignments as a messenger angel to give understanding to humans such as Daniel, Mary, and Joseph when they were confused about what was happening.

"But to which of the angels said he at any time, Sit on my right hand, until I make thine enemies thy footstool? Are they not all ministering spirits, sent forth to minister for them who shall be heirs of salvation?" (Hebrews 1:13–14).

Angels, which are mentioned frequently in the Bible, are the same as the ministering spirits mentioned in Hebrews.

"Where wast thou when I laid the foundations of the earth? declare, if thou hast understanding. Who hath laid the measures thereof, if thou knowest? or who hath stretched the line upon it? Whereupon are the foundations thereof fastened? or who laid the corner stone thereof; When the morning stars sang together, and all the sons of God shouted for joy?" (Job 38:4–7).

These verses tell us that God clearly created seraphim, cherubim, archangels, and angels prior to creating the earth on which we now stand. The sons of God mentioned in Job 38:7 are the seraphim, cherubim, archangels, and angels mentioned above.

God is going to vividly show demon powers and all beings with a free will His attributes through the church. God will become a man in Jesus Christ and show His attributes to mankind, seraphim, cherubim, archangels, and angels. These attributes include power, humbleness, patience, kindness, goodness, forgiveness, gentleness, self-control, love, truth, purity, holiness, faithfulness, purpose, and that God wants a personal relationship with us.

God showed His power when He spoke into existence all created beings and things. God showed His humbleness when He left eternity to become a man. God showed His love when Hew endured great pain on the cross to purchase us back into His eternal kingdom.

The Creation of the Universe in which we live

The scientific theories proposed here come from a book authored by D. Russell Humpheys. His book, *Starlight in Time,* was published by Master Books.

Genesis 1 summary—The History of Creation

Day 1   Earth, space, time, light, and matter
Day 2   Atmosphere, waters, and firmament divided
Day 3   Vegetation
Day 4   Sun, moon, stars
Day 5   Sea creatures, birds
Day 6   Mankind, mammals
Day 7   God rested

Day One (Genesis 1:1–5)

"In the beginning God created the heavens and the earth. And the earth was formless and void, and darkness was on the face of the deep. And the spirit of God was moving on the face of the waters" (Genesis 1:1–2).

"For when they maintained this, it escapes their notice that by the word of God the heavens existed long ago and the earth was formed out of water and by water" (II Peter 3:5).

God first created a black hole of liquid water (the deep) by speaking it into existence out of nothing. The size of this black hole of water would be the size and volume of water necessary to hold the mass of the universe.

Because of the great concentration of matter, this ball of water is deep within a black hole. The earth at this point is merely a formless, undefined region of water at the center of the deep, empty of inhabitant or feature. The deep is rotating slowly, and there is no visible light at its surface.

Because the enormous mass of the whole universe is contained in a ball of (relatively) small size, the gravitational force on the deep is very strong—more than a million trillion g's. This force compresses the deep very rapidly toward the center, making it extremely hot and dense. The heat rips apart the water molecules, atoms, and even the nuclei into elementary particles.

"And God said, 'Let there be light'; and there was light" (Genesis 1:3).

Thermonuclear fusion reactions begin, forming heavier nuclei from lighter ones and liberating huge amounts of energy. As a consequence, an intense light illuminates the interior, breaking through to the surface and ending the darkness there.[46]

"And God saw that the light was good; and God separated the light from the darkness. And God called the light day, and the darkness He called night. And there was evening and there was morning, one day" (Genesis 1:4–5).

God has laid out human history into seven millennia, corresponding to the days of creation. On day one, God said, "Let there be light." This light is a picture of goodness and darkness is a picture of evil. When God speaks, He brings light and life to the creation.

God gave Eve to Adam. Adam and Eve had a choice to be faithful to God or rebel against God.

"Thou turnest man to destruction and sayest, Return ye children of men" (Psalm 90:3).

I believe God made the universe in seven literal days. I also believe each day in Genesis 1 is a prophecy of future events which will unfold from the creation of Adam and Eve and for the seven thousand years that follow.

After the creation of man early in the first millennium, Adam and Eve rebelled against God. Redemption is the heart of God's plan. God was not surprised by the fall of mankind and had purposes for it. A part of that plan was for free-will, created beings to know the consequences of rebellion.

> God turned man to destruction and calls us to return to Him. The *Encyclopedia of Jewish Religion 1986* states the belief that each day in the creation week represents 1,000 years to God (263).[47]

"But, beloved, be not ignorant of this one thing, that one day is with the Lord as a thousand years, and a thousand years as one day" (I Peter 3:8).

"For a thousand years in thy sight are but as yesterday when it is past, and as a watch in the night" (Psalm 90:4).

"And even in the beginning of the creation He makes mention of the sabbath. And God made in six days the works of His hands; and He finished them on the seventh day, and He rested the seventh day, and sanctified it. Consider, my children, what that signifies, He finished them in six days. The meaning of it is this; that in six thousand years the Lord God will bring all things to an end. For with Him one day is a thousand yeas; as himself testifieth, saying, Behold this day shall be as a thousand yeas. Therefore, children, in six days, that is in six thousand years, all things be accomplished. And what is that He saith, And He rested the seventh day: He meaneth this; that when His Son shall come, and abolish the season

---

46 D. Russesll Humphreys. *Starlight and Time, 32–33.*
47 J. R. Church. *Prophecy in the News,* January, 1995.

of the Wicked One, and judge the ungodly; and shall change the sun and the moon, and the stars; then He shall gloriously rest in that seventh day" (Barnabas 13:3–6).[48]

The book of Barnabas is not a book of the Bible; however, its authorship ranges from AD 300, possibly going back to the times of Christ. This is not to be considered inspired by God. These quotes from Barnabas are only included to show that many people believe there is prophecy in the creation account and not just an historical fact.

4000–2000 BC

It was two thousand years from Adam to Abraham; in this period of time occurred the fall of mankind, the building of the great pyramid in Giza, Noah's flood, and the tower of Babel.

2000 BC–AD 1

It was approximately two thousand years from Abraham to Christ. In this period of time were Abraham, Isaac, Jacob, and Joseph. The Hebrews were also enslaved in Egypt, and the deliverance of God was led by Moses. The period of the judges was followed by King Saul, King David, and King Solomon. The major Egyptian, Assyrian, Babylonian, Mede-Persian, Greek, and the beginning of the Roman Empires all occurred in this time period. The birth of Christ was approximately 3 BC.

AD 1–present

The last two thousand years included the life of Christ and the church age, as well as the dispersion and regathering of the Jews to Israel.

I believe the seventh millennium of mankind will be fulfilled by the second coming of Jesus Christ in what is called The Millennium.

Day Two (Genesis 1:6–7)

"And God said, 'Let there be a firmament in the midst of the waters, and let it divide the waters from the waters.' And God made the firmament, and divided the waters which were under the firmament from the waters which were above the firmament: and it was so" (Genesis 1:6–7).

"Which alone spreadeth out the heavens, and treadeth upon the waves of the sea" (Job 9:8).

"Who coverest thyself with light as with a garment: who stretchest out the heavens like a curtain" (Psalm 104:2).

"He hath made the earth by his power, he hath established the world by his wisdom, and hath stretched out the heavens by his discretion" (Jeremiah 10:12).

---

48   *The Lost Books of the Bible,* (Bell Publishing Company, 1979) 160–161.

God first made this black hole of water and separated and stretched it making this black hole of water into the time, space, matter, and the physical universe in which we live.

God stretched out all of the stars, planets, and galaxies faster than the speed of light, making the illusion of an old universe when it fact, it is just thousands of years old. During the first two days of the creation week, God changed the water into the elements listed on a standard periodic chart. This would include uranium, gold, silver, helium, etc.

"And God called the firmament Heaven. And the evening and the morning were the second day" (Genesis 1:8).

> These heavens are interstellar space. Since the sun has not yet been created, the Spirit of God continues to be the light source close to the rotating waters below, giving them a light and dark side. The expansion started at the beginning of this day will continue until at least the end of the fourth day.[49]

> As a prophecy of the future, after every day of the Creation Week except for Day Two, God said it was good. This means that God did not claim that the fall of mankind in the second day was good.[50]

However, the battle between the sons of light (followers of Christ) and the sons of darkness (anyone who doesn't follow Christ) is a spiritual truth in the first few verses of Genesis. You should want to be a Son of Light, which is a Son of God.

Day Three (Genesis 1:9–13)

"And God said, Let the waters under the heaven be gathered together unto one place, and let the dry land appear: and it was so" (Genesis 1:9).

Rapid radioactive decay occurs, possibly as a consequence of the rapid stretching of space. The resulting heating forms the earth's crust and makes it buoyant relative to the mantle rock below it, causing the crust to rise above the waters, thus gathering the waters into ocean basins. Dr. D. Russell Humphreys, Ph.D. hypothesizes that rapid volume cooling of molten rock deep within the earth also occurs, again as a result of the rapid expansion of space, solidifying the rock.

"And God called the dry land Earth; and the gathering together of the waters called he Seas: and God saw that it was good. And God said, "Let the earth bring forth grass, the herb yielding seed, and the fruit tree yielding fruit after his kind, whose seed is in itself, upon the earth": and it was so. And the earth brought forth grass, and herb yielding seed after his kind, and the tree yielding fruit, whose seed was in itself, after his kind: and God saw that it was good. And the evening and the morning were the third day" (Genesis 1:10–13).

---

49 D. Russell Humphreys. *Starlight and Time,* 34–36.
50 J. R. Church. *Prophecy in the News,* 8.

God makes plants on the newly formed land.

> The continuing expansion of space causes the waters above the heavens to reach the event horizon and pass beyond it. This causes the amount of matter within the event horizon to begin decreasing, which in turn causes the event horizon to being rapidly shrinking toward the earth. There are no stars yet, only clusters of hydrogen, helium, and other atoms left behind in the expanse by the rapid expansion.[51]

> In the Third Day of the Creation Week, vegetation was created and brought forth to fill the earth. During the third millennium of the world, mankindbegan to replenish the earth after the Flood and the Tower of Babel.[52]

Toward the beginning of the third millennium of mankind, God worked through Abraham, and a covenant with the Hebrews was made by God.

Day Four (Genesis 1:14–19)

"And God said, Let there be lights in the firmament of the heaven to divide the day from the night; and let them be for signs, and for seasons, and for days, and years. And let them be for lights in the firmament of the heaven to give light upon the earth: and it was so" (Genesis 1:14–15).

The shrinking event horizon reaches earth early on the morning of the fourth day. During this ordinary day as measured on earth, billions of years' worth of physical processes take place in the distant cosmos. In particular, gravity has time to make distant clusters of hydrogen, and helium atoms were compact.

"And God made two great lights; the greater light to rule the day, and the lesser light to rule the night: he made the stars also. And God set them in the firmament of the heaven to give light upon the earth,and to rule over the day and over the night, and to divide the light from the darkness: and God saw that it was good. And the evening and the morning were the fourth day" (Genesis 1:16–19).

> Early on the fourth morning, God coalesces the clusters of atoms into stars and thermonuclear fusion ignites in them. The newly-formed stars find themselves grouped together in galaxies and clusters of galaxies. As the fourth day proceeds on earth, the more distant stars age billions of years, while their lights also has the same billions of years to travel to the earth. While the light is on its way, space continues to expand, relativistically stretching out the light waves and shifting the wavelengths toward the rd side of the spectrum. Stars which are now farthest away have the greatest redshift, because the waves have been stretched the most. This progressive redshift is exactly what is observed.[53]

---

51   D. Russell Humphreys. *Starlight and Time*, 36–37.
52   J. R. Church. *Prophecy in the News*, 25.
53   D. Russell Humphreys. *Starlight and Time*, 37–38.

Basically I believe that what Dr. Russell Humphrey is saying is this: If the universe operates on earth central time, the earth is about 6,000 years old.[54]

> The fourth day of creation corresponds to the fourth millennium; Solomon's temple was built at the beginning of the fourth millennium, and all of the Old Testament Prophets after Samuel gave us the signs of the times. In the fourth day of the Creation Week, God gave two lights—the greater, our sun, and the lesser, our moon. The sun is a type and picture of Jesus Christ who was born at the end of the fourth millennium who is the greater light. The moon reflects the light of the sun as Christians should reflect the light of the Lord Jesus Christ.[55]

Day Five (Genesis 1:20–23)

> On day five of the Creation Week, God filled the air with birds and the seas with fish and told them to multiply. Christians are to be fishers of men, and the waters appear to be a picture of the Holy Spirit which indwelled the Church on the Feast of Pentecost. On the back of many cars is seen the fish symbol which has been a Christian symbol for 2,000 years.[56]

Day Six (Genesis 1:24–31)

> On day six of the Creation Week, God made the land animals and mammals and created mankind in His image. God said in both day five and day six to multiply, and since the birth of Christ, the population of mankind rose from well less than 200,000 million people in AD 30 to over 6 billion people today. The earth's population has grown thirty times in just the last 2,000 years. In the last 50 years, the earth's population has increased from 3 billion people to over 6 billion people.[57]

The Completed Universe (Genesis 1:31)

"And God saw every thing that he had made, and, behold, it was very good. And the evening and the morning were the sixth day" (Genesis 1:31).

> God stops the expansion before the evening of the sixth day.[58]

Day Seven (Genesis 2:1–3)

"Thus the heavens and the earth were finished, and all the host of them. And on the seventh day God ended his work which he had made; and he rested on the seventh day from all his work which he had

---

54   D. Russell Humphreys. *Starlight and Time,* 79.
55   J. R. Church. *Prophecy in the News,* 26.
56   J. R. Church. *Prophecy in the News,* 26.
57   J. R. Church. *Prophecy in the News,* 27.
58   D. Russell Humphreys. *Starlight and Time,* 38.

made. And God blessed the seventh day, and sanctified it: because that in it he had rested from all his work which God created and made" (Genesis 2:1–3).

On day seven of the creation week, God rested. God was not tired but was stating He was finished. This is a picture of the millennial rest and a picture of the millennium after the second coming of Christ.

A brief summary of the ages would include trials, failures, and successes of mankind. God works through His plan for the ages. God is always on plan A; there is no plan B.

The creation week itself is also a prophecy of the trials and failures of mankind.

In the first millennium of the creation, mankind's first failure was to disobey the commandment not to eat of the tree of the knowledge of good and evil. Adam and Eve failed this test, and mankind lost its innocence.

In the second millennium came Noah's flood. There was no written Bible, and man's thoughts were nothing but evil continuously. Mankind lived by its own evil conscience, and mankind failed again.

In the third millennium, Abraham was followed by Moses approximately 450 years later. During this time, the law was given to Moses. Almost all of mankind continually failed God. However, Abraham did believe God after many trials. Moses also obeyed God's voice. During this third millennium of mankind, the state of Israel was formed. The law was given, but Israel disobeyed God frequently.

At the beginning of the fourth millennium of mankind, the people of Israel demanded a king like the pagan nations of the world. God allowed Israel to have a king. Saul, David, and Solomon were the first three kings of Israel. Their history was marked with much military victory and by the building of the first temple in Jerusalem. However, under successive kings, Israel fell into deep sin. Toward the end of the fourth millennium of mankind, Jesus Christ was born.

Approximately twenty-seven years into the fifth millennium, Jesus began His ministry and was crucified approximately three and one-half years later. After His resurrection, the church age began. The church age runs through the fifth and sixth millennium of mankind. In the last two millennia, the gospel has been taken to the world.

At the end of the sixth millennium, the earth's population reached 6 billion people in October of 1999, and man developed the technology to destroy the planet. Christians have what is called the blessed hope, which is the resurrection of the saints.

Day One—Innocence—The Fall of Adam and Eve—4000–3000 BC
Day Two—Human Conscience—The Failure of Mankind and Noah's Flood—3000–2000 BC
Day Three—Human Government and the Law—Abraham—Moses—2000–1000 BC
Day Four—The Promise of the Messiah through the Prophets—1000–1 BC
Day Five—Grace and the Church Age—AD 1–1000
Day Six—Mankind Fills the Earth with Sin Again—AD 1000–2000
Day Seven—Millennial Rest—AD 2000–present

Over and over again throughout the Bible, numbers are used by God to emphasize a biblical truth. The Bible was written over a 1,400-year period of time. There was no manual on how to write the Bible, and yet numbers in the Bible have the same meaning throughout. This is just one of many reasons why I believe the Bible.

One—*Unity*—One God
Two—*Division*—Witness—Union
Three—*Resurrection*—Completeness
Four—*The Creation*—North, South, East, West
Five—*Grace*—God's Goodness
Six—*Sin*—Man—Antichrist—Mankind Created on the Sixth Day
Seven—*Rest*—Completion
Eight—*New Things*—Resurrection
Ten—*The Law*—The Ten Commandments
Twelve—*Governmental Perfection*—Twelve Disciples—Twelve Apostles—Twelve Tribes of Israel
Forty—*Trials*—Probation Period—Testing
Fifty—*Holy Spirit*—Pentecost
Sixty-Six—*Idol Worship*
One Hundred Twenty—*Divine Period of Probation*

Event	Day 1	Day 2	Day 3	Day 4	Day 5	Day 6	Day 7
God created	Earth Space Time Light Matter	Atmosphere Divided waters Firmament	Dry land Plants Vegetation	Sun Moon Stars	Sea Fowl Creatures	Land Animals Mankind	Rested
Prime colors	Ultraviolet	Blue	Green	Yellow	Orange	Red	White
Colors of the rainbow	Light Light and darkness	Water	Plants	Light	Cold-blooded animals	Warm-blooded animals	God Resurrection
Number	Unity	Division Divided the atmosphere and firmament	Resurrection Completeness Trinity	The creation North East South West	God's goodness	Sin Man Evil	Rest Completion
Major event in that millennium	Fall of Adam and Eve	Failure of mankind Noah's flood (water)	Human government The law Abraham's covenant It was good	The birth of Christ (The light of the world)	The church age (symbolized by the fish)	Mankind fills the earth (sin)	Second coming of Christ
Millennium	First 4000–3000 BC	Second 3000–2000 BC	Third 2000–1000 BC	Fourth 1000–1 BC	Fifth AD 1–1000	Sixth AD 1000–2000	Seventh AD 2000–3000

God has a purpose and plan for the ages. There is a timetable of events and progressive revelation throughout the ages. Throughout the ages God reveals His power, love, justice, nature, plans, and purposes.

Various Bible chronologies place the abrupt creation of Adam and Eve at approximately six thousand years ago. God has been unfolding His plans and purposes through the ages. God has dealt with mankind in different ways over the past six thousand years. Most Bible chronologists place Noah's flood 1,656 years after the creation of Adam.

4000 BC	Creation of Adam and Eve
2800–2200 BC	Great pyramid of Egypt (Giza)—possibly built by Enoch prior to the flood
2344 BC	Noah's flood–1,656 years after the creation of Adam
2200 BC	Tower of Babel, Egyptian civilizations (also called Sumer), possibly the great pyramid of Egypt (Giza)
1980 BC	Abraham
1930–1900 BC	Sodom and Gomorrah destroyed
1880–1800 BC	Isaac, Jacob, Joseph
1830–1400 BC	Hebrew slavery in Egypt
1460–1340 BC	Moses and the Exodus
1340–1050 BC	The Judges
1051–1011 BC	Saul rules over Israel
1011–971 BC	David rules over Judah and then over all Israel
971–931 BC	Solomon rules over Israel
	Israel and Judah split after the rule of Solomon
725 BC	Assyrians conquer Egypt and the northern ten tribes of Israel
575 BC	Babylonians conquer Jerusalem and the southern two tribes of Israel (Judah and Benjamin)
505 BC	Medo-Persians conquer the Babylonians
The Jews are allowed to return to Jerusalem and rebuild after their seventy-year captivity	
321 BC	Greece conquers the Medo-Persians
63 BC–300 AD	Roman Empire

Genesis 1:28–Dominion Given to Man–4000 BC

"And God blessed them, and God said unto them, Be fruitful, and multiply, and replenish the earth, and subdue it: and have dominion over the fish of the sea, and over the fowl of the air, and over every living thing that moveth upon the earth" (Genesis 1:28).

God gave dominion over the earth to mankind. Fallen man could not blend in with animals if he tried. God gave us dominion, and with our fallen nature, we will destroy it.

"These are the generations of the heavens and of the earth when they were created, in the day that the LORD God made the earth and the heavens, And every plant of the field before it was in the earth, and every herb of the field before it grew: for the LORD God had not caused it to rain upon the earth, and there was not a man to till the ground. But there went up a mist from the earth, and watered the whole face of the ground" (Genesis 2;4–6).

Many creationists believe that there was a water canopy around the earth prior to Noah's flood. This would increase oxygen supply to the body and keep away harmful rays from the sun. Many believe this explains the extended ages of people listed in Genesis 1–6.

Genesis 2:15–17—Tree of Knowledge of Good and Evil

"And the LORD God took the man, and put him into the garden of Eden to dress it and to keep it. And the LORD God commanded the man, saying, 'Of every tree of the garden thou mayest freely eat: But of the tree of the knowledge of good and evil, thou shalt not eat of it: for in the day that thou eatest thereof thou shalt surely die'" (Genesis 2:15–17).

God gave Adam and Eve only one rule. To disobey God would be rebellion. They chose rebellion, which is the cause of all of our problems.

Genesis 2:20–25—Making of Eve

"And Adam gave names to all cattle, and to the fowl of the air, and to every beast of the field; but for Adam there was not found an help meet for him. And the LORD God caused a deep sleep to fall upon Adam, and he slept: and he took one of his ribs, and closed up the flesh instead thereof; And the rib, which the LORD God had taken from man, made he a woman, and brought her unto the man. And Adam said, 'This is now bone of my bones, and flesh of my flesh: she shall be called Woman, because she was taken out of Man.' Therefore shall a man leave his father and his mother, and shall cleave unto his wife: and they shall be one flesh. And they were both naked, and man and his wife, and were not ashamed" (Genesis 2:20–25).

Adam did not have to learn facts and information over a long period of time. Like placing a computer disc filled with information, God abruptly places a great amount of information and knowledge into Adam's brain. Adam did not just pull names out of the air when he named the animals. The names for the animals on earth were foreordained by God. A person currently uses about 10 percent of his brain. I believe in the beginning, mankind used a much higher percentage of his brain.

God made Eve from the rib of Adam. God did not make Eve from the heel of man but from the rib. A man is to protect his wife.

Genesis 3:1–7—Serpent Deceives Eve

"Now the serpent was more subtil than any beast of the field which the LORD God had made. And he said unto the woman, 'Yea, hath God said, Ye shall not eat of every tree of the garden?' And the woman said unto the serpent, 'We may eat of the fruit of the trees of the garden: But of the fruit of the tree which is in the midst of the garden, God hath said, "Ye shall not eat of it, neither shall ye touch it, lest ye die."' And the serpent said unto the woman, 'Ye shall not surely die: For God doth know that in the day ye eat thereof, then your eyes shall be opened, and ye shall be as gods, knowing good and evil.' And when the woman saw that the tree was good for food, and that is was pleasant to the eyes, and a tree to be desired to make one wise, she took of the fruit thereof, and did eat, and gave also unto her husband with her; and he did eat. And the eyes of them both were opened, and they knew that they were naked; and they sewed fig leaves together, and made themselves aprons" (Genesis 3:1–7)

The serpent used the lust of the flesh (good for food), the lust of the eyes (pleasant to the eyes), and the pride of life (desire to make one wise) to deceive Eve. Adam willingly went into rebellion.

Genesis 3:13–15—Prophecy of Jesus

"And the LORD God said unto the woman, 'What is this that thou hast done?' And the woman said, 'The serpent beguiled me, and I did eat.' And the LORD God said unto the serpent, 'Because thou hast done this, thou art cursed above all cattle, and above every beast of the field; upon thy belly shalt thou go, and dust shalt thou eat all the days of thy life: And I will put enmity between thee and the woman, and between thy seed and her seed; it shall bruise thy head, and thou shalt bruise his heel'" (Genesis 3:13–15).

This is the first of over 300 prophecies of the first coming of Jesus Christ. Enmity here means that God is instituting a bitter battle between those who will be saved and the powers of hell on this earth.

Subject	Seed of a woman	**Prophet**	Moses	**Year Prophesied**	1400 BC
Old Testament Prophesy	Genesis 3:15 "And I will put enmity between thee and the woman, and between thy seed and her seed; it shall bruise thy head, and thou shalt bruise his heel."				
New Testament Fulfillment	Galatians 4:4 "But when the fulness of the time was come, God sent forth his Son, made of a woman, made under the law."				

Genesis 4:8–10—Cain kills Abel—3950 BC

"And Cain talked with Abel his brother: and it came to pass, when they were in the field, that Cain rose up against Abel his brother, and slew him. And the LORD said unto Cain, 'Where is Abel thy brother?' And he said, 'I know not: Am I my brother's keeper?' And he said, 'What hast thou done? the voice of thy brother's blood crieth unto me from the ground'" (Genesis 4:8–10).

This is the first murder of mankind. In the last 100 years alone, it is estimated that 200 million men and women have been killed by wars and murders. Probably twice that number or more have been violently killed in the last six thousand years.

"So ye shall not pollute the land wherein ye are: for blood it defileth the land: and the land cannot be cleansed of the blood that is shed therein, but by the blood of him that shed it" (Numbers 35:33).

Again, the purpose of the first and second coming of Jesus Christ is to stop the shedding of blood, rebellions, and cycles of wars throughout all eternity. Abel's blood cried out from the ground for justice. Living by Christian principles and the indwelling of the Holy Spirit gives us the power to forgive others.

The Puzzle of the Advanced Ancient Cultures

J. R. Church wrote the following:

> Writing about the antediluvian children of Seth, Flavius Josephus notes: "All these proved to be of good dispositions. They also inhabited the same country without dissentions, and in happy condition, without any misfortunes falling upon them, till they died. They also were the inventors of that peculiar sort of wisdom which is concerned with the heavenly bodies and their order. And that their inventions might not be lost before they were sufficiently known, upon Adam's prediction that the world was to be destroyed at one time by the force of fire, and at another time by the violence and quantity of water, they made two pillars; the one of brick, the other of stone: they inscribed their discoveries on them both, that in case the pillar of brick should be destroyed by the flood, the pillar of stone might remain, and exhibit those discoveries to mankind; and also inform them that there was another pillar of brick erected by them. Now this remains in the land of Siriad to this day" (Antiquities I, II, 3).
>
> Here we find that the ancient inventors of astronomy built two huge monuments prior to the Flood. They did this for the specific purpose of sending their knowledge forward in time, through the Flood and fire to come. Josephus calls Egypt by its Greek name, "Siriad." Clearly, he believed that the Great Pyramid of Giza had been built before the Flood.

It survived—but what of the other judgment foretold by Adam? It is the fire yet to come. What does the Bible tell us about it and the nature of the judgments that surround it? Certainly, the destructive force of divine fire is a theme found in various religions around the world. If Josephus' account is to be taken seriously, the Jews attributed the origins of this belief to Adam himself. The Flood came, destroying the ancient brick monument designed to withstand fire. It left the stone monument, whose complex mathematics are breathtaking in their description of the earth and solar system.

To this day, no one has devised a method whereby the monumental pyramid might be built using today's technology. Thought it is not generally known, the Great Pyramid is literally built to optical tolerances. When the Arabs breached its outer wall in the eighth century, they discovered salt deposits in its inner chambers, suggesting that it had once been immersed under the ocean for a time.

Even today, salt crystals can be found in the Queen's Chamber. Josephus is not the only scholar who believes that the antediluvian astronomers built the pyramids as an exhibit of their knowledge. Growing numbers of investigators say that its mathematical perfection suggests a higher form of knowledge. It is a sort of time capsule, waiting for human understanding to redevelop to the extent that its principles can once again be understood.

Also, according to Josephus, it was built to inform mankind that there had been "another pillar of brick erected by them." So far, that bit of knowledge remains just a curious footnote. No doubt, there are still many astonishing discoveries with a pyramid, awaiting their turn for disclosure at the proper time.

The judgment by an overwhelming flood has come and gone, dramatically accomplishing its work of judgment. But the ancients, heeding Adam's prophetic warning, also expected a future fiery judgment.[59]

Noah's Flood and Noah's Ark as a Type of Christ

Genesis 4:22—Years of Rebellion—1,656 years

"And Zillah, she also bore Tubalcain, an instructor of every artificer in brass and iron: and the sister of Tubalcain was Naamah" (Genesis 4:22).

This is the first mention of brass and iron in the Bible. Tubalcain was one of the last generations mentioned before the flood. They took their knowledge and transformed iron into swords and devices of murder. The earth was filled with violence, and God destroyed the earth with the great flood, leaving only Noah, his three sons, and all their wives.

---

59   J. R. Church. *Prophecy in the News*, 3, 10.

Genesis 6:3–5—Evil Thoughts Continually

"And the LORD said, 'My spirit shall not always strive with man, for that he also is flesh: yet his days shall be an hundred and twenty years.' There were giants in the earth in those days; and also after that, when the sons of God came in unto the daughters of men, and they bare children to them, the same became mighty men which were of old, men of renown. And GOD saw that the wickedness of man was great in the earth, and that every imagination of the thoughts of his heart was only evil continually" (Genesis 6:3–5).

In reality, there are billions of people on the earth right now, and the imaginations of many are only evil continually.

Genesis 7:11–13—The Flood—2344 BC

"In the six hundredth year of Noah's life, in the second month, the seventeenth day of the month, the same day were all the fountains of the great deep broken up, and the windows of heaven were opened. And the rain was upon the earth forty days and forty nights. In the selfsame day entered Noah, and Shem, and Ham, and Japheth, the sons of Noah, and Noah's wife, and the three wives of his sons with them, into the ark" (Genesis 7:11–13).

When Noah was 600 years old, God caused the flood. The number six is always associated with mankind and death.

"And they that went in, went in male and female of all flesh, as God had commanded him: and the LORD shut hum in" (Genesis 7:16).

"Which sometime were disobedient, when once the longsuffering of God waited in the days of Noah, while the ark was a preparing, wherein few, that is, eight souls were saved by water. The like figure whereunto even baptism doth also now save us (not the putting away of the filth of the flesh, but the answer of a good conscience toward God,) by the resurrection of Jesus Christ" (I Peter 3:20–21).

Noah's ark literally existed. Noah's ark is a picture or a type of Christ. For instance, there was only one door to the ark by which to enter. There is only one way to salvation, and that is through the person of Jesus Christ. Jesus, speaking about Himself, said that He was the door (John 10:9). Elsewhere, Jesus, speaking of Himself, said He is the way. Just as with the ark, if you are found in Christ at the time of your physical death, you will be saved from destruction as those who entered the ark. Also as the ark rose above the earth, after six months, it came back down to the earth. At the resurrection of the saints, believers will leave the earth and return to the earth at a later time.

Water baptism is a picture of being raised from the dead. There was safety inside the ark, even though destruction was all around the earth. God provided for all in the ark, even if it was a bumpy ride. A book by the name of *Noah's Ark: A Feasibility Study* was written by John Woodmorappe. This book is over three hundred pages long and outlines how Noah's ark could have contained all the animals. The story of Noah kept me from believing the Bible for years. Don't let this happen to you. Fitting the animals in the ark is feasible. The jump from non-life to life without God is what is not feasible. Furthermore, the historical account of Noah's flood was written by Moses approximately 1,400 years before Christ. Moses did not understand that the ark would be a type of Christ. This is one more reason I believe the Bible.

Throughout ancient civilizations around the world, flood accounts similar to Noah's flood are frequently found. They all have the common theme of God destroying the world with water because of the sin of mankind. The reason for all of these flood accounts with similar themes is because the flood actually happened.

Genesis 9:1—Fill the Earth

"And God blessed Noah and his sons, and said unto them, 'Be fruitful, and multiply, and replenish the earth'" (Genesis 9:1).

"And Noah awoke from his wine, and knew what his younger son [Ham] had done unto him. And he said, 'Cursed be Canaan; a servant of servants shall he be unto his brethren.' And he said, 'Blessed be the LORD God of Shem; and Canaan shall be his servant. God shall enlarge Japheth, and he shall dwell in the tents of Shem; and Canaan shall be his servant.' Noah lived after the flood three hundred and fifty years. And all the days of Noah were nine hundred and fifty years: and he died" (Genesis 9:24–29).

> Genesis 9:25–27 shows the tripartite nature of mankind. Every person has a physical, mental, and spiritual component. One of these components tends to dominate the other two. People dominated by the physical would be athletes, laborers, machinists, soldiers, etc. People dominated by the intellectual things of life would be scientists, teachers, accountants, and the like. People motivated by spiritual things would be pastors or others who think about eternal things.
>
> Ham was to be dominated by the physical, Shem by the spiritual, and Japheth by the intellectual. Ham was addressed through Canaan, who was prophesied to be a servant of Shem and Japheth, not a slave but a helper. Jesus said in Luke 22:26, "The greatest in the Kingdom of God is servant of all." A descendant of Ham, Nimrod, built the Tower of Babel, which was an engineering feat.
>
> Hamitic Peoples: Sumeria, Phoenicia, Egyptian, Shiner (probably equivalent to Sumer), Nimrod and the Tower of Babel, Cush, Egypt, Phut, Ethiopia, Libya, Somalia, Canaanites, probably China and American Indians.
>
> Japhetic Peoples: Greece, Germany, England, most of Europe, Gomer, Magog, Madai, Javan, Tubal, Indo European, Crimea, Russia, Togarmar, and Tarshish (possibly Spain).
>
> Semitic Peoples: Israel and Arabic Peoples through Abraham and Ishmael, Medes, and Assyrians.[60]

---

60   Henry M. Morris. *God and the Nations*, 49–50, 53–59.

Shem was to be a blessing, and the genealogy of Jesus Christ comes through Shem. Jesus Christ blessed all the peoples of all the nations in His birth, life, death, burial, and resurrection. Shem was alive approximately 2300 years before the birth of Christ. Prophesying through Noah, God said He would enlarge Japheth. Most of the world's wealth is in lands occupied by the descendants of Japheth. His descendants became the colonial powers of Europe, and the first universities in the world were originated in Europe and North America.

The Tower of Babel

Genesis 11:4–9—Tower of Babel—2250 BC

"And they said, 'Go to, let us build us a city and a tower, whose top may reach unto heaven; and let us make us a name, lest we be scattered abroad upon the face of the whole earth.' And the LORD came down to see the city and the tower, which the children of men builded. And the LORD said, 'Behold, the people is one, and they have all one language; and this they begin to do: and now nothing will be restrained from them, which they have imagined to do. Go to, let us go down, and there confound their language, that they may not understand one another's speech.' So the LORD scattered them abroad from thence upon the face of all the earth: and they left off to build the city. Therefore is the name of it called Babel; because the LORD did there confound the language of all the earth: and from thence did the LORD scatter them abroad upon the face of all the earth" (Genesis 11:4–9).

Prior to the Tower of Babel, there was only one language. After the confusion of languages, there were probably seventy languages that have evolved into close to seven thousand languages now on the earth.

Acts 17:25–27—Purpose of the Nations, that Some would Seek and Follow God

"Neither is worshipped with men's hands, as though he needed any thing, seeing he giveth to all life, and breath, and all things; And hath made of one blood all nations of men for to dwell on all the face of the earth, and hath determined the times before appointed, and the bounds of their habitation; That they should seek the Lord, if haply they might feel after him, and find him, though he be not far from every one of us" (Acts 17:25–27).

The purpose of languages and nations is that some would seek and follow God. Most rations will not follow God. A one-world economy and one-world government will again be confused by God in the near future.

The Puzzle of Ancient Man

As remains of ancient cultures around the world are examined and carefully studied, a recurring theme or pattern emerges. Cultures appear to emerge in a high state of technical development and then decline after a period of time. Also associated with ancient cultures are concepts of astrology and an interest in astronomical measurement and the construction of large monuments for astronomical measurement.

As is the case for the Incas, cultures around the world appear to have originated at about the same time of roughly five thousand years ago (3000 BC). They appear with an already developed high level of technical development. Pyramids, for example, are not unique to Egypt, but a pyramid belt is found around the world, including the Americas and Asia. How are these things to be explained?

The puzzle is that there is little, if any, evidence to support the idea that these ancient cultures experimented with engineering design. There is a lack of evidence pointing to a step-by-step development of the technology possessed by ancient cultures. Instead, each culture appears full-blown right from its beginning. Because of this lack of evidence for a trial-and-error developmental sequence, in the non-Biblical view it is assumed that an earlier society must have made the developments in a slow gradual evolutionary manner and it was then wiped out somehow by a catastrophe which destroyed any evidence of those developments.[61]

Chapter 10 of Genesis provides a detailed account of the scattering out from Babel, and of the nations which eventually developed from those scattered. Some scattered to the area which became known as Egypt. Although they scattered as did other groups, they carried with them the pagan and counterfeit religion of Nimrod. The early Egyptians immediately began to build pyramids. As is well known, one of the big puzzles for secular (non-Biblical) archaeology has been the origin of the Egyptian pyramids. They are technically sophisticated structures. Yet no evidence has been discovered of experimentation leading up to pyramid building.[62]

There seems to be no evidence to show how the technology needed for pyramid building was acquired or developed. How did the required technology arise? The first and earliest pyramids are the best. Later ones were inferior copies. Quality continued to decline until pyramids eventually were no longer built.

The pyramid age had come to an end, having lasted for a little more than a century. Pyramids were still being erected for about a thousand years, but they rapidly became smaller and shoddier, and it is quite clear that with the third Giza pyramid the zest had gone out of pyramid building forever.[63]

The early pyramids were of exceedingly high quality both mathematically and architecturally. Even today with our supposedly high modern technology, we do not know or understand how the pyramids were built. There has been seemingly no end of ideas and speculations as to how the pyramids were built, but no one really knows for certain.

61   Donald E. Chittick. *The Puzzle of Ancient Man,* 11–12.
62   Donald E. Chittick. *The Puzzle of Ancient Man,* 77–78.
63   Graham Hancock. *Fingerprints of the Gods* (New York: Crown Trade Paperback, 1995) 135–136.

Those who have studied the pyramids also note that they were very precisely aligned with astronomical objects. The founders would have retained from Babel much of its culture, including its technology. Thus there was no need to experiment and develop technology used for building pyramids. When Scripture is taken seriously, as giving an actual and true account of history, the puzzle of sudden origin of Egyptian pyramids vanishes. Archaeological reality is seen to be in agreement with the Bible.[64]

Great knowledge would have transferred from pre-flood days to the days after the flood. Pre-flood mankind lived very long lives and would have been unbelievably intelligent. This knowledge would pass from Noah and his sons to the new, post-flood world. This explains the highly developed Egyptian Empire. The Egyptian Empire was more scientifically sophisticated than were the Israeli, Assyrian, Babylonian, Persian, Greek, and Roman Empires that succeeded them.

The reason knowledge would have been so advanced in pre-flood times is because of the extended ages listed in the Bible. It sounds as if quite possibly there was a water canopy around the earth, which explains the greatly lengthened ages of pre-flood mankind.

The *Houston Chronicle* ran a lengthy article titled "Battle of Stonehenge." According to the author, "even in the academic world, scholars still cannot agree on how—or why—Bronze Age man built a meticulous network of earthen dikes and 50-ton rocks. Was Stonehenge an early fortress? A temple? Given that some of the stones cast specific shadows at daybreak on the summer and winter solstices, many think it was a giant calendar."[65]

Creationists have the answer as to how Stonehenge was built. Pre-flood technology was transferred to post-flood times. Stonehenge was built within 500 years after the flood and probably within 400 years of the Tower of Babel.

The Seven Wonders of the Ancient World and Other Great World Empires and Monuments

1. Pyramids of Egypt: ~2800–2100 BC
2. Hanging Gardens in Babylon: ~600 BC
3. Temple of Diana in Ephesus: ~550 BC
4. Statue of Jupiter Olympus: ~425 BC
5. The Mausoleum: ~350 BC
6. The Colossus at Rhodes: ~300 BC
7. Pharos at Alexandria: ~275 BC

Only the great pyramids in Egypt are still standing today, and they are the oldest of the Seven Wonders of the Ancient World. All of the Seven Wonders of the Ancient World are over two thousand years old. All of the great world empires have been in the last four thousand years. The above civilizations seemed to be more advanced than those civilizations from AD 300–1500.

---

64   Donald E. Chittick. *The Puzzle of Ancient Man,* 80.
65   Carl Honore. "Battle of Stonehenge." *Houston Chronicle,* January 27, 2002.

The reason I put the Seven Wonders of the World in this book is to point out the sophistication of ancient empires. Three thousand years ago, David wrote that the average life span was seventy years. One thousand years ago, it was close to half of that number while mankind was in the middle of the Dark Ages.

God reveals the secret things. The great scientific advances we have made in the past 100 years have helped the spreading of the gospel. The purpose of phones is for believers in Christ to pick them up and invite their friends and co-workers to church.

2200–700 BC	Egyptian Empire
1800 BC	Stonehenge—England
1500–1050 BC	Shang Dynasty—China
1200–300 BC	Olmec—Now Mexico
770 BC	Zhou Dynasty—China
750–300 BC	Greece
600–BC–AD 500	Various Indian Empires
500 BC	City of Carthage
325 BC	Maurya Empire—India
200 BC	Great Wall in China
500 BC–AD 400	Roman Empire
90 BC–AD 18	Parthian Empire—India
AD 300–900	The Mayans—Yucatan Peninsula
375	Ming Dynasty—China
AD 630–present	Various Islamic Empires
AD 900–1300	Kings started appearing in Europe
AD 1095–1200	The Crusades
AD 1400–1540	Inca Empire—Andes and Aztec Empires in South America
AD 1796–1815	Napoleonic France

The Lives of Abraham, Sarah, Isaac, and Jacob—1980–1800 BC

James 2:23—Abraham Called the Friend of God

"And the scripture was fulfilled which saith, Abraham believed God, and it was imputed unto him for righteousness: and he was called the Friend of God" (James 2:23).

Abraham is the only person in the Bible called the friend of God.

Genesis 12:1–3—The Promise of Abram

"Now the LORD had said unto Abram, Get thee out of thy country, and from thy kindred, and from thy father's house, unto a land that I will shew thee: And I will make of thee a great nation, and I will bless thee, and make thy name great; and thou shalt be a blessing: And I will bless them that bless thee, and curse him that curseth thee: and in thee shall all families of the earth be blessed" (Genesis 12:1–3).

Here Abram is told by God to leave his country; God tells Abram that he would be given a promised land and made a great nation. Furthermore, God would bless the nations that blessed Abram and curse the nations that cursed Abram's descendents—this includes both literal descendents and spiritual descendents of Abram. All the nations of the earth will ultimately be blessed by the nation of Israel.

Subject	Seed of Abraham	**Prophet**	Moses	**Year Prophesied**	1400 BC
Old Testament Prophesy	Genesis 12:3 "And I will bless them that bless thee, and curse him that curseth thee: and in thee shall all families of the earth be blessed."				
New Testament Fulfillment	Matthew 1:1 "The book of the generation of Jesus Christ, the Son of David, the son of Abraham."				

Genesis 15:12–13—God's Covenant with Abram

"And when the sun was going down, a deep sleep fell upon Abram; and, lo, an horror of great darkness fell upon him. And he said unto Abram, Know of a surety that thy seed shall be a stranger in a land that is not theirs, and shall serve them; and they shall afflict them four hundred years" (Genesis 15:12–13).

God put Abram to sleep. This signifies that in covenants, in reality, God does all the work. God has to save us from our sins; we cannot save ourselves. This is also a prophecy of Hebrew slavery in Egypt to his descendants.

Genesis 15:17–18—God's Covenant with Abram

"And it came to pass, that, when the sun went down, and it was dark, behold a smoking furnace, and a burning lamp that passed between those pieces. In the same day the LORD made a covenant with Abram, saying, Unto thy seed have I given this land, from the river of Egypt unto the great river, the river Euphrates" (Genesis 15:17–18).

A covenant is a contract, testament, or agreement that is either between God and man or between two people. When God makes a covenant, He always performs what He promises. Covenants are described in the Bible as cutting of the flesh and passing between the pieces in a confederation or league with the other party.

The word *covenant* is used over 220 times in the Bible. When a covenant is pledged in blood, it is called a *blood covenant*. Moses gave us the Law, and Jesus gave us grace and truth.

The Old Testament is the old covenant law, and the New Testament is a covenant of grace known as the New Covenant. When God makes a covenant, it is eternal. God will keep His side of a covenant in spite of the fact that man cannot keep his side of any agreement with God because man has a sinful nature from the fall of Adam and Eve.

In the New Testament, Jesus' blood is the New Covenant sacrifice, and He is the New Covenant Himself. This is God's agreement—that God in the flesh, Jesus Christ, will pay the penalty for our sins. We are required to place the salvation of our souls by grace and faith in the finished work that Jesus Christ did on the cross approximately 1970 years ago.

The land that Israel will eventually occupy will be from Egypt to the Euphrates River in Iraq and Jordan, as well as parts of Syria.

Genesis 16:10–12—Abram, Hagar, Ishmael, and their Descendants

"And the angel of the LORD said unto her, 'I will multiply thy seed exceedingly, that it shall not be numbered for multitude.' And the angel of the LORD said unto her, 'Behold, thou art with child, and shalt bear a son, and shalt call his name Ishmael; because the LORD hath heard thy affliction. And he will be a wild man; his hand will be against every man, and every man's hand against him; and he shall dwell in the presence of all his brethren" (Genesis 16:10–12).

Sarah was unable to bear children. Neither she nor Abraham would believe God's promises that Sarah would bear Abraham a son. Abraham took Hagar for a handmaiden, and they had a child named Ishmael. Ishmael was not the child that God promised. In Genesis 16:12, the Bible states that the descendents of Ishmael would be like a wild man and that his descendents would be against every man. Mohammed, who started the religion of Islam, is a descendent of Ishmael. Currently Islam is at war against the Hindus in India, the Christians and animists in Africa, the secular humanists in Europe, and the Christians in the USA, fulfilling this prophecy.

Numerous wars between Islamic countries have also taken place in the last fifty years, killing millions of people. Iraq was at war with Iran in the 1980s. Iraq invaded Kuwait in the early 1990s, starting the Gulf war. Islam has been at war with Israel with major conflicts in 1948, 1956, 1967, 1973, and 1982, followed by a state of war that has been in effect since the mid-1990s.

Genesis 19:23–25—God Destroys Sodom and Gomorrah—1900 BC

"The sun was risen upon the earth when Lot entered into Zoar. Then the LORD rained upon Sodom and upon Gomorrah brimstone and fire from the LORD out of heaven; And he overthrew those cities, and all the plain, and all the inhabitants of the cities, and that which grew upon the ground" (Genesis 19:23–25).

Ezekiel 16:49–50—Why God Destroyed Sodom and Gomorrah

"Beheld, this was the iniquity of thy sister Sodom, pride, fulness of bread, and abundance of idleness was in her and in her daughters, neither did she strengthen the hand of the poor and needy. And they were haughty, and committed abomination before me: therefore I took them away as I saw good" (Ezekiel 16:49–50).

The Bible defines itself. The Bible tells us that Sodom was destroyed because of sin, homosexuality, pride, gluttony, idle time (which leads to drunkenness and sexual sins), and the fact that the people of Sodom did not help the poor and needy. This sounds like many of the major cities in the USA today.

Genesis 21:1–2—The Birth of Isaac

"And the LORD visited Sarah as he had said, and the LORD did unto Sarah as he had spoken. For Sarah conceived, and bare Abraham a son in his old age, at the set time of which God had spoken to him" (Genesis 21:1–2).

Subject	Seed of Isaac	**Prophet**	Moses	**Year Prophesied**	1400 BC
Old Testament Prophesy	Genesis 17:19 "And God said, 'Sarah thy wife shall bear thee a son indeed; and thou shalt call his name Isaac: and I will establish my covenant with him for an everlasting covenant, and with his seed after him.'"				
New Testament Fulfillment	Luke 3:34 "Which was the son of Jacob, which was the son of Isaac, which was the son of Abraham, which was the son of Thara, which was the son of Nachor."				

God predestined the time of Isaac's birth and all of its blessings.

Genesis 22:1–2, 6–12—The Faith of Abraham Confirmed

"And it came to pass after these things, that God did tempt Abraham, and said unto him, 'Abraham:' and he said, 'Behold, here I am.' And he said, 'Take now thy son, thine only son Isaac, whom thou lovest, and get thee into the land of Moriah; and offer him there for a burnt offering upon one of the mountains which I will tell thee of' …. And Abraham took the wood of the burnt offering, and laid it upon Isaac his son; and he took the fire in his hand, and a knife; and they went both of them together. And Isaac spake unto Abraham his father, and said, 'My father:' and he said, 'Here am I, my son.' And he said, 'Behold the fire and the wood: but where is the lamb for a burnt offering?' And Abraham said, 'My son, God will provide himself a lamb for a burnt offering:' so they went both of them together. And they came to the place which God had told him of; and Abraham built an altar there, and laid the wood in order, and bound Isaac his son, and laid him on the altar upon the wood. And Abraham stretched forth his hand, and took the knife to slay his son. And the angel of the LORD called unto him out of heaven, and said, 'Abraham, Abraham': and he said, 'Here am I.' And he said, 'Lay not thine hand upon the lad, neither do thou any thing unto him: for now I know that thou fearest God, seeing thou hast not withheld thy son, thine only son from me'" (Genesis 22:1–2, 6–12).

Moriah is the location of the temple mount in Jerusalem. This is where Solomon's first temple was located, as well as Herod's temple. It is the same general location of the crucifixion of Jesus Christ. The Islamic dome of the rock could be in the exact location that Abraham was stopped from offering up Isaac as a sacrifice. Here Abraham is a picture, type, and shadow of God the Father, and Isaac, the sacrifice, was a picture of Christ. God stopped Abraham from sacrificing his son; however, God did not stop the crucifixion of His Son, Jesus Christ.

This is the same location that David bought the threshingfloor in Jerusalem.

II Samuel 24:24–25—The Purchase of the Threshingfloor

"And the king said unto Araunah, 'Nay; but I will surely buy it of thee at a price: neither will I offer burnt offerings unto the LORD my God of that which doth cost me nothing.' So David bought the threshingfloor and the oxen for fifty shekels of silver. And David built there an altar unto the LORD, and offered burnt offerings and peace offerings. So the LORD was intreated for the land, and the plague was stayed from Israel" (II Samuel 24:24–25).

It is fitting to be called the threshingfloor. In Zechariah 12:2, God says He will make Jerusalem a burdensome stone to the nations that gather against Jerusalem and cut them to pieces. This is what is happening right now.

Isaac is the father of Jacob, who fathered the twelve tribes of Israel.

Genesis 25:23–24—The Offspring of Isaac—Jacob and Esau

"And the LORD said unto her, 'Two nations are in thy womb, and two manner of people shall be separated from thy bowels; and the one people shall be stronger than the other people; and the elder shall serve the younger.' And when her days to be delivered were fulfilled, behold, there were twins in her womb" (Genesis 25:23–24).

Isaac had two sons, Jacob and Esau. The custom is for the firstborn to receive a greater blessing. However, in the Bible, it is almost always the other way around. The older is frequently not the son of promise. The Arabs come from both Ishmael and Esau, because Esau's descendants intermarried with the descendants of Ishmael (Genesis 28:9).

   a. Cain, the older, killed Abel.
   b. Ishmael was older than Isaac, but Isaac was the son of promise.
   c. Esau, the older, sold his birthright to Jacob, the younger.
   d. In the parable of the prodigal son, the younger, rebellious son is given a second great blessing.
   e. In this earth, first you have a physical birth, and when you get saved, you receive a spirit gift from heaven—that being the Holy Spirit from the throne of God.

   The Jews, in contrast (isolated in Egypt for 400 years and brought as an identifiable ethnic group into the promised land), are the descendants of Abraham through his son Isaac and grandson Jacob, whose name God changed to Israel. The promise of the land and of the Messiah was renewed by God to Isaac: "Unto thee, and unto thy seed, I will give all these countries … in thy seed shall all the nations of the earth be blessed" (Genesis 26:3–4). Also, to Jacob (Israel) God said, "the land whereon thou liest, to thee will I give it, and to thy seed ... and in thy seed shall all the families of the earth be blessed" (Genesis 28:13–14).[66]

When a person lives by faith, they are blessed. God will and has blessed the earth through the descendents of Abraham, Isaac, and Jacob. The genealogy of Jesus Christ came through these men.

Subject	Seed of Jacob	**Prophet**	Moses	**Year Prophesied**	1400 BC
Old Testament Prophesy	Numbers 24:17 "I shall see him, but not now: I shall behold him, but not nigh: there shall come a Star out of Jacob, and a Sceptre shall rise out of Israel, and shall smite the corners of Moab, and destroy all the children of Sheth."				
New Testament Fulfillment	Matthew 1:2 "Abraham begat Isaac; and Isaac begat Jacob; and Jacob begat Judas and his brethren."				

The Life of Joseph

Genesis 37:6–8—Joseph Dreams of Greatness—1800 BC

"And he said unto them, 'Hear, I pray you, this dream which I have dreamed: For, behold, we were binding sheaves in the field, and, lo, my sheaf arose, and also stood upright; and, behold, your sheaves stood round about, and made obeisance to my sheaf.' And his brethren said to him, 'Shalt thou indeed reign over us? or shalt thou indeed have dominion over us?' And they hated him yet the more for his dreams, and for his words" (Genesis 27:6–8).

Genesis 37:18–20, 24, 27–28—Joseph is Sold into Egyptian Slavery

"And when they saw him afar off, even before he came near unto them, they conspired against him to slay him. And they said one to another, 'Behold, this dreamer cometh. Come now therefore, and let us slay him, and cast him into some pit, and we will say, Some evil beast hath devoured him: and we shall see what will become of his dreams' .... And they took him, and cast him into a pit: and the pit was empty, there was no water in it .... 'Come, and let us sell him to the Ishmeelites, and let not our hand be upon him; for he is our brother and our flesh.' And his brethren were content. Then there passed by Midianites merchantmen; and they drew and lifted up Joseph out of the pit, and sold Joseph to the Ishmeelites for twenty pieces of silver: and they brought Joseph into Egypt" (Genesis 37:18–20, 24, 27–28).

Genesis 39:1–4—Joseph Given Authority over Egypt

"And Joseph was brought down to Egypt; and Potiphar, an officer of Pharaoh, captain of the guard, an Egyptian, bought him of the hands of the Ishmaelites, which had brought him down thither. And

---

66   David Hunt. *The Berean Call.*

the LORD was with Joseph, and he was a prosperous man; and he was in the house of his master the Egyptian. And his master saw that the LORD was with him, and that the LORD made all that he did to prosper in his hand. And Joseph found grace in his sight, and he served him: and he made him overseer over his house, and all that he had to put into his hand" (Genesis 39:1–4).

Genesis 45:1–9—Joseph Is Revealed to His Brothers

"Then Joseph could not refrain himself before all them that stood by him; and he cried, 'Cause every man to go out from me.' And there stood no man with him, while Joseph made himself known unto his brethren. And he wept aloud: and the Egyptians and the house of Pharaoh heard. And Joseph said unto his brethren, 'I am Joseph; doth my father yet live?' And his brethren could not answer him; for there were troubled at his presence. And Joseph said unto his brethren, 'Come near to me, I pray you.' And they came near. And he said, 'I am Joseph your brother, whom ye sold into Egypt. Now therefore be not grieved, nor angry with yourselves, that he sold me hither: for God did send me before you to preserve life. For these two years hath the famine been in the land: and yet there are five years, in the which there shall neither be earing nor harvest. And God sent me before you to preserve you a posterity in the earth, and to save your lives by a great deliverance. So now it was not you that sent me hither, but God: and he hath made me a father to Pharaoh, and lord of all his house, and a ruler throughout all the land of Egypt. Haste ye, and go up to my father, and say unto him, Thus saith thy son Joseph, God hath made me lord of all Egypt: come down unto me, tarry not'" (Genesis 45:1–9).

Genesis 50:15–21—What Was Meant for Evil, God Meant It for Good

"And when Joseph's brethren saw that their father was dead, they said, 'Joseph will peradventure hate us, and will certainly requite us all the evil which we did unto him.' And they sent a messenger unto Joseph, saying, 'Thy father did command before he died, saying, So shall ye say unto Joseph, Forgive, I pray thee now, the trespass of thy brethren, and their sin; for they did unto thee evil: and now, we pray thee, forgive the trespass of the servants of the God of thy father.' And Joseph wept when they spake unto him. And his brethren also went and fell down before his face; and they said, 'Behold, we be thy servants.' And Joseph said unto them, Fear not: for am I in the place of God? But as for you, ye thought evil against me; but God meant it unto good, to bring to pass, as it is this day, to save much people alive. Now therefore fear ye not: I will nourish you, and your little ones.' And he comforted them, and spake kindly unto them" (Genesis 50:15–21).

Joseph as a Type of Christ

Joseph is a type of Christ. Joseph was sold as a slave for twenty pieces of silver. Jesus was sold and betrayed for thirty pieces of silver. Joseph was rejected by his brothers. Later, Joseph saved his brothers from death. Joseph was a picture of the first and second coming of Jesus Christ. Abel, Jacob, Joseph, Moses, and David were shepherds; Jesus is our shepherd. Joseph's father loved Joseph more than any other of his sons. God the Father loves God the Son, Jesus Christ. Joseph told people what would happen in the future. His prophecies were always 100 percent correct. Jesus' prophecies are always 100 percent correct. Joseph and Jesus both had servant's hearts and were a blessing to others. Joseph and Jesus were both falsely accused and did not defend themselves. Both were tried by the Gentiles. Joseph was imprisoned with a butler and the chief of the bakers. Jesus was surrounded by two thieves on the cross. The baker was put to death, and the butler was freed. The thief on the cross who professed Jesus as God was given freedom in that he went to paradise that day of his death. The other thief on the cross who mocked Jesus was separated to hell.

Joseph got out of prison and was given authority over all of Egypt. Jesus was raised from the dead on the third day and continued His authority over heaven and earth. Joseph was not recognized by his brothers. Jesus was not recognized by His Jewish brothers as the Messiah. Joseph saved his brothers from death and then made himself known to his brothers. His brothers knew they had mistreated Joseph and that Joseph was giving them grace. At the second coming of Jesus Christ, Jesus will save Israel and make Himself known to all again.

Joseph as a type of Christ is well established. However, Moses—who was the author of Genesis—did not know ahead of time of this fact. In Isaiah 46:10, God stated He would declare the end from the beginning. Joseph as a type of Christ is an example of God controlling time, matter, and space and the events that occur on earth. Again, this is why I believe the Bible.

Genesis 49:9–11—Prophecy of Jesus

"Judah is a lion's whelp: from the prey, my son, thou art gone up: he stooped down, he couched as a lion, and as an old lion; who shall rouse him up? The sceptre shall not depart from Judah, nor a lawgiver from between his feet, until Shiloh come; and unto him shall the gathering of the people be. Binding his foal unto the vine, and his ass's colt unto the choice vine; he washed his garments in wine, and his clothes in the blood of grapes" (Genesis 49:9–11).

Jesus has historically been called the Lion from the Tribe of Judah.

Subject	From the Tribe of Judah	Prophet	Moses	Year Prophesied	1400 BC
Old Testament Prophesy	Genesis 49:10 "The sceptre shall not depart from Judah, nor a lawgiver from between his feet, until Shiloh come; and unto him shall the gathering of the people be."				
New Testament Fulfillment	Luke 3:33 "Which was the son of Aminadab, which was the son of Aram, which was the son of Esrom, which was the son of Phares, which was the son of Juda."				

Moses and the Exodus

Book of Exodus—1450–1400 BC

Paul summarizes in Acts 7 much of the books of Genesis and Exodus. It would be worth your time to read Acts 7.

Exodus 5:1–2—Moses Encounters Pharaoh

"And afterward Moses and Aaron went in, and told Pharaoh, 'thus saith the LORD God of Israel, Let my people go, that they may hold a feast unto me in the wilderness.' And Pharaoh said, 'Who is the LORD, that I should obey his voice to let Israel go? I know not the LORD, neither will I let Israel go'" (Exodus 5:1–2).

Numbers 12:8—God Speaks to Moses Mouth to Mouth

"With him will I speak mouth to mouth, even apparently, and not in dark speeches; and the similitude of the LORD shall he behold: wherefore then were ye not afraid to speak against my servant Moses?" (Numbers 12:8)

God spoke to Moses in a way unique to man. God revealed the feasts of the Lord, the temple, and the Ten Commandments to Moses. God spoke mouth to mouth with Moses, which signifies the degree and the importance of the truths given to Moses by God.

"Now the sojourning of the children of Israel, who dwelt in Egypt, was four hundred and thirty years" (Exodus 12:40).

Plagues on Egypt

1. Waters into blood
2. Frogs
3. Lice
4. Swarms of flies and insects
5. All cattle die (except for Hebrews' cattle)
6. Boils
7. Very heavy hail
8. Locusts
9. Thick darkness
10. Death of firstborn

Exodus 13:15—1400 BC—The Law of the Firstborn

"And it came to pass, when Pharaoh would hardly let us go, that the LORD slew all the firstborn in the land of Egypt, both the firstborn of man, and the firstborn of beast: therefore I sacrifice to the LORD all that openeth the matrix, being males; but all the firstborn of my children I redeem" (Exodus 13:15).

Exodus 14:13–14, 21–22, 28–30—God Delivers the Hebrews from Egyptian Slavery

"And Moses said unto the people, 'Fear ye not, stand still, and see the salvation of the LORD, which he will shew to you to day: for the Egyptians whom ye have seen to day, ye shall see them again no more for ever. The LORD shall fight for you, and ye shall hold your peace' …. And Moses stretched out his hand over the sea; and the LORD caused the sea to go back by a strong east wind all that night, and made the sea dry land, and the waters were divided. And the children of Israel went into the midst of the sea upon the dry ground: and the waters were a wall unto them on their right hand, and on their left … And the waters returned, and covered the chariots, and the horsemen, and all the host of Pharaoh that came into the sea after them; there remained not so much as one of them. But the children of Israel walked upon dry land in the midst of the sea; and the waters were a wall unto them on their right hand, and on their left. Thus the LORD saved Israel that day out of the hand of the Egyptians; and Israel saw the Egyptians dead upon the sea shore" (Exodus 14:13–14, 21–22, 28–30).

God tells His people not to be afraid when things look impossible. God miraculously separated the sea, ushered the Hebrews to safe land, and killed the Egyptians, who were attempting to kill the Hebrews.

The Passover in the Old Testament is rich in symbolism, types, and shadows, and it literally occurred. The Passover remembers Israel in slavery in Egypt. Prior to salvation, a Christian is a slave to sin. The Passover remembers the affliction of slavery. A Christian remembers the addictions and the hopelessness prior to being saved.

The Egyptian Pharaoh is a picture of Lucifer, who does not want to let you go and is trying to kill you. In the Old Testament Passover, the father of the house would cut the throat of the Passover lamb. The father would then apply the blood of the lamb on the door of his house—on the top and the sides. The family members were forbidden to leave their house. The angel of death was coming that night to kill all the firstborn except for those who had the blood of the lamb on their doorposts. God would protect these houses. When a person is saved, he becomes a Christian and is covered by the blood of Jesus Christ.

The Feast of Unleavened Bread remembers Israel leaving Egypt. In the New Testament, this parallels Jesus' body in the grave for three days. The soul of Jesus—which is the soul of God—did not remain in the grave; only the body remained in the grave. On the third day, God raised Jesus with a new, flesh-and-bone, resurrected body that will never die or decay.

After the Passover, the Hebrews left their houses to go into the wilderness to worship God. The Egyptians pursued them. God parted the Red Sea and provided a way of escape for the Hebrews. Moses and God's people passed through the Red Sea to the other side safely. Pharaoh and his armies pursued Moses and God's people, and Pharaoh and his armies were destroyed as the seas came together again.

The Feasts of the Lord

The feasts of the Lord are rehearsals of the first and second coming of Jesus Christ, the Messiah. There are seven major Old Testament feasts of the Lord with parallel fulfillment in the New Testament.

The first three spring feasts are in the first month of the Jewish calendar. These feasts generally take place in April and May over a period of seven consecutive days. These feasts are rehearsals concerning the first coming of Jesus Christ.			
Feast	Old Testament prophecy	Time span until fulfillment	New Testament fulfillment

1. The Passover	The killing of the Passover lambs Exodus 12:5–8 Approximately 1370 BC	Same day of year Approximately 1,400 years later	Crucifixion and death of Christ Hebrews 9:11–14 Approximately AD 30–32
2. Feast of Unleavened Bread	The seriousness of the consequences of sin Exodus 13:3–7	Same days of year Approximately 1,400 years later	The seriousness of the consequences of sin and a Holy Walk I Corinthians 5:8
3. Feast of Firstfruits	Moses leading the people through the Red Sea—deliverance from certain death by Pharaoh Exodus 14	Same time period of year approximately 1,400 years later	Jesus' resurrected body rises from the dead I Corinthians 15:20
***			
The fourth spring feast is known as Pentecost, and it occurred fifty days after the Feast of Firstfruits. In the Old Testament, the Hebrews received the Ten Commandments from God, and in the New Testament, believers receive the Holy Spirit from God.			
4. Feast of Pentecost or Feast of Weeks	Exodus 19:9–25 Exodus 20 God verbally speaks to the Hebrews from Mt. Sinai God verbally gives the Ten Commandments to the Hebrews	Same day of year approximately 1,400 years later	The descent and outpouring of the Holy Spirit stated in Acts 1–2 The New Testament church age begins Approximately AD 30
***			
The three fall feasts are in the seventh month of the Jewish calendar. These generally take place in September and October. These feasts are rehearsals concerning the second coming of Jesus Christ and the Millennium. The Fall Feasts deal with national cleansing.			
5. Feast of Trumpets or Rosh Hashanah	Signals new year Numbers 10	To be fulfilled in the near future	Israel's regathering in faith
6. Day of Atonement or Yom Kippur	Day the High Priest makes atonement for national sin Leviticus 23:26–32	To be fulfilled in the near future	Cleansing by Christ Romans 11:20

7. Feast of Booths or Feast of Tabernacles	Commemorates forty yeas of wilderness wandering Leviticus 23:33–44	To be fulfilled possibly at the end of the Millennium	Rest and reunion in Christ Zechariah 14:16–18

Subject	A Prophet	Prophet	Moses	Year Prophesied		1400 BC
Old Testament Prophesy		Deuteronomy 18:15 "The Lord thy God will raise up unto thee a Prophet from the midst of thee, of thy brethren, like unto me; unto him ye shall harken"				
New Testament Fulfillment		Acts 3:20, 22 "And he shall send Jesus Christ, which before was preached unto you: For Moses truly said unto the fathers, A prophet shall the Lord your God raise up unto you of your brethren, like unto me; him shall ye hear in all things whatsoever he shall say unto you"				

The Feasts of the Lord as Fulfilled in Jesus Christ

Jesus as a fulfillment of the seven major Jewish feasts is one of the most compelling reasons to believe that Jesus was God in the flesh. The life of Jesus fulfilling these feasts of the Lord is the most underutilized tool in explaining the gospel. It is my favorite witnessing tool.

The literal Passover lambs that were killed by the Hebrews are a picture of Jesus being crucified on Passover. The Feast of Unleavened Bread corresponds to Jesus' body in the grave after the crucifixion. The Feast of Firstfruits, which celebrates the deliverance of the Hebrews from the Egyptians, parallels what the Apostle Paul stated when he said Jesus was our first fruit, which is the resurrection of Jesus Christ.

In the Old Testament, Pentecost was God speaking the Ten Commandments to the Hebrews at Mt. Sinai. The Church was born on the same day approximately 1400 years later on Pentecost with the outpouring and indwelling of the Holy Spirit into the bodies of believers.

The fulfillment of these feasts by Jesus Christ at the first coming occurred while Israel was still a country under Gentile control. Forty years later, in AD 70, the Romans destroyed most of Jerusalem and began the dispersion of the Jews from Israel. With the regathering of the Jews to Israel approximately two thousand years later (two days to God), Jesus will be fulfilling the Feasts of Trumpets, the Day of Atonement, and the Feast of Booths at His second coming and events at the end of the millennium.

I get excited writing about these truths and wish ministers of the gospel would preach and teach more often concerning the feasts of the Lord. The purpose of the first coming of Jesus Christ is for personal salvation—our personal relationship with God.

The purpose of the second coming of Jesus Christ is for national salvation of Israel and for the world. The powers of hell will be bound and further limited until the great white throne of judgment. This is prior to hell being thrown into the lake of fire. This is a place you do not want to go. Please go back to the salvation chapter of this book and call upon the name of the Lord if you have not already. A sample prayer is there; however, the prayer you have on your heart right now would be even better. Stop now and accept Jesus Christ as Lord and Savior if you don't know Him. If you know Him, praise Him for His wisdom, power, and purposes.

Moses as a Type of Christ

Moses was clearly a picture and type of Christ. Both Moses and Jesus were Israelites. At the birth of Moses and at the birth of Jesus, the nation was under Gentile rule. At the time of the birth of Moses, the Egyptians were killing Hebrew children at their birth so the Egyptians would not be outnumbered by the Hebrews. After the birth of Jesus, Herod attempted to kill Jesus. Herod was unsuccessful but had many male children put to death. Moses was adopted by Pharaoh's daughter, and in a way, he had no father. Jesus' mother was Mary, but He did not have a human father. Jesus has the soul of God, because He is God. Moses led his people out of Egypt. Mary and Joseph fled to Egypt so Jesus would not be murdered. After the death of Herod, God called His son Jesus out of Egypt. Then Mary and Joseph took Jesus back to Israel.

Both Moses and Jesus understood at an early age their unique missions. Both Moses and Jesus were rejected at times by their brethren. Moses was a shepherd of sheep for many years. Jesus is our Great Shepherd. Both performed miracles. Moses and Aaron had a mighty rod. The Bible says in Psalm 2:9, "Thou shalt break them with a rod of iron" (thou shalt dash them in pieces like a potter's vessel).

Both were greatly opposed and threatened by their brethren. Both Moses and Jesus had a forgiving spirit, were very meek (power under control), and displayed great leadership. Moses sent out twelve spies; Jesus had twelve disciples. Moses appointed seventy men to be elders of the people; Jesus selected the seventy in Luke 10:1.

Moses died before the Hebrews went into the Promised Land. Had Jesus not died on the cross for our sins, we could not have eternal life. Moses built a tabernacle; Jesus is building a church—a temple not made with hands. Moses was at the Mount of Transfiguration in Matthew 17:3. Therefore, Moses came back to earth after his death. At the second coming of Jesus Christ, Jesus will place His feet on earth once again.

This is just another example of God declaring the end from the beginning. These types and shadows did not happen by chance.

The Old Testament Laws

There are 613 laws in the first five books of the Bible. About half of these laws deal with our relationship with God, Old Testament temple sacrifices, and duties and are rehearsals for the first and second coming of Jesus Christ. The other half of these laws deal with man's relationship with man.

The Jew was required to believe that God exists and to love, fear, and serve God. They are required to imitate God and to sanctify His name.

For detailed information on Old Testament law, read *Jewish Roots* by Daniel Juster.

Man's Relationship to God	Man's Relationship to Man
The Temple and its Priests	Community
Animal Sacrifices (Rehearsals of the Crucifixion of Jesus Christ)	War
	Business & Business Loans
Vows	Family
Ritual Purity	Judicial
Donations to the Temple	Salves
Sabbatical Year	Concerning consumption of animals
Feasts of the Lord	Torts
Idolatry	Dietary Laws
Sacrifices	Agriculture
Nazarite Vows	Justice
The Monarchy	Incest and Other Forbidden Relationships

The following is a brief summary of the laws listed in the first five books in the Old Testament. These are some of the laws, not all of the laws. Give to the poor, lend to the poor without interest, pay your employees on time, help man or beast which is overloaded, love lost people, weights and measures must be accurate, respect the wise, honor and fear your parents, thieves must be punished, you must not practice the occult, don't listen to gossip, women are not to dress as men and men are not to dress as women, don't mark or tattoo your skin, don't mix seed, don't erase God's name from the holy text or destroy institutions devoted to worshipping God, don't allow the body of someone hanged to remain overnight, don't break your word, don't be a glutton, don't hassle people who cannot pay you back, don't kidnap, don't steal, don't remove a landmark, don't defraud a person, don't afflict the widow or orphan, don't covet other persons' possessions, don't mislead a person, don't injure another person's trade, return things, don't accept bribes, don't favor the poor in criminal law, don't give false testimony, don't murder, don't convict on circumstantial evidence, don't tell tales or hold a grudge, don't take revenge, don't curse people, don't commit adultery, only have sexual relations with your lawful wife, don't have sexual relations with a menstruous wife.[67]

In the early 1960s, two-thirds of Americans believed in moral absolutes. Thirty years later, that number decreased to one-third of Americans believing in moral absolutes. To believe in moral absolutes is to believe that God created the dimensions of time, matter, and space and that therefore, God has the power and the right to decide what is good and what is evil. To believe in moral absolutes also means that you believe that God takes an interest in every event going on in all of His creation and has control of the future.

---

67   Daniel Juster. *Jewish Roots: A Foundation of Biblical Theology* (DAVAR Publishing) 261–287.

The results of breaking the Ten Commandments and the rapid decrease of Americans believing in moral absolutes are the cause broken families, abortions, lower SAT scores, the phenomenal increase of government and personal debt, and widespread financial bankruptcy, as well as underfunded social security, Medicare, and pension programs. This nation will also lose wars in the future, and losing wars is a time-honored way for God to get a nation's attention.

The Ten Commandments can be summarized as follows: no other gods, no idols, don't take the Lord's name in vain, remember sabbath, honor parents, don't murder, don't commit adultery, don't steal, don't lie, and don't covet.

The cost of sin to the economy of the USA easily tops $1 trillion per year. Federal, state, and local law enforcement, prison systems, and the like cost our nation over $500 billion per year. The reason people are in prison is because they broke one of the Ten Commandments (murder, rape, theft, lying, and coveting in general). These are all covered by the Ten Commandments, which many school systems do not allow to be posted on the walls in their hallways.

Sexually transmitted diseases cost the medical industry well over tens of billions of dollars per year. The cost of broken marriages due to adultery compounded over the last fifty years is too much to calculate. Many more billions are spent on insurance and medical fraud, theft that is never reported, etc. This can all be summed up in Proverbs 14:34: "Righteousness exalteth a nation: but sin is a reproach to any people."

The Cities of Refuge as a Type of Christ

The land of Canaan, which is now Israel, was divided among the twelve tribes of Israel. The tribe of Levi is a priestly tribe and was not given a specific land but was awarded forty-eight cities, of which six cities were designated as cities of refuge. When a man kills another man by accident, this is called manslaughter, not murder. If you broke a law, you would either pay back the person with money, or in essence become a slave for a period of time until you could pay off your debt. In the case of murder, you would be put to death.

> If someone slew another person by accident the slayer could flee to a city of refuge. If the slayer could convince the city elders that there was no premeditation he must remain in the city and not leave. The relatives and friends of the person that was murdered could not enter the city to avenge the death.

> "Because he should have remained in the city of his refuge until the death of the high priest: but after the death of the high priest the slayer shall return unto the land of his possession" (Numbers 35:28).

> What this means is that once the current high priest in Jerusalem died, the person who committed manslaughter could then leave the city of refuge and be free to travel and work and return to his homeland. To a Christian, Jesus is our creator, king, and high priest.

When Jesus was crucified the first words that Jesus stated were, "Father forgive them; for they know not what they do" (Luke 23:34). A saved person is under a manslaughter conviction, not a death sentence.

For a person who puts their faith in Jesus Christ and becomes born again, Jesus Christ becomes our city of refuge and our high priest. When we accept Jesus as our Lord and Savior, the death penalty is taken away from us, and we are free.[68]

Summaries of Joshua, Judges, Ruth, I Samuel, II Samuel, and I Kings

The Book of Joshua—1380 BC

Shortly after the death of Moses, Joshua took Israel out of the wilderness to occupy the land given by God. Joshua led Israel across the Jordan River into Canaan. As Joshua grew old, God told Joshua how to divide the land between the twelve tribes of Israel. The battle of Jericho was won by Joshua.

The Book of Judges and the Cycles of Nations—1375–1050 BC

In the Book of Judges, Israel falls into deep sin and idolatry and has a few godly judges and heroes like Gideon. The Book of Judges describes cycles of apostasy (falling away from God), gross sin, idolatry, oppression, and occasional deliverance. Judges describes that cycles of repentance and deliverance are followed by falling away from God. Judges 21:25, the last verse in the book of Judges, describes the whole book. This verse describes all civilizations and the fact that they all will eventually fall: "In those days there was no King in Israel: every man did that which is right in his own eyes."

God promises blessings when a people and a nation believe in the God of the first sentence in the Bible.

There is a cycle of nations and a pattern for nations and people who are blessed by God. That cycle begins with God blessing a particular nation or individuals, and after a few generations—or in the case of an individual, after a few months or years—a nation or individual will take for granted the blessings of God and rebel against God by doing evil. After a period of time, God begins a time of judgment followed by either repentance or more judgments. When repentance occurs, this will be followed by revival and rest.

The Book of Ruth—1150 BC

The Book of Ruth takes place during the times of Judges, before there was an earthly king over Israel. It was a time of Israel falling away from God again. The book is about a Gentile woman, Ruth, who forsakes her pagan heritage. A man by the name of Boaz (a kinsman redeemer) marries Ruth, and they have a son named Obed. Obed is the grandfather of David, and Ruth is the great-grandmother of David. David is in the lineage of Jesus Christ, both on the side of Joseph and Mary. However, remember that Jesus was conceived by the Holy Ghost. Ruth displayed the characteristics of New Testament

---

68   Chuck Missler. *Hidden Treasures in the Biblical Text* (Koinonia House) 101–104.

Christianity and Naomi, Ruth's former mother-in-law, was typical of Israel, who lost her land and lived among the Gentiles. In the end, Naomi returned to Israel, and Ruth, with her marriage to the kinsman redeemer, received the greater inheritance.

I Samuel—1040–1000 BC

I Samuel covers the last judge over Israel, who was Samuel. This book also covers the first king of Israel, who was Saul, and contains the battle of David defeating Goliath.

II Samuel—1000–925 BC

II Samuel covers major events of King David's forty-year reign over Israel.

I Kings—975–850 BC

I Kings records the times of King Solomon, who was the son of King David. King Solomon built the first temple in Israel.

The Old Testament Temple as a Type of Christ, as is the Body and Soul of a Believer in Christ

The Old Testament temple and the tabernacle are also pictures of salvation.

"Know ye not that ye are the temple of God, and that the Spirit of God dwelleth in you?" (I Corinthians 3:16)

The Old Testament temple has three major sections consisting of the Outer Court, the Holy Place, and the Holy of Holies. The Old Testament temple is also a picture of the soul of a believer in Christ.

Jesus is the door, the way, and the portal into the temple. A person gets into the temple through the person of Jesus Christ.

"I am the door: by me if any man enter in, he shall be saved, and shall go in and out, and find pasture" (John 10:9).

"Behold, I stand at the door, and knock: if any man hear my voice, and open the door, I will come in to him, and will sup with him, and he with me" (Revelation 3:20).

"And let them make me a sanctuary; that I may dwell among them. According to all that I shew thee, after the pattern of the tabernacle, and the pattern of all the instruments thereof, even so shall ye make it" (Exodus 25:8–9).

"Who serve unto the example and shadow of heavenly things, as Moses was admonished of God when he was about to make the tabernacle: for, See, saith he, that thou make all things according to the pattern shewed to thee in the mount" (Hebrews 8:5).

"Then David gave to Solomon his son the pattern of the porch, and of the houses thereof, and of the treasuries thereof, and of the upper chambers thereof, and of the inner parlours thereof, and of the place of the mercy seat, And the pattern of all that he had by the spirit, of the courts of the house of the LORD, and of all the chambers round about, of the treasuries of the house of God, and of the treasuries of the dedicated things: Also for the courses of the priests and the Levites, and for all the work of the service of the house of the LORD, and for all the vessels of service in the house of the LORD" (I Chronicles 28:11–13).

"And the Word was made flesh, and dwelt among us, (and we beheld his glory, the glory as of the only begotten of the Father), full of grace and truth" (John 1:14).

In the New Testament, the body of a believer in Christ is now the residing place of the Holy Spirit and thus becomes the temple of God.

"Know ye not that ye are the temple of God, and that the Spirit of God dwelleth in you? If any man defile the temple of God, him shall God destroy; for the temple of God is holy, which temple ye are" (I Corinthians 3:16–17).

The Outer Court

"For such an high priest became us, who is holy, harmless, undefiled, separate from sinners, and made higher than the heavens; Who needeth not daily, as those high priests, to offer up sacrifice, first for his own sins, and then for the people's: for this he did once, when he offered up himself" (Hebrews 7:26–27).

Jesus is pictured above as both the High Priest and the sacrificial lamb—the Lamb of God.

In the outer court area is the brazen altar. The brazen altar is a picture of the cross. Jesus is the sacrificed one and our justification. This happens when we make Jesus Lord and Savior of our lives. The animal sacrifices of the Old Testament were a type and shadow of Christ as our Passover lamb. Jesus Christ is the great *I AM* mentioned in the book of Exodus. To a Christian, Jesus is the creator, king, high priest, and the lamb of God. At the Brazen Altar, animals would be sacrificed as atonement for sin.

"Peter saith unto him, 'Thou shalt never wash my feet.' Jesus answered him, 'If I wash thee not, thou hast no part with me'" (John 13:8).

Jesus stated, "If I do not wash you, you have no part with Me."

A second instrument is the brazen laver, which is also in the outer court. Jesus cleanses us, sanctifies us, and separates us from our sin. We are washed in the water of His Word. Priests used the brazen laver for ceremonial cleaning.

The Holy Place

"Then spake Jesus again until them, saying, 'I am the light of the world: he that followeth me shall not walk in darkness, but shall have the light of life'" (John 8:12).

In the Holy Place are the golden lampstand, the table of shewbread, and the altar of incense. The golden lampstand symbolizes that Jesus is the light of the world. Christians are to be the light of the world and are to be pure in actions, intensions, and thoughts.

"And Jesus said unto them, 'I am the bread of life: he that cometh to me shall never hunger; and he that believeth on me shall never thirst'" (John 6:35).

The table of shewbread is a picture of Jesus being our provider who sustains us and communes with us. God supplies daily provisions and gives us a deeper understanding of Himself and the ability to walk by faith. We are to be in God's presence continually and read His Word daily. Jesus is our bread of life.

"O taste and see that the Lord is good: blessed is the man that trusteth in him" (Psalm 34:8).

"Wherefore he is able also to save them to the uttermost that come unto God by him, seeing he ever liveth to make intercession for them" (Hebrews 7:25).

The Altar of Incense is a picture of Jesus interceding for us. This represents the prayers of God's people. To walk in the holy Places of God, we must pray. This is where Christians become dangerous to the workings of Satan. Christians should not just want to be saved, but to be led continuously by the Holy Spirit.

The Holy of Holies

In the Holy of Holies is the living presence of God, the Ark of the Covenant, and the Mercy Seat.

"Whom God hath set forth to be propitiation through faith in his blood, to declare his righteousness for the remission of sins that are past, through the forbearance of God; To declare, I say, at this time his righteousness: that he might be just, and the justifier of him which believeth in Jesus" (Romans 3:25–26).

This is the full glory of God. The Ark of the Covenant is represented by Jesus and the fullness of the Godhead. The Mercy Seat is the Throne of God. The Ark of the Covenant contains the golden pot of manna, Aaron's rod, and the written Ten Commandments given to Moses on Mt. Sinai. God is our lawgiver and authority. The blood of the sacrifice was placed on the mercy seat. Jesus is a picture of the mercy seat.

The golden pot of manna symbolizes God's supernatural provisions for the saints as well as Jesus being the bread of life sent from heaven. Aaron's rod is a picture of God's authority. Our goal as Christians is to live in the Holy of Holies. We must strive to hear clearly from God and speak and do what He wants us to speak and do. Christians are to be fruitful and disciplined by God, speaking God's words continuously.

"Jesus saith unto him, 'I am the Way, the Truth and the Life, no man cometh unto the Father, but by me'" (John 14:6).

Outer Court	=	The Way—Covered by the blood of Jesus Christ
Holy Place	=	The Way and the Truth—Bible reading, prayer life, and good works
Holy of Holies	=	The Way, the Truth, and the Life—Disciple of Christ, hearing God's Voice, and eventually seeing God face-to-face and touching Him

"I beseech you therefore, brethren, by the mercies of God, that ye present your bodies a living sacrifice, holy, acceptable unto God, which is your reasonable service. And be not conformed to this world: but be ye transformed by the renewing of your mind, that ye may prove what is that *good*, and *acceptable*, and *perfect*, will of God" (Romans 12:1–2).

Outer Court	=	Good Will of God	=	Covered by the blood of Jesus
Holy Place	=	Acceptable Will of God	=	Bible reading, prayer life, light of the world
Holy of Holies	=	Perfect Will of God	=	A God-disciplined life, obeying the Holy Spirit of God, hearing from God

Outer Court	=	Passover	=	Covered by the blood of Jesus
Holy Place	=	Pentecost	=	The indwelling of the Holy Spirit
Holy of Holies	=	Tabernacles	=	Resting in Christ and obeying the Holy Spirit

Holy of Holies	The Holy Place	Outer Court
Ark of the Covenant	Golden lampstand Light of the World (Sight)	Brazen altar Covered by the blood
Golden Pot of Manna Supernatural Provisions	Table of shewbread Word of God (Taste)	Brazen laver Cleansed from sin
Mercy Seat Throne of God	Altar of incense Prayer life (Smell)	
Aaron's Rod God-Disciplined Life (Touch)	The Torn Veil Our five senses include sight, taste, smell, touch, and hearing	
Ten Commandments Obedience to God (Hearing)		Outer court=natural light
John 14:6		
Life	Truth	Way

Romans 12:1–2		
Perfect	Acceptable	Good
Feast of Tabernacles	Pentecost	Passover
Revelation 15:1–8 The sea of glass and fire—the judgment seat of Christ		

1. The moral law is the Ten Commandments, which are written in stone.
2. The civil law applies moral law to specific situations.
3. The ceremonial laws cover the priesthood and are types and shadows of the first and second comings of Jesus Christ.

Conscience	Noah's Flood		Judgment by water
Blood Covenant	Outer Court	1400–1 BC	Cleansing
Church Age	Holy Place	AD 30–2000	Regeneration
Millennium	Holy of Holies	Future event to end of age	Resurrection

The Old Testament temple is a picture of a believer's body, soul, and spirit, as well as many other symbolic truths. There are three major sections to the Old Testament temple—the Outer Court, the Holy Place, and the Holy of Holies. You are triune in that you have a body, soul, and spirit. All people fall into one of four categories.

1. You are lost (have not trusted Jesus Christ as Lord and Savior), in rebellion to God, and spiritually outside of the temple of God.
2. You are in the good will of God.
3. You are in the acceptable will of God.
4. You are in the perfect will of God.

When a person gets saved, he is either in the good, acceptable, or perfect will of God. He is covered by the blood, which is the finished work of Jesus Christ on the cross. For this to occur, you must come through the person of Jesus Christ, who is the gate and the way to eternal life. The Outer Court was where the shedding of innocent blood occurred. In the Old Testament, it was the shedding of the blood of lambs and other animals that occurred in the Outer Court of the Temple, and this was a picture of things to come. Jesus fulfilled this prophecy as the Passover lamb. The Outer Court was illuminated with natural light from the sun. A Christian is to learn to live by faith and not by natural light. It is good to be saved, but if you are living by natural light, that is all you are good for.

The golden lampstand, the table of shewbread, and the altar of incense is inside and under the cover of the Holy Place. I believe this corresponds to three of our five senses being sight, taste, and smell. The golden lampstand symbolizes that we are to be the light of the world (sight) through our works, deeds, and words. The table of shewbread is symbolized by the Word of God—the Bible. The Bible says to "taste and see that the Lord is good." The only way to grow in the Lord is to read His Word. The altar of incense concerns our prayers (smell) as our prayers go up to heaven. Our works, deeds, words, reading the Bible, and prayer life are only what is just acceptable to God.

God wants us to be in His perfect will. To be in God's perfect will, we have to stop and wait to hear from the Lord and let Him touch our lives. God wants us to be sold out to Him and have a totally God-disciplined life so that we will hear from Him moment by moment throughout the day. God's perfect will is that He supplies our needs in a supernatural way and we are totally dependent on Him, have a quiet time daily to hear from Him, and then do all He desires us to do.

God desires us to be absolutely surrendered to Him. Again, another major purpose in this life is to always choose the way of faith. Please review the graphs, Bible verses, and parallels listed in the previous two pages of this section. The Holy Spirit of God can speak to your soul, and you will learn the deep things of God without further commentary.

Summaries of Psalms, Proverbs, Ecclesiastes, and the Song of Solomon

Book of Psalms—1400–425 BC

The book of Psalms has design and order in it even though it is not evident just on the surface. The graph below outlines the general themes of the Psalms.[69]

Psalm	Corresponds to	Theme
Psalms 1–41	Genesis	Life and Election
Psalms 42–72	Exodus	Redemption
Psalms 73–89	Leviticus	Sanctification
Psalms 90–106	Numbers	Testing and Experience
Psalms 107–150	Deuteronomy	Divine Government

Book of Proverbs—950 BC

King Solomon was the author of the book of Proverbs. Proverbs is a collection of wise sayings that can direct us to do the right thing and have right attitudes. I believe Proverbs can be condensed into these categories and in this order.

1.	Obey, fear, and believe God.	12.	Train your children in the ways of the Lord.
2.	Seek wisdom and understanding from God.	13.	Don't fear evil.
3.	The wicked will be destroyed and the righteous delivered.	14.	Believe God created all things.
4.	Honor your parents.	15.	Don't be prideful.
5.	Work hard—don't be slothful.	16.	Don't lie.

---

69 J. R. Church. *Hidden Prophecies in the Psalms*, 15.

6.	Be slow to speak.	17.	Don't get drunk.
7.	Don't be foolish.	18.	Be slow to anger.
8.	Pray for righteous rulers.	19.	Defines poor marriage (lack of communication).
9.	Help the poor.	20.	Don't love pleasure.
10.	Don't worry or fret about not being right.	21.	Desire a good name over riches.
11.	Don't conspire with the wicked (pick good friends).	22.	Don't envy.

The book of Proverbs' basic theme is that the beginning of knowledge is the fear of God. Fear is a good motivator. Before my salvation, I knew if there was a god, I was going to Hell. The more I understand the Bible, the more I both love and obey God and fear Him. I fear the verse in the Bible that says God will judge every idle word you speak; this is good. Perfect love towards God will give the power needed to keep from speaking idle words.

The Book of Ecclesiastes—925 BC

The book of Ecclesiastes is attributed to King Solomon, as well as the Song of Solomon.

Israel, under King Solomon, was the most powerful kingdom on earth. Israel was strong because King Solomon's father, King David, had a heart for God. King Solomon was the wisest, richest, and most powerful person on earth. However, without obeying the voice of God and God's Holy Spirit, all becomes vanity and empty. King Solomon had seven hundred wives and three hundred concubines. The effect this had on his offspring resulted in Israel being split into a northern and a southern kingdom.

The Book of The Song of Solomon—950 BC

The Song of Solomon is a type and shadow. This book is full of symbolism showing the relationship of love between man and wife as a symbol of the love between God and mankind. Israel is the bride of God.

The approximate years of the rules of Saul, David, and Solomon over Israel:

1051–1011 BC—Saul
101 –971 BC—David
971–931 BC—Solomon

The Kings of Israel and Judah and the Twelve Tribes of Israel

Divided Kingdom			
Israel—Northern Ten Tribes	931–722 BC	Judah—Southern Two Tribes	931–586 BC
Jeroboam	Bad	Rehoboam	Bad/Good
Nadab	Bad	Abijah	Bad
Baasha	Bad	Asa	Good/Bad

Elah	Bad	Jehoshaphat	Good
Zimri	Bad	Jehoram	Bad
Tibni	Bad	Ahaziah	Bad
Omri	Bad	Queen Athaliah	Bad
Ahab	Bad	Joash	Good
Ahaziah	Bad	Amaziah	Mostly Good
Joram	Bad	Uzziah	Good
Jehu	Bad	Jotham	Good
Jehoahaz	Bad	Ahaz	Bad
Jehoash	Bad	Hezekiah	Good
Jeroboam II	Bad	Manasseh	Bad/Good
Zechariah	Bad	Amon	Bad
Shallum	Bad	Josiah	Good
Menahem	Bad	Jehoahaz	Bad
Pekahiah	Bad	Jehoiakim	Bad
Pekah	Bad	Jehoiachin	Bad
Hoshea	Bad	Zedekiah	Bad[70]

Northern Tribes		Southern Tribes	
1.	Reuben	1.	Benjamin
2.	Gad	2.	Judah
3.	Manasseh		
4.	Issachar		
5.	Naphtali		
6.	Ephraim		
7.	Asher		
8.	Dan		
9.	Zebulon		
10.	Simeon		
Levi—the tribe of Levi was not given a specific area of land in Israel. Levi was the tribe of priests in both the northern and southern tribes.			

After King Solomon, the northern ten tribes had particularly evil kings until their dispersion and defeat by the Assyrians. The southern two tribes of Israel had mostly evil kings. However, eventually the sins of the southern tribes were even greater than those of the northern tribes until Babylonian captivity.

---

70 (Torrance, CA: Rose Publishing)

Simeon and Levi had a zeal for God. Ephraim and Manasseh are children of Joseph, the son of Jacob. They were the offspring of Joseph's Gentile wife.

The Book of II Kings—850–550 BC

II Kings records the ten northern tribes of Israel and the two southern tribes of Israel from approximately 850–550 BC. The northern kings of Israel were all particularly evil, and Israel was defeated by Assyria around 722 BC. The southern two tribes of Judah and Benjamin fell into captivity around 586 BC. Many of the northern ten tribes were dispersed into the nations of the earth, and some returned to Israel from their captivity. A remnant of Judah returned from their Babylonian captivity.

The Book of I Chronicles—1000 BC

I Chronicles also covers the time of King David. This book lists the genealogy from Adam to David.

The Book of II Chronicles—931–586 BC

II Chronicles primarily covers the southern kingdom of Judah from 981 BC to the destruction of Jerusalem, which resulted in the Babylonian captivity. II Chronicles does not describe the Babylonian captivity. This book jumps seventy years from the destruction of Jerusalem to the destruction of the Babylonians, who were overthrown by the Persians. Cyrus was the King of Persia, and after he defeated the Babylonians, Artaxeres commanded the temple to be rebuilt in Jerusalem.

Leviticus 25:4–5—Sabbath Rest

"But in the seventh year shall be a sabbath of rest unto the land, a sabbath for the LORD: thou shalt neither sow thy field, nor prune thy vineyard. That which groweth of its own accord of thy harvest thou shalt not reap, neither gather the grapes of thy vine undressed: for it is a year of rest unto the land" (Leviticus 25:4–5).

II Chronicles 36:21—Babylonian Captivity

"To fulfil the word of the LORD by the mouth of Jeremiah, until the land had enjoyed her sabbaths: for as long as she lay desolate she kept sabbath, to fulfil threescore and ten years" (II Chronicles 36:21).

Many biblical scholars believe that Daniel understood that for 420 years from the time of Solomon's temple until the time of Daniel and the Babylonian captivity that Israel never kept the Sabbath. Israel had not rested the land every seven years as God had told them to do.

God allowed (directed) the Babylonians to overrun Israel. For God to gain back the Sabbath years lost would take seventy years, thus Daniel understood the Babylonian captivity would be for seventy years (Leviticus 25:4–5). God frequently works in 490-year cycles, which are ten jubilee cycles (10 x 49 = 490) (7 x 7 = one jubilee cycle).

The Book of Ezra—500–450 BC

Ezra covers the exodus from Babylon back to Jerusalem. Only a remnant returned.

Ezra 1:1–2—The Proclamation to Rebuild the Temple in Jerusalem

"Now in the first year of Cyrus king of Persia, that the word of the LORD by the mouth of Jeremiah might be fulfilled, the LORD stirred up the spirit of Cyrus king of Persia, that he made a proclamation throughout all his kingdom, and put it also in writing, saying, 'Thus saith Cyrus king of Persia, The LORD God of heaven hath given me all the kingdoms of the earth; and he hath charged me to build him an house at Jerusalem, which is in Judah'" (Ezra 1:1–2).

Other Non-Biblical Philosophers

Buddha—530 BC—India

Gautama Buddha was the founder of Buddhism. He taught that suffering was a part of life and that one could get to nirvana (nothingness or annihilation) by mental or moral self-purification. My interpretation of Buddhism is that in India in 400 BC, life was miserable. God wrote eternity in Buddha's soul, but no one told him about the God of Israel. He came up with a philosophy to get away from the sorrows of this earth to perfect spiritual fulfillment. Buddhists are primarily located in eastern Asia.

Confucius—520 BC—China

Confucianism is a philosophy based on piety, kindness, righteousness, intelligence, and faithfulness. It is a philosophy which formed much of Chinese society. It is just a philosophy, though. It does not explain the origins or purpose of mankind.

Plato—347 BC—Greece

Platoism is a philosophy. Plato lived during the time of Alexander the Great in Greece. He believed that man had a soul. I believe he is the father of secular humanism and mere human reasoning.

The purpose of briefly reviewing other religions is to show that their origins are relatively recent. The major non-Christian religious origins are in the past 2,500 years. Mohammed lived in the AD 600s. Islam is further explored in the New Testament chapter.

I believe Hinduism is the oldest of the non-Christian religions. It is the only religion that does not have a particular person as its originator. I believe Lucifer himself started Hinduism in the Garden of Eden, and all other non-Christian religions are, in essence, an offshoot of it. This includes Latter-Day Saints and Jehovah's Witnesses, even though these two religions believe in a resurrection and not reincarnation.

Further, biblical Christianity is not a religion, but a personal relationship with God, the creator of heaven and earth through the person of God in the flesh, Jesus Christ.

The Book of Nehemiah—425 BC

Nehemiah deals with the rebuilding of the walls around Jerusalem after a remnant of the tribes of Judah, Benjamin, and Levi return to Jerusalem. This occurred after the Babylonian captivity. Nehemiah was greatly opposed by Judah's enemies.

Nehemiah 2:17–18—Rebuilds the Wall around Jerusalem

"Then said I unto them, 'Ye see the distress that we are in, how Jerusalem lieth waste, and the gates thereof are burned with fire: come, and let us build up the wall of Jerusalem, that we be no more a reproach.' Then I told them of the hand of my God which was good upon me; as also the king's words that he had spoken unto me. And they said, 'Let us rise up and build.' So they strengthened their hands for this good work" (Nehemiah 2:17–18).

Nehemiah and God's people completed the rebuilding of the wall, and the people grew closer to God by the reading of the law. These people not only heard the Word, but they also began to obey the Word.

The Book of Esther—475 BC

Most people from the southern tribes of Israel (Judah and Benjamin) did not return to Jerusalem. Israel was still under direct Gentile control after the Babylonians were defeated by the Medes and the Persians.

It is important to remember that from the time of the destruction of Jerusalem by the Babylonians around 586 BC until AD 1948, the Jews did not have sovereign control over Jerusalem. From 586 BC until AD 1948, the Babylonians, the Medes and Persians, the Greeks, the Romans, and various European and Middle Eastern empires had control over the city of Jerusalem. The Jews were allowed to rebuild the temple only because the Persians allowed it. The Persians were defeated by the Greek Empire under Alexander the Great. The Greeks were defeated by the Romans. God used the Romans to disperse the Jews from Israel from AD 70 until AD 125. Israel ceased to be a nation until AD 1948.

In the book of Esther, there was a plot to kill all the Jews. Instead of the Jews being killed, the plotters were killed, and the Feast of Purim was initiated.

A Chronology of Old Testament Prophets and to Whom They Prophesied

Israel = Northern Ten Tribes   Judah = Southern Two Tribes   Nineveh is in Syria

Time	Prophet	Prophesied to
850 BC	Elijah	Israel
825 BC	Elisha	Israel
775 BC	Jonah	Nineveh
750 BC	Hosea	Israel
750 BC	Amos	Israel

725 BC	Isaiah	Judah
725 BC	Micah	Judah
650 BC	Nahum	Concerning Nineveh
625 BC	Zephaniah	Judah
600 BC	Jeremiah & Lamentations	Judah
600 BC	Habakkuk	Judah
575 BC	Ezekiel	Exiles in Babylonia
575 BC	Obadiah	Concerning Edom
550 BC	Daniel	In Babylon
525 BC	Joel	Judah
525 BC	Haggai	Judah
525 BC	Zechariah	Judah
475 BC	Malachi	Judah[71]

Prophecies of the First Coming of Christ in Chronological Order of the Life of the Prophet

Subject	Declared Son of God	Prophet	David	Year Prophesied	~1000 BC
Old Testament Prophesy		Psalm 2:7 "I will declare the decree: the Lord hath said unto me, 'Thou art my Son; this day have I begotten thee.'"			
New Testament Fulfillment		Matthew 3:17 "And lo a voice from heaven, saying, 'This is my beloved Son, in whom I am well pleased.'"			

Subject	Adored by Infants	Prophet	David	Year Prophesied	~1000 BC
Old Testament Prophesy		Psalm 8:2 "Out of the mouth of babes and sucklings has thou ordained strength because of thine enemies, that thou mightest still the enemy and the avenger."			
New Testament Fulfillment		Matthew 21:15, 16 "And when the chief priests and scribes saw the wonderful things that he did, and the children crying in the temple, and saying, 'Hosanna to the son of David'; they were sore displeased, And said unto him, 'Hearest thou what these say?' And Jesus saith unto them, 'Yea; have ye never read, Out of the mouth of babes and sucklings thou has perfected praise?'"			

Subject	To be Resurrected	Prophet	David	Year Prophesied	~1000 BC

---

71 (Torrance, CA: Rose Publishing)

Old Testament Prophesy	Psalm 16:10 "For thou wilt not leave my soul in hell; neither wilt thou suffer thine Holy One to see corruption." Psalm 49:15 "But God will redeem my soul from the power of the grave: for he shall receive me."
New Testament Fulfillment	Mark 16:6, 7 "And he saith unto them, 'Be not affrighted: Ye seek Jesus of Nazareth, which was crucified: he is risen; he is not here: behold the place where they laid him. But go your way, tell his disciples and Peter that he goeth before you into Galilee: there shall ye see him, as he said unto you.'"

Subject	Forsaken by God	Prophet	David	Year Prophesied	~1000 BC
Old Testament Prophesy	Psalm 22:1 "My God, my God, why hast thou forsaken me? why art thou so far from helping me, and from the words of my roaring?"				
New Testament Fulfillment	Matthew 27:46 "And about the ninth hour Jesus cried with a loud voice, saying, 'Eli, Eli, lama sabach thani?' that is to say, 'My God, My God, why hast thou forsaken me?'"				

Subject	Scorned and Mocked	Prophet	David	Year Prophesied	~1000 BC
Old Testament Prophesy	Psalm 22:7, 8 "All they that see me laugh me to score: they shoot out the lip, they shake the head, saying, He trusted on the Lord that he would deliver him: let him deliver him, seeing he delighted in him."				
New Testament Fulfillment	Luke 23:35 "And the people stood beholding. And the rulers also with them derided him, saying, 'He saved others; let him save himself, if he be Christ, the chosen of God.'"				

Subject	Soldiers Gambled for His Garment	Prophet	David	Year Prophesied	~1000 BC
Old Testament Prophesy	Psalm 22:17, 18 "I may tell all my bones: they look and stare upon me. They part my garments among them, and cast lots upon my vesture."				
New Testament Fulfillment	Matthew 27:35, 36 "And they crucified him, and parted his garments, casting lots: that it might be fulfilled which was spoken by the prophet, They parted my garments among them, and upon my vesture did they cast lots. And sitting down they watched him there."				

Subject	No Bones Broken	Prophet	David	Year Prophesied	~1000 BC

Old Testament Prophesy	Psalm 34:20
	"He keepeth all his bones: not one of them is broken."
New Testament Fulfillment	John 19:32–33, 36
	"Then came the soldiers, and brake the legs of the first, and of the other which was crucified with him. But when they came to Jesus, and saw that he was dead already, they brake not his legs: For these things were done, that the scripture should be fulfilled: A bone of Him shall not be broken."

Subject	Accused by False Witness	Prophet	David	Year Prophesied	~1000 BC
Old Testament Prophesy	Psalm 35:11				
	"False witnesses did rise up; they laid to my charge things that I knew not."				
New Testament Fulfillment	Mark 14:57, 58				
	"And there arose certain, and bare false witness against him, saying, We heard him say, 'I will destroy this temple that is made with hands, and within three days I will build another made without hands.'"				

Subject	Hated without Reason	Prophet	David	Year Prophesied	~1000 BC
Old Testament Prophesy	Psalm 35:19				
	"Let not them that are mine enemies wrongfully rejoice over me: neither let them wink with the eye that hate me without a cause."				
New Testament Fulfillment	John 15:24, 25				
	"If I had not done among them the works which none other man did, they had not had sin: but now have they both seen and hated both me and my Father. But this cometh to pass, that the work might be fulfilled that is written in their law, They hated me without cause."				

Subject	Betrayed by a Close Friend	Prophet	David	Year Prophesied	~1000 BC
Old Testament Prophesy	Psalm 41:9				
	"Yea, mine own familiar friend, in whom I trusted, which did eat of my bread, hath lifted up his heel against me."				
New Testament Fulfillment	Luke 22:47–48				
	"And while he yet spake, behold a multitude, and he that was called Judas, one of the twelve, went before them, and drew near unto Jesus to kill him. But Jesus said unto him, 'Judas, betrayest thou the Son of man with a kiss?'"				

Subject	Anointed and Eternal	Prophet	David	Year Prophesied	~1000 BC

Old Testament Prophesy	Psalm 45:6–7 "Thy throne, O God, is for ever and ever, the sceptre of thy kingdom is a right sceptre. Thou lovest righteousness, and hatest wickedness: therefore God, thy God, hath annointed thee with the oil of gladness above thy fellows." Psalm 102:25–27 "Of old hast thou laid the foundation of the earth: and the heavens are the work of thy hands. They shall perish, but thou shalt endure: yea, all of them shall wax old like a garment; as a vesture shalt thou change them, and they shall be changed: But thou art the same, and thy years shall have no end."
New Testament Fulfillment	Hebrews 1:8–12 "But unto the Son he saith, 'Thy throne, O God, is for ever and ever: a scepter of righteousness is the scepter of Thy kingdom. Thou hast loved righteousness, and hated iniquity; therefore God, even Thy God, hath anointed thee with the oil of gladness, above thy fellows. And Thou, Lord, in the beginning hast laid the foundation of the earth; and the heavens are the works of Thine hands: they shall perish; but thou remainest; and they shall all wax old as doth a garment; and as a vesture shalt Thou fold them up, and they shall be changed; but Thou art the same, and Thy years shall not fail.'"

Subject	His Ascension to God's Right Hand	Prophet	David	Year Prophesied	~1000 BC
Old Testament Prophesy		Psalm 68:18 "Thou hast ascended on high, thou hast led captivity captive: thou hast received gifts for men; yea, for the rebellious also, that the Lord God might dwell among them."			
New Testament Fulfillment		Mark 16:19 "So then after the Lord had spoken unto them, he was received up into heaven, and sat on the right hand of God." I Corinthians 15:4 "And that he was buried, and that he rose again the third day according to the scriptures." Ephesians 4:8 "Wherefore he saith, When he ascended up on high, he led captivity captive, and gave gifts unto men."			

Subject	Reproached	Prophet	David	Year Prophesied	~1000 BC
Old Testament Prophesy		Psalm 60:9 "For the zeal of thine house hath eaten me up; and the reproaches of them that reproached thee are fallen upon me."			

New Testament Fulfillment	Romans 15:3
	"For even Christ pleased not himself: but, as it is written, The reproaches of them that reproached thee fell on me."

Subject	Speaks in Parables	Prophet	David	Year Prophesied	~1000 BC
Old Testament Prophesy	Psalm 78:2–4 "I will open my mouth in a parable: I will utter dark sayings of old: Which we have heard and known, and our fathers have told us. We will not hide them from their children, shewing to the generation to come the praises of the Lord, and his strength, and his wonderful works that he hath done."				
New Testament Fulfillment	Matthew 13:34–35 "All these things spake Jesus unto the multitude in parables; and without a parable spake he not unto them: That it might be fulfilled which was spoken by the prophet, saying, I will open my mouth in parables; I will utter things which have been kept secret from the foundation of the world."				

Subject	Prayer for His Enemies	Prophet	David	Year Prophesied	~1000 BC
Old Testament Prophesy	Psalm 109:4 "For my love they are my adversaries: but I give myself unto prayer."				
New Testament Fulfillment	Luke 23:34 "Then said Jesus, 'Father, forgive them; for they know not what they do.' And they parted his raiment, and cast lots."				

Subject	Priest after Order of Melchizedek	Prophet	David	Year Prophesied	~1000 BC
Old Testament Prophesy	Psalm 110:4 "The Lord hath sworn, and will not repent. Thou art a priest for ever after the order of Melchizedek."				
New Testament Fulfillment	Hebrews 5:5–6 "So also Christ glorified not himself to be made an high priest; but he that said until him, 'Thou art my Son, to day have I begotten thee.' As he saith also in another place, 'Thou art a priest for ever after the order of Melchizedek.'"				

Subject	Flight to Egypt	Prophet	Hosea	Year Prophesied	~750 BC
Old Testament Prophesy	Hosea 11:1 "When Israel was a child, then I loved him, and called my son out of Egypt."				

New Testament Fulfillment	Matthew 2:14–15 "When he arose, he took the young child and his mother by night, and departed into Egypt: And was there until the death of Herod: that it might be fulfilled which was spoken of the Lord by the prophet, saying. 'Out of Egypt have I called my son.'"

Subject	To be Born of a Virgin	Prophet	Isaiah	Year Prophesied	~725 BC
Old Testament Prophesy		Isaiah 7:14 "Therefore the Lord himself shall give you a sign; Behold, a virgin shall conceive, and bear a son, and shall call his name Immanuel."			
New Testament Fulfillment		Luke 1:26–27, 30–31 "And in the sixth month the angel Gabriel was sent from God unto a city of Galilee, named Nazareth, To a virgin espoused to a man whose name was Joseph, of the house of David; and the virgin's name was Mary. And the angel said unto her, 'Fear not, Mary: for thou hast found favour with God. And, behold, thou shalt conceive in thy womb, and bring forth a son, and shalt call his name JESUS.'"			

Subject	Galilean Ministry	Prophet	Isaiah	Year Prophesied	~725 BC
Old Testament Prophesy		Isaiah 9:1–2 "Nevertheless the dimness shall not be such as was in her vexation, when at the first he lightly afflicted the land of Zebulun and the land of Naphtali, and afterward did more grievously afflict her by the way of the sea, beyond Jordan, In Galilee of the nations. The people that walked in darkness have seen a great light: they that dwell in the land of the shadow of death, upon them hath the light shined."			
New Testament Fulfillment		Matthew 4:13–16 "And leaving Nazareth, he came and dwelt in Capernaum, which is upon the sea coast, in the borders of Zabulon and Nephthalim: That it might be fulfilled which was spoken by Esaias the prophet, saying, The land of Zabulon, and the land of Nephthalim, by the way of the sea, beyond Jordan, Galilee of the Gentiles; The people which at in darkness saw great light; and to them which sat in the region and shadow of death light is sprung up."			

Subject	Heir to the Throne of David	Prophet	Isaiah	Year Prophesied	~725 BC

Old Testament Prophesy	Isaiah 9:7 "Of the increase of his government and peace there shall be no end, upon the throne of David, and upon his kingdom, to order it, and to establish it with judgment and with justice from henceforth even for ever. The zeal of the Lord of hosts will perform this."
New Testament Fulfillment	Luke 1:32–33 "He shall be great, and shall be called the Son of the Highest: and the Lord God shall give unto him the throne of his father David: And he shall reign over the house of Jacob for ever; and of his kingdom there shall be no end."

Subject	The Way Prepared	Prophet	Isaiah	Year Prophesied	~725 BC
Old Testament Prophesy		Isaiah 40:3–5 "The voice of him that crieth in the wilderness, Prepare ye the way of the Lord, make straight in the desert a highway for our God. Every valley shall be exalted, and every mountain and hill shall be made low: and the crooked shall be made straight, and the rough places plain: And the glory of the Lord shall be revealed, and all flesh shall see it together: for the mouth of the Lord hath spoken it."			
New Testament Fulfillment		Luke 3:3–6 "And he came into all the country about Jordan, preaching the baptism of repentance for the remission of sins; As it is written in the book of the words of Esaias the prophet, saying, The voice of one crying in the wilderness, Prepare ye the way of the Lord, make his paths straight. Every valley shall be filled, and every mountain and hill shall be brought low; and the crooked shall be made straight, and the rough ways shall be made smooth; And all flesh shall see the salvation of God."			

Subject	Spat Upon and Smitten	Prophet	Isaiah	Year Prophesied	~725 BC
Old Testament Prophesy		Isaiah 50:6 "I gave my back to the smiters, and my cheeks to them that plucked off the hair: I hid not my face from shame and spitting."			
New Testament Fulfillment		Matthew 26:67 "Then did they spit in his face, and buffeted him; and other smote him with the palms of their hands."			

Subject	Not Believed	Prophet	Isaiah	Year Prophesied	~725 BC
Old Testament Prophesy		Isaiah 53:1 "Who hath believed our report? and to whom is the arm of the Lord revealed."			

New Testament Fulfillment	John 12:37–38 "But though he had done so many miracles before them, yet they believed not on him: That the saying of Esaias the prophet might be fulfilled, which he spake, Lord, who hath believed our report? and to whom hath the arm of the Lord been revealed?"

Subject	Rejected by His Own People, the Jews	Prophet	Isaiah	Year Prophesied	~725 BC
Old Testament Prophesy	Isaiah 53:3 "He is despised and rejected of men; a man of sorrows, and acquainted with grief: and we hid as it were our faces from him; he was despised; and we esteemed him not."				
New Testament Fulfillment	John 1:11 "He came unto his own, and his own received him not." Luke 23:18 "And they cried out all at once, saying, 'Away with this man, and release unto us Barabbas.'"				

Subject	Vicarious Sacrifice	Prophet	Isaiah	Year Prophesied	~725 BC
Old Testament Prophesy	Isaiah 53:5 "But he was wounded for our transgressions; he was bruised for our iniquities: the chastisement of our peace was upon him, and with his stripes we are healed."				
New Testament Fulfillment	Romans 5:6, 8 "For when we were yet without strength, in due time Christ died for the ungodly. But God commendeth his love toward us, in that, while we were yet sinners, Christ died for us."				

Subject	Silent to Accusations	Prophet	Isaiah	Year Prophesied	~725 BC
Old Testament Prophesy	Isaiah 53:7 "He was oppressed, and he was afflicted, yet he opened not his mouth: he is brought as a lamb to the slaughter, and as a sheep before her shearers is dumb, so he openeth not his mouth."				
New Testament Fulfillment	Mark 15:4–5 "And Pilate asked him again, saying, 'Answerest thou nothing? behold how many things they witness against thee.' But Jesus yet answered nothing, so that Pilate marvelled."				

Subject	Buried with the Rich	Prophet	Isaiah	Year Prophesied	~725 BC

Old Testament Prophesy	Isaiah 53:9 "And he made his grave with the wicked, and with the rich in his death; because he had done no violence, neither was any deceit in his mouth."
New Testament Fulfillment	Matthew 27:57–60 "When the even was come, there came a rich man of Arimathea, named Joseph, who also himself was Jesus' disciple. He went to Pilate, and begged the body of Jesus. Then Pilate commanded the body to be delivered. And when Joseph had taken the body, he wrapped it in a clean linen cloth. And laid it in his own new tomb, which he had hewn out in the rock: and he rolled a great stone to the door of the sepulchre, and departed."

Subject	Crucified with Malefactors	Prophet	Isaiah	Year Prophesied	~725 BC
Old Testament Prophesy		Isaiah 53:12 "Therefore will I divide him a portion with the great, and he shall divide the spoil with the strong; because he hath poured out his soul unto death: and he was numbered with the transgressors; and he bare the sin of many, and made intercession for the transgressors."			
New Testament Fulfillment		Luke 22:37 "For I say unto you, that this that is written must yet be accomplished in me. And He was reckoned among the transgressors: for the things concerning me have an end."			

Subject	To Heal the Brokenhearted	Prophet	Isaiah	Year Prophesied	~725 BC
Old Testament Prophesy		Isaiah 61:1–2 "The Spirit of the Lord God is upon me; because the Lord has anointed me to preach good tidings unto the meek; he hath sent me to bind up the brokenhearted, to proclaim liberty to the captives, and the opening of the prison to them that are bound; To proclaim the acceptable year of the Lord, and the day of vengeance of our God; to comfort all that mourn."			
New Testament Fulfillment		Luke 4:18–19 "The Spirit of the Lord is upon me, because he hath anointed me to preach the gospel to the poor; he hath sent me to heal the brokenhearted, to preach deliverance to the captives, and recovering of sight to the blind, to set at liberty them that are bruised. To preach the acceptable year of the Lord."			

Subject	Born in Bethlehem	Prophet	Micah	Year Prophesied	~725 BC

Old Testament Prophesy	Micah 5:2 "But thou, Bethlehem Ephratah, though thou be little among the thousands of Judah, yet out of thee shall he come forth unto me that is to be ruler in Israel; whose goings forth have been from of old, from everlasting."
New Testament Fulfillment	Luke 2:4–5, 7 "And Joseph also went up from Galilee, out of the city of Jazareth, into Judaea, unto the city of David, which is called Bethlehem; (because he was of the house and lineage of David:) To be taxed with Mary his espoused wife, being great with child. And she brought forth her firstborn son, and wrapped him in swaddling clothes, and laid him in a manger; because there was no room for them in the inn."

Subject	Slaughter of the Innocents	Prophet	Jeremiah	Year Prophesied	~600 BC
Old Testament Prophesy	Jeremiah 31:15 "Thus saith the Lord; A voice was heard in Ramah, lamentation, and bitter weeping; Rahel weeping for her children refused to be comforted for her children, because they were not."				
New Testament Fulfillment	Matthew 2:16–18 "Then Herod, when he saw that he was mocked of the wise men, was exceeding wroth, and sent forth, and slew all the children that were in Bethlehem, and in all the coasts thereof, from two years old and under, according to the time which he had diligently enquired of the wise men. Then was fulfilled that which was spoken by Jeremy the prophet, saying, In Rama was there a voice heard, lamentation, and weeping, and great mourning, Rachel weeping for her children, and would not be comforted, because they are not."				

Subject	Time for His Birth	Prophet	Daniel	Year Prophesied	~550 BC
Old Testament Prophesy	Daniel 9:25 "Know therefore and understand, that from the going forth of the commandment to restore and to build Jerusalem unto the Messiah the Prince shall be seven weeks, and three score and two weeks: the street shall be built again, and, the wall, even in the troublous times."				
New Testament Fulfillment	Luke 2:1–2 "And it came to pass in those days, that there went out a decree from Caesar Augustus, that all the world should be taxed. (And this taxing was first made when Cyrenius was governor of Syria.)"				

Subject	Triumphal Entry	Prophet	Zechariah	Year Prophesied	~525 BC

Old Testament Prophesy	Zechariah 9:9 "Rejoice greatly, O daughter of Zion; shout, O daughter of Jerusalem: behold, thy King cometh unto thee: he is just, and having salvation; lowly, and riding upon an ass, and upon a colt the foal of an ass."
New Testament Fulfillment	Mark 11:7, 9, 11 "And they brought the colt to Jesus, and cast their garments on him; and he sat upon him, And they that went before, and they that followed, cried, saying, 'Hosanna; Blessed is he that cometh in the name of the Lord': And Jesus entered into Jerusalem, and into the temple: and when he had looked round about upon all things, and now the eventide was come, he went out unto Bethany with the twelve."

Subject	Betrayed for Thirty Pieces of Silver	Prophet	Zechariah	Year Prophesied	~525 BC
Old Testament Prophesy		Zechariah 11:12 "And I said unto them, 'If ye think good, give me my price; and if not, forbear.' So they weighed for my price thirty pieces of silver."			
New Testament Fulfillment		Matthew 26:14–15 "Then one of the twelve, called Judas Iscariot, went unto the chief priests. And said unto them, 'What will ye give me, and I will deliver him unto you?' And they covenanted with him for thirty pieces of silver."			

Subject	His Side Pierced	Prophet	Zechariah	Year Prophesied	~525 BC
Old Testament Prophesy		Zechariah 12:10 "And I will pour upon the house of David, and upon the inhabitants of Jerusalem, the spirit of grace and of supplications: and they shall look upon me whom they have pierced, and they shall mourn for him, as one mourneth for his only son, and shall be in bitterness for him, as one that is in bitterness for his firstborn."			
New Testament Fulfillment		John 19:34 "But one of the soldiers with a spear pierced his side: and forthwith came there out blood and water."			

Subject	Pierced through Hands and Feet	Prophet	Zechariah	Year Prophesied	~525 BC

Old Testament Prophesy	Zechariah 12:10 "And I will pour upon the house of David, and upon the inhabitants of Jerusalem, the spirit of grace and of supplications: and they shall look upon me whom they have pierced, and they shall mourn for him, as one mourneth for his only son, and shall be in bitterness for him, as one that is in bitterness for his firstborn."
New Testament Fulfillment	John 20:27 "Then saith he to Thomas, 'Reach hither thy finger, and behold my hands; and reach hither thy hand, and thrust it into my side, and be not faithless, but believing.'"

Subject	Preceded by a Forerunner	Prophet	Malachi	Year Prophesied	~475 BC
Old Testament Prophesy		Malachi 3:1 "Behold, I will send my messenger, and he shall prepare the way before me: and the Lord, whom ye seek, shall suddenly come to his temple, even the messenger of the covenant, whom ye delight in: behold, he shall come, saith the Lord of hosts."			
New Testament Fulfillment		Luke 7:24, 27 "And when the messengers of John were departed, he began to speak unto the people concerning John, 'What went ye out into the wilderness for to see? A reed shaken with the wind? This is he, of whom it is written, Behold, I sent my messenger before thy face, which shall prepare thy way before thee.'"			

The Seventieth Week of Daniel

Daniel 9:24–27—Prophecy of the First and Second Comings of Jesus Christ

"Seventy weeks are determined upon thy people and upon thy hold city, to finish the transgression, and to make an end of sins, and to make reconciliation for iniquity, and to bring in everlasting righteousness, and to seal up the vision and prophecy, and to anoint the most Holy. Know therefore and understand, that from the going forth of the commandment to restore and to build Jerusalem unto the Messiah the Prince shall be seven weeks, and threescore and two weeks: the street shall be built again, and the wall, even in troublous times. And after threescore and two weeks shall Messiah be cut off, but not for himself: and the people of the prince that shall come shall destroy the city and the sanctuary; and the end thereof shall be with a flood, and unto the end of the war desolations are determined. And he shall confirm the covenant with many for one week: and in the midst of the week he shall cause the sacrifice and the oblation to cease, and for the overspreading of abominations he shall make it desolate, even until the consummation, and that determined shall be poured upon the desolate" (Daniel 9:24–27).

Daniel 9:24–27 are among the most difficult verses in the Bible to understand. Six events are mentioned in Daniel 9:24 as follows:

1. To finish the transgression
2. To make an end of sins
3. To make reconciliation for iniquity
4. To bring in everlasting righteousness
5. To seal up the vision and prophecy
6. To anoint the most Holy

These events were and will be totally fulfilled with the first and second coming of Jesus Christ.

Verse 25 states from the going forth of the commandment to restore and build Jerusalem will be seven weeks and threescore and two weeks. Seven weeks is 49 years (7 x 7 = 49). Threescore and two weeks is 434 years (62 x 7 = 434). (434 + 49 = 483 years)

To a Jew in Old Testament times, these weeks meant weeks of years. The word in Hebrew is Shavout, meaning weeks of years. Shavout is a word with a meaning of being a multiplier of a number.

During this time, the King of Persia directed and allowed the rebuilding of Jerusalem (7 x 7 = 49). This is a jubilee cycle, forty-nine years, wherein all land went back to its original owner if it had been sold. In Daniel's time, calendars were based on a 360-day year. Using these truths from around 445 BC to AD 32 would be 173,880 days, which is sixty-nine weeks of years, which is 483 years mentioned above. This would take us up to the very day that Jesus was crucified (173,880 days ÷ 360 days in a year = 483 years).

From the outpouring of the Holy Spirit on Pentecost, which was fifty days after the resurrection of Jesus Christ, to the present, is the Church Age. Some time in the near future, the seventieth week will commence and/or continue and end with the second coming of Jesus Christ.

The seventieth week will be seven years long; add this to 483 years, equals 490 years or ten jubilee cycles.

Artaxertes decrees the restoration of Jerusalem.

↙

		Seventieth Week
	Church Age	
← 483 years →	← ~2,000 years →	←→ 7 year tribulation
		Future event
~447–445 BC. AD 32		
Crucifixion of Jesus Christ		483 + 7 = 490 years[72]

Other prophecy teachers believe that Daniel's seventieth week was partially fulfilled with the resurrection of Jesus Christ in the middle of Daniel's seventieth week. This would leave a 3.5-year tribulation in the near future to complete Daniel's seventieth week. Still others believe Daniel's seventieth week was completed in the first century AD 3.5 years after the resurrection.

Some others believe Daniel's seventieth week, instead of being 490 years old, could also have a second meaning of 4,900 years. This thought is that Daniel's seventieth week, instead of being 7 x 70, is 70 x 70 = 4,900 years. This thought is that from the time of God's covenant with Abraham in about 1920 BC in Genesis 15 until 4,900 years later, about 950 years in the future, will be the time God brings this earth to an end and creates a new heaven and a new earth.

I am not dogmatic about these kinds of difficult verses. What I do know is that God has an exact timetable for the end of the age. After the second coming of Christ, we will understand details of the second coming just as we now understand the details of His first coming. I enjoy studying all different views of difficult verses in the Bible from those who study and believe the gospel of Jesus Christ. The word *gospel* means "good news."

---

72   Chuck Missler. *Hidden Treasures in the Biblical Text* (Koinonia House) pp.43–46.

An Overview of the New Testament

The reason I believe the Bible is because I can see that the author of the Bible (God) created the dimension of time. This is what Bible prophecy is all about. God created matter. God separated the matter, creating the dimension of space, and started it rotating, creating the dimension of time.

Previously, we have seen that many Old Testament heroes were pictures and types of Christ. It can be easily proven that Jesus Christ is personally fulfilling the feasts of the Lord in that He was the Passover lamb, crucified for our sins, our firstfruits fulfilled in His resurrection, and sending the Holy Spirit on Pentecost. All of this fulfills the first four feasts of the Lord in Exodus in the killing of the Passover lambs, the serious consequences of sin, the deliverance of the Hebrews from Egypt (sin), and the giving the Ten Commandments verbally by God at Mt. Sinai.

The Old Testament temple consisted of three parts—the Outer Court, the Holy Place, and the Holy of Holies. In the Old Testament temple, we can see prophecies of Jesus Christ in the Outer Court, where blood sacrifices occurred. We can see God in the Holy Place and its fulfillment when Jesus sent the Holy Spirit to dwell in believers on Pentecost in the New Testament, which was around AD 30–32. I believe the fall feasts will be fulfilled in events surrounding the second coming of Jesus and the millennium.

We see that Jesus Christ fulfilled prophecy in His genealogy, circumstances around His birth and life, and by His crucifixion and resurrection. The major direct prophecies of Jesus Christ were written from about 1000 BC through 475 BC. David and Isaiah penned the most prophecies, but Hosea, Micah, Jeremiah, Zechariah, and Malachi, which are books in the Old Testament, also wrote detailed prophecies.

There are detailed prophecies about the time of Jesus' birth. I believe the wise men knew the Old Testament, knew the approximate time of the birth of the Savior, and were looking for that birth. The reason the wise men were wise is because they came and worshipped Jesus. There were prophecies of the time of Jesus Christ's birth, His birth in Bethlehem from a virgin, and their fleeing to Egypt to escape death. There are prophecies of His life and ministry.

There are very detailed prophecies of Jesus Christ's triumphal entry into Jerusalem on Palm Sunday, betrayal by a close friend for thirty pieces of silver, being hated without a reason, falsely accused, scorned, mocked, spat on, and silent to accusers. His crucifixion between two sinners was given in detail. His clothes being gambled for; His hands, feet, and side being pierced; and being forsaken by God on the cross were all prophesied hundreds of years earlier.

The resurrection was prophesied, as was the declaration of Christ being the Son of God. His ascension to the right hand of God the Father and His being of the priesthood in the Order of Melchizedek were also prophesied.

These are the reasons I believe the Bible. I have purposed in my life not to deny Christ. Again, I see Jesus Christ throughout the Bible in His genealogy and major Bible characters as types of Christ. The feasts of the Lord, the temple of the Lord, and all of the detailed prophecies of His birth, life, ministry, trials, crucifixion, and His resurrection were prophesied hundreds of years earlier.

Jesus Christ was 100 percent God and 100 percent man when He walked on the earth two thousand years ago. He is the King and creator of the universe, as well as our High Priest who intercedes for mankind and specifically for His saints. He died for the sins of the world—but a person has to decide for himself whether or not to accept the free gift of salvation.

We will study Jesus' life, teachings, deeds, and works in the pages ahead. In Luke 22:26, Jesus said, "The greatest in the Kingdom of Heaven is servant of all." The word *Christ* means "anointed one" or "Messiah."

The Themes of the Four Gospels

"And the first beast was like a lion, and the second beast like a calf, and the third beast had a face as a man, and the fourth beast was like a flying eagle. And the four beasts had each of them six wings about him; and they were full of eyes within: and they rest not day and night, saying, Holy, holy, holy, Lord God Almighty, which was, and is, and is to come" (Revelation 4:7–8).

The Book of Matthew	Jesus as the Son of David	Lion of the Tribe of Judah	Royalty and King
The Book of Mark	Jesus as a Servant	Calf	Beast of Burden/Our Provider/Sacrificial Living
The Book of Luke	Jesus as the Son of Man	Man	The Humanity of Jesus
The Book of John	Jesus as the Son of God	Flying Eagle	Sees Everything from Above

Each of the seraphim (four beasts) represents an attribute of Jesus Christ in each of the four gospels. God as creator and king of the universe is outlined in the books of John and Matthew, respectively. His humanity is underscored in Luke. In the book of Mark, Jesus is a servant, continuously healing people. The calf is a beast of burden and is sacrificed for the purposes of ceremonial cleansing. Jesus is the Lamb of God. The Book of Mark is, I believe, frequently overlooked. When you are truly God (we aren't), it's easy to create the universe from nothing. What God did in the person of Jesus Christ is to show by example how He wants us to act in eternity. The servant, humble and gentle spirit with controlled strength, is God's desire for your soul. However, the major concept that God wants you to understand is His unsearchable love that He has for you—whether you are lost or saved.

The Genealogy of Jesus Christ

Luke 3:23–38—Genealogy of Jesus Christ

"And Jesus himself began to be about thirty years of age, being (as was supposed) the son of Joseph, which was the son of Heli, Which was the son of Matthat, which was the son of Levi, which was the son of Melchi, which was the son of Janna, which as the son of Joseph, Which was the son of Mattathias, which was the son of Amos, which was the son of Naum, which was the son of Esli, which was the son of Nagge, Which was the son of Maath, which was the son of Mattathias, which was the son of Semei, which was the son of Joseph, which was the son of Juda, Which was the son of Joanna, which was the son of Rhesa, which was the son of Zorobabel, which was the son of Salathiel, which was the son of Neri, Which was the son of Melchi, which was the son of Addi, which was the son of Cosam, which was the son of Elmodam, which was the son of Er, Which was the son of Jose, which was the son of Eliezer, which was the son of Jorim, which was the son of Matthat, which was the son of Levi, Which was the son of Simeon, which was the son of Juda, which was the son of Joseph, which was the son of Jonan, which was the son of Eliakim, Which was the son of Melea, which was the son of Menan, which was the son of Mattatha, which was the son of Nathan, which was the son of David, Which was the son of Jesses, which was the son of Obed, which was the son of Booz, which was the son of Salmon, which was the son of Naasson, Which was the son of Aminadab, which was the son of Aram, which was the son of Esrom, which was the son of Phares, which was the son of Juda Which was the son of Jacob, which was the son of Isaac, which was the son of Abraham, which was the son of Thara, which was the son of Nachor, Which was the son of Saruch, which was the son of Ragau, which was the son of Phalec, which was the son of Heber, which was the son of Sala, Which was the son of Cainan, which was the son of Arphaxad, which was the son of Sem, which was the son of Noe, which was the son of Lamech, Which was the son of Mathusala, which was the son of Enoch, which was the son of Jared, which was the son of Maleleel, which was the son of Cainan, Which was the son of Enos, which was the son of Seth, which was the son of Adam, which was the son of God" (Luke 3:23–38).

I heard Ed Young, pastor of Second Baptist Church in Houston, tell a story of a missionary in China. This missionary preached many great sermons, but no one ever came to believe the gospel. Finally, one day the missionary started reading the genealogy of Jesus Christ to the people, and many people received Christ immediately. Up until that time, they did not know if the preacher was telling a story or was talking about a real person. Jesus is real.

Adam and Eve were real people and were not related to amoebas or monkeys. The genealogy of Jesus Christ covers the time period from approximately 4000–3 BC. Jewish genealogies were kept in the temple, in Jerusalem and the temple was destroyed in AD 70 by the Romans, after the gospels were written. After the birth of Jesus, Jesus had stepbrothers and stepsisters through Joseph and Mary. I believe it was God's design that the genealogies would be destroyed so that people would not be able to claim to be a stepbrother or stepsister to the Son of God in future generations.

Luke 2:13–15—Heavenly Host Praises God at the Birth of Jesus—3–2 BC

"And suddenly there was with the angel a multitude of the heavenly host praising God, and saying, 'Glory to God in the highest, and on earth peace, good will toward men.' And it came to pass, as the angels were gone away from them into heaven, the shepherds said one to another, 'Let us now go even unto Bethlehem, and see this thing which is come to pass, which the Lord hath made known unto us'" (Luke 2:13–15).

Even though only a handful of people on the earth witnessed the birth of Jesus, all created beings in the heavens and the powers of hell knew about the birth of Jesus as it occurred.

Matthew 2:11—Wise Men Find Jesus

"And when they were come into the house, they saw the young child with Mary his mother, and fell down, and worshipped him: and when they had opened their treasures, they presented unto him gifts; gold, and frankincense, and myrrh" (Matthew 2:11).

A person is wise when they worship Jesus Christ.

Matthew 2:15–18—The Flight to Egypt and the Massacre of Innocent Babies

"And was there until the death of Herod: that it might be fulfilled which was spoken of the Lord by the prophet, saying, 'Out of Egypt have I called my son.' Then Herod, when he saw that he was mocked of the wise men, was exceeding wroth, and sent forth, and slew all the children that were in Bethlehem, and in all the coasts thereof, from two years old and under, according to the time which he had diligently enquired of the wise men. Then was fulfilled that which was spoken by Jeremiah the prophet, saying, 'In Rama was there a voice heard, lamentation, and weeping, and great mourning, Rachel weeping for her children, and would not be comforted, because they are not'" (Matthew 2:15–18).

These events were one to two years after the birth of Jesus. Babies were being killed at the time of the birth of Moses, at the birth of Jesus Christ, and even now.

Matthew 2:23—Jesus Grown up in Nazareth

"And he came and dwelt in a city called Nazareth: that it might be fulfilled which was spoken by the prophets, He shall be called a Nazarene" (Matthew 2:23).

Luke 2:42–43—AD 10—Scholars Astonished at the Knowledge of Jesus at Age Twelve

"And when he was twelve years old, they went up to Jerusalem after the custom of the feast. And when they had fulfilled the days, as they returned, the child Jesus tarried behind in Jerusalem; and Joseph and his mother knew not of it" (Luke 2:42–43).

Luke 2:49–50—Jesus About His Father's Business

"And he said unto them, 'How is it that ye sought me? wist ye not that I must be about my Father's business?' And they understood not the saying which he spake unto them" (Luke 2:49–50).

The father that Jesus was speaking about was His Father in heaven. We are to be about God's purposes while we are alive on the earth.

The Ministry of Jesus Christ after Age Thirty—AD 28

Luke 3:21–23—AD 27—Jesus was Baptized by John the Baptist

"Now when all the people were baptized, it came to pass, that Jesus also being baptized, and praying, the heaven was opened, And the Holy Ghost descended in a bodily shape like a dove upon him, and a voice came from heaven, which said, Thou art my beloved Son; in thee I am well pleased. And Jesus himself began to be about thirty years of age, being (as was supposed) the son of Joseph, which was the son of Heli" (Luke 3:21–23).

Jesus' formal ministry began at this time. Within 3.5 years after Jesus was baptized, He was crucified on the cross.

Luke 4:1–2—Satan Tempts Jesus

"And Jesus being full of the Holly Ghost returned from Jordan, and was led by the Spirit into the wilderness, Being forty days tempted of the devil. And in those days he did eat nothing: and when they were ended, he afterward hungered" (Luke 4:1–2).

Mark 6:3—Jesus Rejected in Nazareth

Is not this the carpenter, the son of Mary, the brother of James, and Joses, and of Juda, and Simon? and are not his sisters here with us? And they were offended at him" (Mark 6:3).

Mark 1:32–34—Many Healed after Sabbath Sunset

"And at even, when the sun did set, they brought unto him all that were diseased, and them that were possessed with devils. And all the city was gathered together at the door. 34 And he healed many that were sick of divers diseases, and cast out many devils; and suffered not the devils to speak, because they knew him" (Mark 1:32–34).

Jesus proved He was God in the flesh through the miracles He performed while on the earth. God created matter, space, and time from nothing. Therefore, these miracles would be extremely easy to perform. God created the natural world; the natural world must act and perform just as God commands it to do.

In Mark 1:32, the Bible tells us that they brought all in the city with diseases and possessed with devils. Jesus healed thousands in His time on the earth. Seven times in recorded miracles, Jesus showed His creation power. Three times Jesus raised a person from the dead. Twice Jesus fed the multitude by multiplying and creating bread and fish to eat from nothing. One time Jesus turned water into wine. On two different occasions, Jesus healed the blind. On twenty-two occasions, Jesus healed people from infirmities and sicknesses. Six times Jesus displayed power over nature (e.g., rebuking the wind and the sea to stop covering the ship with water which Jesus and His disciples were in). The disciples were amazed that even the winds obeyed Jesus. On three occasions, Jesus showed power over devils by casting them out. These are just the recorded miracles. There were clearly thousands of unrecorded miracles.

Jesus, while on the earth, taught many things, including things about the Kingdom of God. We were created to be friends of God. Jesus taught the nearness of God, that God is good, that we must trust God, that we should believe God, and that we must have faith in God. We must also understand that God is our provider. People make life more difficult than it needs to be.

Matthew 22:36-40—The First and Greatest Commandment

"Master, which is the great commandment in the law? Jesus said unto him, 'Thou shalt love the Lord thy God with all thy *heart*, and with all thy *soul*, and with all thy *mind*. This is the first and great commandment. And the second is like unto it, Thou salt love thy neighbour as thyself. On these two commandments hang all the law and the prophets'" (Matthew 22:36–40).

The Sermon on the Mount is the longest single recorded discord that Jesus spoke. It starts in Matthew 5 and concludes with Matthew 7. The Sermon on the Mount covers about twenty major topics. The Sermon on the Mount starts with the Beatitudes and ends with other basic foundations of biblical Christianity. The Beatitudes show us what our attitudes must be.

Matthew 5:1–3—The Beatitudes

"And seeing the multitudes, he went up into a mountain: and when he was set, his disciples came unto him: And he opened his mouth, and taught them, saying, 'Blessed are the poor in spirit: for theirs is the kingdom of heaven'" (Matthew 5:1–3).

Jesus spoke the Sermon on the Mount sitting down. The word *blessed* means "happy." Happy are the poor in spirit. Sin brings unhappiness. Being led by the Holy Spirit brings happiness. Poor in spirit means not being controlled by this world; it means being led by God, being humble, and being broken by one's own sin. To be poor in spirit does not mean being on the verge of a nervous breakdown and having no courage. Take note when reading the Bible whenever you see the words "kingdom of God" or "kingdom of heaven" that God is introducing us to the deep things of God that lost people cannot understand.

"Blessed are they that mourn: for they shall be comforted" (Matthew 5:4).

Christians are not to be miserable; however, to be saved, we must be downcast and broken over our own sins.

"Blessed are the meek: for they shall inherit the earth" (Matthew 5:5).

The meek are persons with God-controlled strength. Meek does not mean a person who is easy to run over. A meek person is not boastful or defensive.

"Blessed are they which do hunger and thirst after righteousness: for they shall be filled" (Matthew 5:6).

The righteous are not happy until they are in the will of God.

"Blessed are the merciful: for they shall obtain mercy" (Matthew 5:7).

When a person is merciful, they will receive mercy from others and God. Do you want to be loved by people? Then you must love people. We reap what we sow.

"Blessed are the pure in heart: for they shall see God" (Matthew 5:8).

The heart represents what you really believe. You have a pure heart when you are saved and are single-minded towards God.

"Blessed are the peacemakers: for they shall be called the children of God" (Matthew 5:9).

Jesus is the Prince of Peace. A peacemaker does not ask what is fair to himelf. A peacemaker controls his tongue, is slow to speak, and is slow to anger.

"Blessed are they which are persecuted for righteousness' sake: for theirs is the kingdom of heaven. Blessed are ye, when men shall revile you, and persecute you, and shall say all manner of evil against you falsely, for my sake. Rejoice, and be exceeding glad: for great if your reward in heaven: for so persecuted they the prophets which were before you" (Matthew 5:10–12).

The result of being a Christian is you will be persecuted. If people hated Jesus, they will hate you. A Christian's ultimate reward is eternity in heaven.

"Ye are the salt of the earth: but if the salt have lost his savour, wherewith shall it be salted? It is thenceforth good for nothing, but to be cast out, and to be trodden under foot of men. Ye are the light of the world. A city that is set on an hill cannot be hid. Neither do men light a candle, and put it under a bushel, but on a candlestick; and it giveth light unto all that are in the house. Let your light so shine before men, that they may see your good works, and glorify your Father which is in heaven" (Matthew 5:13–16).

Christians are to be the preservative of the earth. A backslidden Christian is good for nothing other than to be ridiculed by those who are lost.

"Think not that I am come to destroy the law, or the prophets: I am not come to destroy, but to fulfil. For verily I say unto you, Till heaven and earth pass, one jot or one tittle shall in no wise pass from the law, till all be fulfilled. Whosoever therefore shall break one of these least commandments, and shall teach men so, he shall be called the least in the kingdom of heaven: but whosoever shall do and teach them, the same shall be called great in the kingdom of heaven" (Matthew 5:17–19).

Jesus states He came to fulfill the law not to do away with the law. In other words, He came to never sin, and thus He was an acceptable sacrifice for our sins.

"For I say unto you, That except your righteousness shall exceed the righteousness of the scribes and Pharisees, ye shall in no case enter into the kingdom of heaven. Ye have heard that it was said by them of old time, Thou shalt not kill; and whosoever shall kill shall be in danger of the judgment: But I say unto you, That whosoever is angry with his brother without a cause shall be in danger of the judgment: and whosoever shall say to his brother, Raca, shall be in danger of the council: but whosoever shall say, Thou fool, shall be in danger of hell fire" (Matthew 5:20–22).

The New Testament raised the standard. The Old Testament tells us not to murder. Jesus raised the standard and tells us not to hate our fellow man and to be forgiving.

"Ye have heard that it was said by them of old time, Thou shalt not commit adultery: But I say unto you, That whosoever looketh on a woman to lust after her hath committed adultery with her already in his heart. And if thy right eye offend thee, pluck it out, and cast it from thee: for it is profitable for thee that one of thy members should perish, and not that thy whole body should be cast into hell And if thy right hand offend thee, cut it off, and cast it from thee: for it is profitable for thee that one of thy members should perish, and not that thy whole body should be cast into hell" (Matthew 5:27–30).

The Old Testament tells us not to commit adultery. Jesus tells us not to look upon a woman with lust. We are to take drastic measures not to sin. This includes actions such as throwing out your TV if your TV causes you to stumble. The remainder of Matthew 5–7 gives us direction on the issues of divorce, taking oaths, retaliation, gifts to the needy, prayer, fasting (abstaining from foods for a period of time), money, judging others, and persistent prayer.

Matthew 6:9–13—The Lord's Prayer

"After this manner therefore pray ye: Our Father which art in heaven, Hallowed be thy name. Thy kingdom come. Thy will be done in earth, as it is in heaven. Give us this day our daily bread. And forgive us our debts, as we forgive our debtors. And lead us not into temptation, but deliver us from evil: For thine is the kingdom, and the power, and the glory, forever. Amen" (Matthew 6:9–13).

Prayer is talking to God. I talk to God all day long. I don't think I go one minute without thinking about what God thinks about the situation I'm thinking about. I pray to God frequently without closing my eyes. I suggest that you pray to God while you are driving alone. I pray every morning with my wife before we go to work (except for Saturdays; we sleep in).

Matthew 7:12—The Golden Rule

"Therefore all things whatsoever ye would that men should do to you, do ye even so to them: for this is the law and the prophets" (Matthew 7:12).

We are to treat others the way we want to be treated.

Matthew 7:13–14—The Narrow Way to Heaven

"Enter ye at the straight gate: for wide is the gate, and broad is the way, that leadeth to destruction, and many there be which go thereat: Because straight is the gate, and narrow is the way, which leadeth unto life and few there be that find it" (Matthew 7:13–14).

Matthew 7:21–23—The Wide Way to Destruction

"Not every one that saith unto me, 'Lord, Lord,' shall enter into the kingdom of heaven; but he that doeth the will of my Father which is in heaven. Many will say to me in that day, 'Lord, Lord, have we not prophesied in thy name? and in thy name have cast out devils? and in thy name done many wonderful works?' And then will I profess unto them, 'I never knew you: depart from me, ye that work iniquity'" (Matthew 7:21–23).

The wide way is the way to hell; the narrow way is the way to heaven. This is a very important truth, but many people will not believe the truth, and you will be hated when you profess the truth. These are some of the scariest verses in the Bible. The vast majority of the people on the earth are not—and never will be—saved.

The Purpose of Parables

In the Bible, a parable is used as a short story with a purpose of telling a Christian truth or a moral lesson. Parables compare one thing to another. Parables reveal truth to Christians and hide truth from unbelievers. Parables show us what God thinks about a matter. They show us that we must follow God now. Also, we are to follow God at all costs, to pay close attention to what God is telling us, and to focus on eternity.

Mark 4:11–20—The Purpose of Parables and the Parable of the Sower

"And he said unto them, 'Unto you it is given to know the mystery of the kingdom of God: but unto them that are without, all these things are done in parables: That seeing they may see, and not perceive; and hearing they may hear, and not understand; lest at any time they should be converted, and their sins should be forgiven them.' And he said unto them, 'Know ye not this parable? and how then will ye know all parables? The sower soweth the word. And these are they by the way side, where the word is sown: but when they have heard, Satan cometh immediately, and taketh away the word that was sown in their hearts. And these are they likewise which are sown on stony ground; who, when they have heard the word, immediately receive it with gladness; And have no root in themselves, and so endure but for a time: afterward, when affliction or persecution ariseth for the word's sake, immediately they are offended. And these are they which are sown among thorns; such as hear the word, And the cares of this world, and the deceitfulness of riches, and the lusts of other things entering in, choke the word, and it becometh unfruitful. And these are they which are sown on good ground; such as hear the word, and receive it, and bring forth fruit, some thirtyfold, some sixty, and some an hundred'" (Mark 4:11–20).

Parables show Christians the deep things of God and the kingdom of heaven. God desires none to perish but all to have eternal life. However, to people who do not seek the kingdom of God, the Bible is a dead letter.

Most people will not believe the Bible. For those searching to know the true and living creator God, God gives them spiritual eyes to see. God also gives spiritual ears to understand the mysteries of the kingdom of God. Listed below are the truths of the Parable of the Sower:

1. Many hear, but few receive God's Word into their hearts.
2. Most are distracted from hearing God because of unbelief.
3. Many believe salvation by the grace of God through faith is just too simple.
4. Most people get distracted too easily and will not take the time to find out what is the truth.
5. Others mock God.
6. Others don't think their heart is ready to believe, and this puts them in great danger of hell's fire.
7. Others hear the Word of God and accept it gladly; then, because of worldly desires, they fall away from God. These people will not study the Bible and will not stand the persecution of being a Christian.
8. Many fall away from Christianity because it is not worth the problems of being a Christian. It's easier to stay home, watch TV, and only be concerned with the cares of this world.
9. Many say the sinner's prayer, but few move along with God.
10. A small number hear the word, receive it, and bring forth the fruit of the Spirit.

A true Christian will hear and respond to the Bible and God's Holy Spirit. A true Christian will bear much fruit—some thirtyfold, some sixtyfold, and some hundredfold. Inheriting the kingdom of God is hearing God's voice and obeying His Word. Fruit is expected and must be plentiful. The Spirit will bring forth a changed life that will bear much fruit.

The Fruit of the Spirit is love, joy, peace, longsuffering, gentleness, goodness, faith, meekness, and temperance; against such, there is no law.

You Must Be Born Again

John 3:3–7—You Must Be Born Again

"Jesus answered and said unto him, 'Verily, verily, I say unto thee, Except a man be born again, he cannot see the kingdom of God.' Nicodemus saith unto him, 'How can a man be born when he is old? can he enter the second time into his mother's womb, and be born?' Jesus answered, 'Verily, verily, I say unto thee, Except a man be born of water and of the Spirit, he cannot enter into the kingdom of God.

That which is born of the flesh is flesh; and that which is born of the Spirit is spirit. Marvel not that I said unto thee, Ye must be born again'" (John 3:3–7).

Jesus said "verily, verily," which means "truly" or "listen." When God says something twice, it means it is immensely important. We must have a new life, a new beginning, and a new nature; we must be born from above. The flesh is flesh and can be seen by the eye. The spirit is spirit and cannot be seen by the naked eye. Jesus said people were so sinful that we needed to be regenerated. We are recreated and regenerated by the Holy Spirit of God at the time of salvation, which is receiving Jesus Christ as Lord and Savior.

Matthew 18:1–6—Who Will be the Greatest in the Kingdom of Heaven

"At the same time came the disciples unto Jesus, saying, 'Who is the greatest in the kingdom of heaven?' And Jesus called a little unto him, and set him in the midst of them. And said, 'Verily I say unto you, Except ye be converted, and become as little children, ye shall not enter into the kingdom of heaven. Whosoever therefore shall humble himself as this little child, the same is greatest in the kingdom of heaven. And whoso shall receive one such little child in my name receiveth me. But whoso shall offend one of these little ones which believe in me, it were better for him that a millstone were hanged about his neck, and that he were drowned in the depth of the sea'" (Matthew 18:1–6).

Ultimately we must come to God with simple, childlike faith. A person must never teach a child to break the Ten Commandments, for this will bring great judgment against them.

Matthew 12:20—Hope for the Backslidden Christian

"A bruised reed shall he not break, and smoking flax shall he not quench, till he send forth judgment unto victory" (Matthew 12:20).

If you are a backslidden Christian, God will not snuff you out. However, today is the day to turn back to God.

John 3:16—For God So Loved the World

"For God so loved the world, that he gave his only begotten Son, that whosoever believeth in him should not perish, but have everlasting life" (John 3:16).

Jesus was begotten. Jesus is God. God is love and loves the whole world. The Holy Spirit regenerates sinful man. Without faith in God, there is no eternal life. At the moment of salvation, a person's sins are forgiven by God.

John 3:17–21—Jesus Did Not Come to Condemn the World

"For God sent not his Son into the world to condemn the world; but that the world through him might be saved. He that believeth on him is not condemned: but he that believeth not is condemned already, because he hath not believed in the name of the only begotten Son of God. And this is the condemnation, that light is come into the world, and men loved darkness rather than light, because their deeds were evil. For every one that doeth evil hateth the light, neither cometh to the light, lest his deeds should be reproved. But he that doeth truth cometh to the light, that his deeds may be made manifest, that they are wrought in God" (John 3:17–21).

Coming into the light is painful as we deal with our sinful habits. God has given all mankind spiritual light to believe in Him and His Son, Jesus Christ. You have the free will to believe in the only begotten Son of God, Jesus Christ—or you can choose to rebel against God.

The Triumphal Entry of Jesus Christ into Jerusalem—AD 30–32—The Spring Feasts of the Lord

"And the disciples went, and did as Jesus commanded them, And brought the ass, and the colt, and put on them their clothes, and they set him thereon. And a very great multitude spread their garments in the way; others cut down branches from the trees, and strawed them in the way. And the multitudes that went before, and that followed, cried, saying, 'Hosanna to the Son of David: Blessed is he that cometh in the name of the Lord; Hosanna in the highest.' And when he was come into Jerusalem, all the city was moved, saying, 'Who is this?' And the multitude said, 'This is Jesus the prophet of Nazareth of Galilee'" (Matthew 21:6–11).

These verses were prophesied by Zechariah in approximately 525 BC. This describes Palm Sunday. The rabbis who performed temple sacrifices of lambs brought lambs from Bethlehem to be sacrificed. These Passover lambs were killed on the same day that Jesus was crucified.

Luke 22:1–6—Judas Conspires with Religious Leaders

"Now the feast of unleavened bread drew nigh, which is called the Passover. And the chief priests and scribes sought how they might kill him; for they feared the people. Then entered Satan into Judas surnamed Iscariot, being of the number of the twelve. And he sent his way, and communed with the chief priests and captains, how he might betray him unto them. And they were glad, and covenanted to give him money. And he promised, and sought opportunity to betray him unto them in the absence of the multitude" (Luke 22:1–6).

These verses were prophesied in Psalm 41:9 approximately one thousand years before the crucifixion.

The Last Supper and the Garden of Gethsemane

Luke 22:7–13—The Disciples Prepare for Passover

"Then came the day of unleavened bread, when the passover must be killed. And he sent Peter and John, saying, 'Go and prepare us the passover, that we may eat.' And they said unto him, 'Where wilt thou that we prepare?' And he said unto them, 'Behold, when ye are entered into the city, there shall a man meet you, bearing a pitcher of water; follow him into the house where he entereth in. And ye shall say unto the goodman of the house, The Master saith unto thee, Where is the guestchamber, where I shall eat the passover with my disciples? And he shall shew you a large upper room furnished: there make ready.' And they went, and found as he had said unto them: and they made ready the passover" (Luke 22:7–13).

Luke 22:14–20—Jesus Institutes the Lord's Supper

"And when the hour was come, he sat down, and the twelve apostles with him. And he said unto them, 'With desire I have desired to eat this passover with you before I suffer: For I say unto you, I will not any more eat thereof, until it be fulfilled in the kingdom of God.' And he took the cup, and gave thanks, and said, 'Take this, and divide it among yourselves: For I say unto you, I will not drink of the fruit of the vine, until the kingdom of God shall come.' And he took bread, and gave thanks, and brake it, and gave unto them, saying, 'This is my body which is given for you: this do in remembrance of me.' Likewise also the cup after supper, saying, 'This cup is the new testament in my blood, which is shed for you'" (Luke 22:14–20).

"For as often as ye eat this bread, and drink this cup, ye do shew the Lord's death till he come" (I Corinthians 11:26).

The Lord's Supper is to memorialize the death of Jesus Christ.

Luke 22:24–26—The Disciples Argue About Who Should Be the Greatest

"And there was also a strife among them, which of them should be accounted the greatest. And he said unto them, 'The kings of the Gentiles exercise lordship over them; and they that exercise authority upon them are called benefactors. But ye shall not be so: but he that is greatest among you, let him be as the younger; and he that is chief, as he that doth serve'" (Luke 22:24–26).

The greatest in the kingdom of heaven will be the servant of all. Our purpose on the earth is to learn to live by faith, not to gain great positions in heaven. Jesus was the Lamb of God as represented by the calf (a servant) in Revelation 4:7.

Luke 22:31–34—Jesus Tells Simon Peter that Peter will Deny Jesus Three Times

"And the Lord said, 'Simon, Simon, behold, Satan hath desired to have you, that he may sift you as wheat: But I have prayed for thee, that thy faith fail not: and when thou art converted, strengthen thy brethren.' And he said unto him, 'Lord, I am ready to go with thee, both into prison, and to death.' And he said, 'I tell thee, Peter, the cock shall not crow this day, before that thou shalt thrice deny that thou knowest me'" (Luke 22:31–24).

Jesus told Peter that Peter would deny Him three times before the morning—and this in fact did occur.

Luke 22:39-48—Jesus Prays in the Garden and is Betrayed and Arrested

"And he came out, and went, as he was wont, to the mount of Olives; and his disciples also followed him. And when he was at the place, he said unto them, 'Pray that ye enter not into temptation.' And he was withdrawn from them about a stone's cast, and kneeled down, and prayed, Saying, 'Father, if thou be willing, remove this cup from me: nevertheless not my will, but thine, be done.' And there appeared an angel unto him from heaven, strengthening him. And being in an agony he prayed more earnestly: and his sweat was as it were great drops of blood falling down to the ground. And when he rose up from prayer, and was come to his disciples, he found them sleeping for sorrow, And said unto them, 'Why sleep ye? rise and pray, lest ye enter into temptation.' And while he yet spake, behold a multitude, and he that was called Judas, one of the twelve, went before them, and drew near unto Jesus to kill him. But Jesus said unto him, 'Judas, betrayest thou the Son of man with a kiss?'" (Luke 22:29–48).

Jesus always did the will of God the Father. Jesus never looked for the easy way out and came as an example for the saints. Jesus Christ stated He would always do the will of the Father. Again, we are to imitate His actions.

Luke 22:54–62—Peter Denies Jesus Three Times

"Then took they him, and led him, and brought him into the high priest's house. And Peter followed afar off. And when they had kindled a fire in the midst of the hall, and were set down together, Peter sat down among them. But a certain maid beheld him as he sat by the fire, and earnestly looked upon him, and said, 'This man was also with him.' And he denied him, saying, 'Woman, I know him not.' And after a little while another saw him, and said, 'Thou art also of them.' And Peter said, 'Man, I am not.' And about the space of one hour after another confidently affirmed, saying, 'Of a truth this fellow also was with him: for he is a Galilaean.' And Peter said, 'Man, I know not what thou sayest.' And immediately, while he yet spake, the cock crew. And the Lord turned, and looked upon Peter. And Peter remembered the word of the Lord, how he had said unto him, 'Before the cock crow, thou shalt deny me thrice.' And Peter went out, and wept bitterly" (Luke 22:54–62).

Peter was the only disciple to stay close to Jesus after He was arrested; however, Peter denied Jesus three times—just as Jesus said he would.

The Trial of Jesus Christ

Luke 22:63–65—Jesus is Mocked and Beaten

"And the men that held Jesus mocked him, and smote him. And when they had blindfolded him, they struck him on the face, and asked him, saying, 'Prophesy, who is it that smote thee?' And many other things blasphemously spake they against him" (Luke 22:63–65).

These events were prophesied by the prophet Isaiah in approximately 725 BC.

Luke 22:66–71—Jesus is Taken to Jewish Religious Leaders

"And as soon as it was day, the elders of the people and the chief priests and the scribes came together, and led him into their council, saying, 'Art thou the Christ? tell us.' And he said unto them, 'If I tell you, ye will not believe: And if I also ask you, ye will not answer me, nor let me go. Hereafter shall the Son of man sit on the right hand of the power of God.' Then said they all, 'Art thou then the Son of God?'

And he said unto them, 'Ye say that I am.' And they said, 'What need we any further witness? for we ourselves have heard of his own mouth'" (Luke 22:66–71).

Jesus is saying here that He is in fact the Son of God. Jesus is a lunatic, a liar, or the Son of God. I believe Jesus is the Son of God.

Luke 23:1–7—Jesus is Taken to Pilate

"And the whole multitude of them arose, and led him unto Pilate. And they began to accuse him, saying, 'We found this fellow perverting the nation, and forbidding to give tribute to Caesar, saying that he himself is Christ a King.' And Pilate asked him, saying, 'Art thou the King of the Jews?' And he answered him and said, 'Thou sayest it.' Then said Pilate to the chief priests and to the people, 'I find no fault in this man.' And they were the more fierce, saying, 'He stirreth up the people, teaching throughout all Jewry, beginning from Galilee to this place.' When Pilate heard of Galilee, he asked whether the man were a Galilaean. And as soon as he knew that he belonged unto Herod's jurisdiction, he sent him to Herod, who himself also was at Jerusalem at that time" (Luke 23:1–7).

Pilate did not want to take responsibility for the situation and wanted Herod to take over. Furthermore, Pilate found no fault in Jesus.

Luke 23:8–25—Jesus is Taken to Herod and the Jews Demand that Jesus be Crucified

"And when Herod saw Jesus, he was exceeding glad: for he was desirous to see him of a long season, because he had heard many things of him; and he hoped to have seen some miracle done by him. Then he questioned with him in many words; but he answered him nothing. And the chief priests and scribes stood and vehemently accused him. And Herod with his men of war set him at nought, and mocked him, and arrayed him in a gorgeous robe, and sent him again to Pilate. And the same day Pilate and Herod were made friends together: for before they were at enmity between themselves. And Pilate, when he had called together the chief priests and the rulers and the people, Said unto them, 'Ye have brought this man unto me, as one that perverteth the people: and, behold, I, having examined him before you, have found no fault in this man touching those things whereof ye accuse him: No, nor yet Herod: for I sent you to him; and, lo, nothing worthy of death is done unto him. I will therefore chastise him, and release him.' (For of necessity he must release one unto them at the feast.) And they cried out all at once, saying, 'away with this man, and release unto us Barabbas' (Who for a certain sedition made in the city, and for murder, was cast into prison.) Pilate therefore, willing to release Jesus, spake again to them. But they cried, saying, 'Crucify him, crucify him.' And he said unto them the third time, 'Why, what evil hath he done? I have found no cause of death in him: I will therefore chastise him, and let him go.' And they were instant with loud voices, requiring that he might be crucified. And the voices of them and of the chief priests prevailed. And Pilate gave sentence that it should be as they required. And he released unto them him that for sedition and murder was cast into prison, whom they had desired; but he delivered Jesus to their will" (Luke 23:8–25).

Herod just wanted to see a miracle; he didn't really want to know the truth. Jesus answered him nothing, which was prophesied in Isaiah 53:7 (written approximately 725 BC). The religious people of Jerusalem were threatened by Jesus and wanted Him dead quickly—at any cost.

Matthew 27:25–35—Barabbas Released and Jesus Mocked and Crucified

"Then answered all the people, and said, 'His blood be on us, and on our children.' Then released he Barabbas unto them: and when he had scourged Jesus, he delivered him to be crucified. Then the soldiers of the governor took Jesus into the common hall, and gathered unto him the whole band of soldiers. And they stripped him, and put on him a scarlet robe. And when they had platted a crown of thorns, they put it upon his head, and a reed in his right hand: and they bowed the knee before him, and mocked him, saying, 'Hail, King of the Jews!' And they spit upon him, and took the reed, and smote him on the head. And after that they had mocked him, they took the robe off from him, and put his own raiment on him, and led him away to crucify him. And as they came out, they found a man of Cyrene, Simon by name: him they compelled to bear his cross. And when they were come unto a place called Golgotha, that is to say, a place of a skull, They gave him vinegar to drink mingled with gall: and when he had tasted thereof, he would not drink. And they crucified him, and parted his garments, casting lots: that it might be fulfilled which was spoken by the prophet, 'they parted my garments among them, and upon my vesture did they cast lots'" (Matthew 27:25–35).

In Matthew 27:25, the people said to put the innocent blood of Jesus Christ on them, and forty years later, the Romans killed hundreds of thousands of Jews (in AD 70). Be careful what you ask for.

For greater detail, go back to the Old Testament section of this book for Old Testament prophecies and their fulfillment in Jesus in the New Testament.

The Last Seven Statements of Jesus Christ on the Cross

Luke 23:32–49—Jesus on the Cross between Two Thieves

"And there were also two other, malefactors, led with him to be put to death. And when they were come to the place, which is called Calvary, there they crucified him, and the malefactors, one on the right hand, and the left. Then said Jesus, 'Father, forgive them; for they know not what they do.' And they parted his raiment, and cast lost. And the people stood beholding. And the rulers also with them derided him, saying, 'He saved others; let him save himself, if he be Christ, the chosen of God.' And the soldiers also mocked him, coming to him, and offering him vinegar. And saying, 'If thou be the king of the Jews, save thyself.' And a superscription also was written over him in letters of Greek, and Latin, and Hebrew, 'THIS IS THE KING OF THE JEWS.' And one of the malefactors which were hanged railed on him, saying, 'If thou be Christ, save thyself and us.' But the other answering rebuked him, saying, 'Dost not thou fear God, seeing thou art in the same condemnation? And we indeed justly; for we receive the due reward of our deeds: but this man hath done nothing amiss.' And he said unto Jesus, 'Lord, remember me when thou comest into thy kingdom.' And Jesus said unto him, 'Verily I say unto thee, To day shalt thou be with me in paradise.' And it was about the sixth hour, and there was a darkness over all the earth until the ninth house. And the sun was darkened, and the veil of the Temple was rent in the midst. And when Jesus had cried with a loud voice, he said, 'Father, into thy hands I commend my spirit': and having said thus, he gave up the ghost. Now when the centurion saw what was done, he glorified God, saying, 'Certainly this was a righteous man.' And all the people that came together to that sight, beholding the things which were done, smote their breasts, and returned. And all his acquaintance, and the women that followed him from Galilee, stood afar off, beholding these things" (Luke 23:32–49).

These verses fulfill the prophecy of Isaiah 53:12.

John 19:25–27—Jesus Cares for His Mother at the Cross

"Now there stood by the cross of Jesus his mother, and his mother's sister, Mary the wife of Cleophas, and Mary Magdalene. When Jesus therefore saw his mother, and the disciple standing by, whom he loved, he saith unto his mother, 'Woman, behold thy son!' Then saith he to the disciple, 'Behold thy mother!' And from that hour that disciple took her unto his own home" (John 19:25–27).

Jesus was looking after the needs of His mother even in His time of great distress.

Matthew 27:45–50—Jesus Fulfills Prophecy on the Cross

"Now from the sixth hour there was darkness over all the land unto the ninth hour. And about the ninth hour Jesus cried with a loud voice, saying 'Eli, Eli, lama sabachthani?' that is to say, 'My God, my God, why hast thou forsaken me?' Some of them that stood there, when they heard that, said, 'This man calleth for Elias.' And straightway one of them ran, and took a sponge, and filled it with vinegar, and put it on a reed, and gave him a drink. The rest said, 'Let be, let us see whether Elias will come to save him.' Jesus, when he had cried again with a loud voice, yielded up the ghost" (Matthew 27:45–50).

This fulfills Psalm 22:1.

John 19:28–30—Jesus Fulfills Prophecy on the Cross

"After this, John knowing that all things were now accomplished, that the scripture might be fulfilled, saith, 'I thirst.' Now there was set a vessel full of vinegar: and they filled a sponge with vinegar, and put it upon hyssop, and put it to his mouth. When Jesus therefore had received the vinegar, he said, 'It is finished': and he bowed his head, and gave up the ghost" (John 19:28–30).

This fulfills Psalm 22:15.

Luke 23:43–46—Jesus Dies on the Cross and the Veil of the Temple Tears Down the Middle

"And there appeared an angel unto him from heaven, strengthening him. And it was about the sixth hour, and there was a darkness over all the earth until the ninth hour. And the sun was darkened, and the veil of the Temple was rent in the midst. And when Jesus had cried with a loud voice, he said, 'Father, into thy hands I commend my spirit': and having said thus, he gave up the ghost" (Luke 23:43–46).

This fulfills Psalm 31:5, written one thousand years earlier by King David.

The following is a summary of Jesus' seven major statements on the cross from the books of Matthew, Luke, and John. Jesus came to be an example for us. Jesus said:

1. *Father, forgive them; for they know not what they do.*

    We are to forgive those who hate us and cause us harm. The ability to forgive others cannot occur without the indwelling of the Holy Spirit.

    "And they stoned Stephen, calling upon God, and saying 'Lord Jesus receive my spirit.' And he kneeled down, and cried with a loud voice, 'Lord, lay not this sin to their charge'" (Acts 7:59–60).

2. *Verily I say unto thee, today shalt thou be with me in paradise.*

    Jesus told the thief on the cross that He would see him in paradise that day. Jesus came to save those who are lost, and He was even saving people while He was on the cross.

3. *"Woman, behold thy son!" Then saith he to His disciple, "Behold thy mother!"*

    While Jesus was on the cross, He was arranging for the wellbeing of His mother.

4. *My God, My God, why hast thou forsaken me?*

    Jesus was pointing back to over one thousand years earlier to David in Psalm 22. While on the cross, Jesus was fulfilling hundreds of Bible prophecies.

    "My God, My God, why hast thou forsaken me? Why art thou so far from helping me, and from the words of my roaring? Oh my God I cry in the daytime but thou hearest not: and in the night season, and am not silent" (Psalm 22:1–2).

5. *I thirst.*

    Jesus said, "I thirst." This again points to prophecy.

    "They gave me also gall for my meat (and in my thirst they gave me vinegar to drink)" Psalm 69:21).

6. *It is finished.*

    Jesus said, "It is finished." He fulfilled all that He was sent to do. Jesus paid for our sins in full; there is nothing we can do to save ourselves. Salvation is by the grace of God through our faith.

7. *Father, into thy hands I commend my spirit.*

    Jesus gave Himself back to His Father in heaven.

The seven statements that Jesus said on the cross have been life-changing for me. I believe they are among the most important verses in the Bible. I think of them daily because of their simplicity. The statements made by Jesus are statements you can review and evaluate at the end of the day. These are questions you can ask yourself.

1) Have I forgiven and prayed for my enemies as Jesus did today?
2) Have I witnessed to help lead people to the Lord as Jesus did to the thief on the cross? Even if you are in great pain and struggling at your job or at home, you can still lead others to Christ. If you are unemployed, you can lead people to the Lord.
3) Have you honored your parents? The best way to honor your parents is to communicate with them in the spirit of humility, honor, friendship, and respect.
4) Do you know the Bible well enough to properly discern the truth of events that occurred during the day?
5) Have you accomplished what God has called you to do, and are you stopping to fellowship and listen to His voice? Would you be ready to meet God if you died tonight? Would your arrival in heaven be nothing but joyous, or would your works, deeds, and words be an embarrassment that is burned up as wood, hay, and stubble on judgment day?

The pain and suffering of Jesus on the cross was immense. Jesus prayed so hard in the Garden of Gethsemane He sweat blood. From the crucifixion account in the Bible, Jesus did not sleep the night before He was crucified. He would have not slept for at least thirty hours before He was nailed to the cross. Jesus would have lost a lot of blood prior to the crucifixion. His beard was plucked out. Jesus was scourged (whipped) with a whip that had metal pieces at the tips. A crown of thorns was placed on His head, and it is reasonable to think that He had a terrible headache. Jesus was crucified at Golgotha, which is located close to the Temple Mount. It was a place to dispose of dead animals, trash, etc., and the smell would have been horrific.

The Romans stripped the clothes off Jesus so He was naked on the cross. There would have been dried blood. Tearing the clothes off of Jesus would have been very painful and humiliating. The purpose of crucifixion was to show the masses not to come against those in earthly authority.

The nails would have been quickly nailed in place. Every part of Jesus' body (head, back, hands, and feet) would have been in severe pain. Every movement on the cross would cause more sharp, terrible pain. Jesus would have had cramps, intense thirst, and deep breathing, and His legs would be swelling. His tongue would have swelled, and His heart would be beating very fast.

Jesus died for the sins of the world—including those of Adolf Hitler and of you. Adolf Hitler did not accept the free gift of eternal life offered by God; will you be like Hitler too?

The Resurrection of Jesus Christ

Matthew 27:51–56—The Graves Were Opened, and Many Saints Arose

"And, behold, the veil of the Temple was rent in twain from the top to the bottom; and the earth did quake, and the rocks rent; And the graves were opened; and many bodies of the saints which slept arose,

And came out of the graves after his resurrection, and went into the holy city, and appeared unto many. Now when the centurion, and they that were with him, watching Jesus, saw the earthquake, and those things that were done, they feared greatly, saying, 'Truly this was the Son of God.' And many women were there beholding afar off, which followed Jesus from Galilee, ministering unto him: Among which was Mary Magdalene, and Mary the mother of James and Joses, and the mother of Zebedee's children" (Matthew 27:51–56).

In Matthew 27:51, the veil of the temple split into two pieces from the top to the bottom at the time of the death of Jesus Christ. This signifies the fact that you do not have to go through your priest or pastor to talk to God or to ask for forgiveness of your sins; you can go directly to God yourself. The verses in Matthew 27:52–53 occurred three days after the veil in the temple split. Jesus is our firstfruit and was raised from the dead first, and after this, many Old Testament saints arose from the dead and appeared to many. In the resurrection of Jesus Christ, He fulfilled the Feast of Firstfruits, which occurred approximately 1,400 years earlier in the time of Moses.

Matthew 27:57–66—Jesus Buried in Joseph's Tomb

"When the even was come, there came a rich man of Arimathaea, named Joseph, who also himself was Jesus' disciple: He went to Pilate, and begged the body of Jesus. Then Pilate commanded the body to be delivered. And when Joseph had taken the body, he wrapped it in a clean linen cloth, And laid it in his own new tomb, which he had hewn out in the rock: and he rolled a great stone to the door of the sepulchre, and departed. And there was Mary Magdalene, and the other Mary, sitting over against the sepulchre. Now the next day, that followed the day of the preparation, the chief priests and Pharisees came together unto Pilate, Saying, 'Sir, we remember that that deceiver said, while he was yet alive, After three days I will rise again. Command therefore that the sepulchre be made sure until the third day, lest his disciples come by night, and steal him away, and say unto the people, He is risen from the dead: so the last error shall be worse than the first.' Pilate said unto them, 'Ye have a watch: go your way, make it as sure as ye can.' So they went, and made the sepulchre sure, sealing the stone, and setting a watch" (Matthew 27:57–66).

The burial place of Jesus was sealed by Pilate so His body could not be stolen.

Matthew 28:1–6, 11–15—Soldiers are Bribed to Say that the Body of Jesus was Stolen

"In the end of the sabbath, as it began to dawn toward the first day of the week, came Mary Magdalene and the other Mary to see the sepulchre. And, behold, there was a great earthquake: for the angel of the Lord descended from heaven, and came and rolled back the stone from the door, and sat upon it. His countenance was like lightning, and his raiment white as snow: And for fear of him the keepers did shake, and became as dead men. And the angel answered and said unto the women, 'Fear not ye: for I know that ye seek Jesus, which was crucified. He is not here: for he is risen, as he said. Come, see the place where the Lord lay' …. Now when they were going, behold, some of the watch came into the city, and shewed unto the chief priests all the things that were done. And when they were assembled with the elders, and had taken counsel, they gave large money unto the soldiers, Saying, 'Say ye, His disciples came by night, and stole him away while we slept. And if this come to the governor's ears, we will persuade him, and secure you.' So they took the money, and did as they were taught: and this saying is commonly reported among the Jews until this day" (Matthew 28:1-6, 11-15).

Had the guards allowed the body of Jesus to be stolen, they would have been put to death rather than to be bribed. I believe many of the religious people who had Jesus crucified were more concerned with keeping their positions of honor and authority than in knowing the truth in Jesus Christ.

Luke 24:9-12—Jesus Risen from the Dead and the Women at the Tomb

"And returned from the sepulchre, and told all these things unto the eleven, and to all the rest. It was Mary Magdalene, and Joanna, and Mary the other of James, and other women that were with them, which told these things unto the apostles. And their words seemed to them as idle tales, and they believed them not. Then arose Peter, and ran unto the sepulchre; and stooping down, he beheld the linen clothes laid by themselves, and departed, wondering in himself at that which was come to pass" (Luke 24:9-12).

The women believed first. If you were going to start a false religion two thousand years ago, you would not start with women being the first witnesses.

"Howbeit we speak wisdom among them that are perfect: yet not the wisdom of this world, nor of the princes of this world, that come to nought: But we speak the wisdom of God in a mystery, even the hidden wisdom, which God ordained before the world unto our glory: Which none of the princes of this world knew: for had they known it, they would not have crucified the Lord of glory" (I Corinthians 2:6-8).

This is also a very interesting verse in the Bible. Had the demons known that God would raise Jesus from the dead, the demons would not have crucified Jesus.

Luke 24:25-32—Jesus Talks to Two Disciples on the Road to Emmaus

"Then he said unto them, 'O fools, and slow of heart to believe all that the prophets have spoken: Ought not Christ to have suffered these things, and to enter into his glory?' And beginning at Moses and all the prophets, he expounded unto them in all the scriptures the things concerning himself. And they drew nigh unto the village, whither they went: and he made as though he would have gone further. But they constrained him, saying, 'Abide with us: for it is toward evening, and the day is far spent.' And he went in to tarry with them. And it came to pass, as he sat at meat with them, he took bread, and blessed it, and brake, and gave to them. And their eyes were opened, and they knew him; and he vanished out of their sight. And they said one to another, 'Did not our heart burn within us, while he talked with us by the way, and while he opened to us the scriptures?'" (Luke 24:25-32).

In Luke 24:27-32, the two disciples loved to learn about the things of the Lord and wanted the Scriptures opened to them. Jesus, after the resurrection and before Pentecost, expounded in the Scriptures from Genesis through the Prophets.

Luke 24:33–43—Jesus Appears to His Disciples

"And they rose up the same hour, and returned to Jerusalem, and found the eleven gathered together, and them that were with them, Saying, 'The Lord is risen indeed, and hath appeared to Simon.' And they; told what things were done in the way, and how he was known of them in breaking of bread. And as they thus spake, Jesus himself stood in the midst of them, and saith unto them, 'Peace be unto you.' But they were terrified and affrighted, and supposed that they had seen a spirit. And he said unto them, 'Why are ye troubled? and why do thoughts arise in your hearts? Behold my hands and my feet, that it is I myself: handle me, and see; for a spirit hath not flesh and bones, as ye see me have.' And when he had thus spoken, he shewed them his hands and his feet. And while they yet believed not for joy, and wondered, he said unto them, 'Have ye here any meat?' And they gave him a piece of a broiled fish, and of a honeycomb. And he took it, and did eat before them" (Luke 24:33–43).

Jesus' resurrected body was one of flesh and bones. Jesus is God, and God is Spirit. However, in the resurrection, we will have a flesh-and-bones body with all of our senses, like Jesus' resurrected body.

Luke 24:44–48—Jesus Explains the Scriptures

"And he said unto them, 'These are the words which I spake unto you, while I was yet with you, that all things must be fulfilled, which were written in the law of Moses, and in the prophets, and in the psalms, concerning me.' Then opened he their understanding, that they might understand the scriptures, And said unto them, 'Thus it is written, and thus it behooved Christ to suffer, and to rise from the dead the third day: And that repentance and remission of sins should be preached in his name among all nations, beginning at Jerusalem. And ye are witnesses of these things'" (Luke 24:44–48).

After His resurrection, Jesus physically showed the disciples the prophecies of His first coming written in the Old Testament. I believe Jesus showed to the disciples the many verses I included in the overview of the Old Testament section of this book. He showed Himself in the first five books of the Bible, prophecies in the Psalms, and prophecies of the Prophets. To me, this is one of the most interesting verses in the Bible. Jesus would have taken out a scroll and literally showed the disciples where He was written about in the first five books of the Bible (the books of Moses), and in the Psalms and in the writings of the Prophets, all of which were written anywhere from 400 to 1,400 years prior to His crucifixion.

John 20:26–29—Thomas Feels the Nailprints

"And after eight days again his disciples were within, and Thomas with them: then came Jesus, the doors being shut, and stood in the midst, and said, 'Peace be unto you.' Then saith he to Thomas, 'Reach hither thy finger, and behold my hands; and reach hither thy hand, and thrust it into my side: and be not faithless, but believing.' And Thomas answered and said unto him, 'My Lord and my God.' Jesus saith unto him, 'Thomas, because thou hast seen me, thou hast believed: blessed are they that have not seen, and yet have believed'" (John 20:26–29).

Thomas called Jesus God. The disciples really understood who Jesus was.

John 20:30–31—All is Written That You Would Believe

"And many other signs truly did Jesus in the presence of his disciples, which are not written in this book: But these are written, that ye might believe that Jesus is the Christ, the Son of God; and that believing ye might have life through his name" (John 20:30–31).

You have life when you believe the Son of God, Jesus Christ.

Acts 1:1–9, 13–14—Jesus Ascends into Heaven—AD 30–32

"The former treatise have I made, O Theophilus, of all that Jesus began both to do and teach, Until the day in which he was taken up, after that he through the Holy Ghost had given commandments unto the apostles whom he had chosen: To whom also he shewed himself alive after his passion by many infallible proofs, being seen of them forty days, and speaking of the things pertaining to the kingdom of God: And, being assembled together with them, commanded them that they should not depart from Jerusalem, but wait for the promise of the Father, which, saith he, ye have heard of me. For John truly baptized with water; but ye shall be baptized with the Holy Ghost not many days hence. When they therefore were come together, they asked of him, saying, 'Lord, wilt thou at this time restore again the kingdom of Israel?' And he said unto them, 'It is not for you to know the times or the seasons, which the Father hath put in his own power. But ye shall receive power, after that the Holy Ghost is come upon you: and ye shall be witnesses unto me both in Jerusalem, and in all Judaea, and in Samaria, and unto the uttermost part of the earth.' And when he had spoken these things, while they beheld, he was taken up; and a cloud received him out of their sight …. And when they were come in, they went up into an upper room, where abode both Peter, and James, and John, and Andrew, Philip, and Thomas, Bartholomew, and Matthew, James the son of Alphaeus, and Simon Zelotes, and Judas the brother of James. These all continued with one accord in prayer and supplication, with the women, and Mary the other of Jesus, and with his brethren" (Acts 1:1–9, 13–14).

Jesus' ascension occurred forty days after the resurrection and ten days before Pentecost, which is the birth of the church age.

The Feast of Pentecost

Acts 2:1–4, 16–21, 36–47—The Coming of the Holy Spirit and Peter's Sermon on Pentecost

"And when the day of Pentecost was fully come, they were all with one accord in one place. And suddenly there came a sound from heaven as of a rushing mighty wind, and it filled all the house where they were sitting. And there appeared unto them cloven tongues like as of fire, and it sat upon each of them. And they were all filled with the Holy Ghost, and began to speak with other tongues, as the Spirit gave them utterance …. But this is that which was spoken by the prophet Joel; 'And it shall come to pass in the lat days,' saith God, 'I will pour out of my Spirit upon all flesh: and your sons and your daughters shall prophesy, and your young men shall see visions, and your old men shall dream dreams: And on my servants and on my handmaidens I will pour out in those days of my Spirit; and they shall prophesy: And I will shew wonders in heaven above, and signs in the earth beneath; blood, and fire, and vapour of smoke: The sun shall be turned into darkness, and the moon into blood, before that great and notable day of the Lord come: And it shall come to pass, that whosoever shall call on the name of the Lord shall be saved' …. Therefore let all the house of Israel know assuredly, that God hath made that same Jesus, whom ye have crucified, both Lord and Christ. Now when they heard this, they were pricked in their heart, and said unto Peter and to the rest of the apostles, 'Men and brethren, what shall we do?' Then Peter said unto them, 'Repent, and be baptized every one of you in the name of Jesus Christ for the remission of sins, and ye shall receive the gift of the Holy Ghost. For the promise is unto you, and to your children, and to all that are afar off, even as many as the Lord our God shall call.' And with many other words did he testify and exhort, saying, 'Save yourselves from this untoward generation.' Then they that gladly received his word were baptized: and the same day there were added unto them about three thousand souls. And they continued stedfastly in the apostles' doctrine and fellowship, and in breaking of bread, and in prayers. And fear came upon every soul: and many wonders and signs were done by the apostles. And all that believed were together, and had all things common; And sold their possessions and goods, and parted them to all men, as every man had need. And they, continuing daily with one accord in the Temple, and breaking bread from house to house, did eat their meat with gladness and singleness of heart, Praising God, and having favour with all the people. And the Lord added to the church daily such as should be saved" (Acts 2:1–4, 16–21, 36–47).

In Acts 2, the Holy Spirit is poured out onto the believers. This was on the Old Testament feast of Pentecost, fulfilling many types and shadows.

Peter stated that whosoever shall call upon the name of the Lord shall be saved, that we must repent and be baptized, and that the believer would receive the Holy Ghost. Signs and wonders followed the disciples, and people got saved every day of the week—not just on Sundays.

The Martyrdom of Stephen and the Conversion of the Apostle Paul

Acts 7:51–60—Stephen Martyred

"Ye stiffnecked and uncircumcised in heart and ears, ye do always resist the Holy Ghost: as your fathers did, so do ye. Which of the prophets have not your fathers persecuted? and they have slain them which shewed before of the coming of the Just One; of whom ye have been now the betrayers and murderers: Who have received the law by the disposition of angels, and have not kept it. When they heard these things, they were cut to the heart, and they gnashed on him with their teeth. But he, being full of the Holy Ghost, looked up stedfastly into heaven, and saw the glory of God, and Jesus standing on the right hand of God, And said, 'Behold, I see the heavens opened, and the Son of man standing on the right hand of God.' Then they cried out with a loud voice, and stopped their ears, and ran upon him with one accord, And cast him out of the city, and stoned him: and the witnesses laid down their clothes at a young man's feet, whose name was Saul. And they stoned Stephen, calling upon God, and saying, 'Lord Jesus, receive my spirit.' And he kneeled down, and cried with a loud voice, 'Lord, lay not this sin to their charge.' And when he had said this, he fell asleep" (Acts 7:51–60).

Stephen used Jesus as an example. When Jesus was crucified, He said, "Father, forgive them; they know not what they do." Had Jesus commanded a thousand angels to come down and destroy all the people crucifying Him, Stephen would have used that as an example and called upon God to destroy the people stoning himself. If those who crucified Jesus and stoned Stephen had been destroyed immediately, then we would not be put in a position to learn patience and forgiveness of those who hate us.

Acts 9:1–6—Saul Converted and Becomes the Apostle Paul

"And Saul, yet breathing out threatenings and slaughter against the disciples of the Lord, went unto the high priest, And desired of him letters to Damascus to the synagogues, that if he found any of this way, whether they were men or women, he might bring them bound unto Jerusalem. And as he journeyed, he came near Damascus: and suddenly there shined round about him a light from heaven: And he fell to the earth, and heard a voice saying unto him, 'Saul, Saul, why persecutest thou me?' And he said, 'Who art thou, Lord?' And the Lord said, 'I am Jesus whom thou persecutest: it is hard for thee to kick against the pricks.' And he trembling and astonished said, 'Lord, what wilt thou have me to do?' And the Lord said unto him, 'Arise, and go into the city, and it shall be told thee what thou must do'" (Acts 9:1–6).

Saul became the apostle Paul. Paul wrote approximately 30 percent of the New Testament and was from the tribe of Benjamin. The conversion of Paul occurred a few years after the crucifixion of Jesus Christ.

Bible Verses of Encouragement and Instruction for Believers in Christ

1. Believe God's Word, the Bible.
2. Allow the Holy Spirit to teach and lead you.
3. Trust God to the point that you immediately obey when you hear His voice.

The purpose of this section is to train yourself to believe God's Word, allow it to change you, trust God, and know that all things work together for good for those who love God.

"Knowing this, that our old man is crucified with him, that the body of sin might be destroyed, that henceforth we should not serve sin" (Romans 6:6).

"I am crucified with Christ: nevertheless I live; yet not I, but Christ liveth in me: and the life which I now live in the flesh I live by the faith of the Son of God, who loved me, and gave himself for me" (Galatians 2:20).

"So then faith cometh by hearing, and hearing by the word of God" (Romans 10:17).

"But without faith it is impossible to please him: for he that cometh to God must believe that he is, and that he is a rewarder of them that diligently seek him" (Hebrews 11:6).

"For by grace are ye saved through faith: and that not of yourselves: it is the gift of God: Not of works, lest any man should boast" (Ephesians 2:8–9).

Within five minutes of reading Ephesians 2:8–9, I called upon the Lord to be saved.

"Jesus answered and said unto him, 'Verily, verily, I say unto thee, Except a man be born again, he cannot see the kingdom of God'" (John 3:3).

"Whosoever therefore shall confess me before men, him will I confess also before my Father which is in heaven" (Matthew 10:32).

"Therefore if any man be in Christ, he is a new creature: old things are passed away; behold, all things are become new" (II Corinthians 5:17).

"Study to shew thyself approved unto God, a workman that needeth not to be ashamed, rightly dividing the word of truth" (II Timothy 2:15).

"If we say that we have fellowship with him, and walk in darkness, we lie, and do not the truth: But if we walk in the light, as he is in the light, we have fellowship one with another, and the blood of Jesus Christ his Son cleanseth us from all sin. If we say that we have no sin, we deceive ourselves, and the truth is not in us. If we confess our sins, he is faithful and just to forgive us our sins, and to cleanse us from all unrighteousness. If we say that we have not sinned, we make him a liar, and his word is not in us" (I John 1:6–10).

Encouragement and Praise

"I can do all things through Christ which strengtheneth me" (Philippians 4:13).

"But as it is written, Eye hath not seen, nor ear heard, neither have entered in to the heart of man, the things which God hath prepared for them that love him" (I Corinthians 2:9).

"And we know that all things work together for good to them that love God, to them who are the called according to his purpose" (Romans 8:28).

"What shall we then say to these things? If God be for us, who can be against us?" (Romans 8:31)

"We are troubled on every side, yet not distressed; we are perplexed, but not in despair, Persecuted, but not forsaken; cast down, but not destroyed" (II Corinthians 4:8–9).

"For our light affliction, which is but for a moment, worketh for us a far more exceeding and eternal weight of glory" (II Corinthians 4:17).

"For with God nothing shall be impossible" (Luke 1:37).

"I will bless the LORD at all times: his praise shall continually be in my mouth" (Psalm 34:1).

"The righteous cry, and the LORD heareth, and delivereth them out of all their troubles. The LORD is nigh unto them that are of a broken heart; and saveth such as be of a contrite spirit. Many are the afflictions of the righteous: but the LORD delivereth him out of them all" (Psalm 34:17–19).

"But my God shall supply all your need according to his riches in glory by Christ Jesus" (Philippians 4:19).

"For the LORD God is a sun and shield: the LORD will give grace and glory: no good thing will he withhold from them that walk uprightly" (Psalm 84:11).

Fruit of the Spirit

"But the fruit of the Spirit is love, joy, peace, longsuffering, gentleness, goodness, faith, Meekness, temperance: against such there is no law. And they that are Christ's have crucified the flesh with the affections and lusts" (Galatians 5:22–24).

"Thou believest that there is one God; thou does well: the devils also believe, and tremble. But wilt thou know, O vain man, that faith without works is dead?" (James 2:19–20).

Walk with the Lord

"But I say unto you, That every idle word that men shall speak, they shall give account thereof in the day of judgment. For by thy words thou shalt be justified, and by thy words thou shalt be condemned" (Matthew 12:36–67).

"But seek ye first the kingdom of God, and his righteousness; and all these things shall be added unto you. Take therefore no thought for the morrow: for the morrow shall take thought for the things of itself. Sufficient unto the day is the evil thereof" (Matthew 6:33–34).

"Submit yourselves therefore to God. Resist the devil, and he will flee from you" (James 4:7).

Peace

"Come unto me, all ye that labour and are heavy laden, and I will give you rest. Take my yoke upon you, and learn of me; for I am meek and lowly in heart: and ye shall find rest unto your souls. For my yoke is easy, and my burden is light" (Matthew 11:28–30).

"There is therefore now no condemnation to them which are in Christ Jesus, who walk not after the flesh, but after the Spirit. For the law of the Spirit of life in Christ Jesus hath made me free from the law of sin and death" (Romans 8:1–2).

"Be careful for nothing; but in every thing by prayer and supplication with thanksgiving let your requests be made known unto God. And the peace of God, which passeth all understanding, shall keep your hearts and minds through Christ Jesus. Finally, brethren, whatsoever things are true, whatsoever things are honest, whatsoever things are just, whatsoever things are pure, whatsoever things are lovely, whatsoever things are of good report: if there be any virtue, and if there be any praise, think on these things" (Philippians 4:6–8).

"For we brought nothing into this world, and it is certain we can carry nothing out. And having food and raiment let us be therewith content. But they that will be rich fall into temptation and a snare, and into many foolish and hurtful lusts, which drown men in destruction and perdition. For the love of money is the root of all evil: which while some coveted after, they have erred from the faith, and pierced themselves through with many sorrows" (I Timothy 6:7–10).

"For God hath not given us the spirit of fear; but of power, and of love, and of a sound mind" (II Timothy 1:7).

Believers in Christ need to have their minds renewed with biblical truths. Below are portions of the above scriptures that you might want to consider repeating until your mind has been renewed and you truly believe them.

- I am a new creation in Christ; the old has passed away, and all things are new.
- There is now no condemnation in Christ.
- God has not given me a spirit of fear, but of power and love and a sound mind.
- All things work together for good, because I love God.
- If God is with me, who can be against me?
- I am persecuted, but not forsaken.
- I am cast down, but not destroyed.
- My affliction is but for a moment.
- I cannot comprehend what great things God has in store for me.
- God will deliver me from all my afflictions.
- God will supply all my needs according to His riches.
- God has not withheld one good thing from me.
- With God, nothing is impossible.
- I can do all things through Christ who strengthens me.

The Church Age

"Now when they had gone throughout Phrygia and the region of Galatia, and were forbidden of the Holy Ghost to preach the word in Asia, After they were come to Mysia, they assayed to go into Bithynia: but the Spirit suffered them not. And they passing my Mysia came down to Troas. And a vision appeared to Paul in the night; There stood a man of Macedonia, and prayed him, saying, 'Come over into Macedonia, and help us'" (Acts 16:6–9).

The course of world events was established in these verses. Had the Holy Spirit directed Paul to go into Asia or Africa, and had these people received and accepted Paul's words, the wealth of the nations would have been concentrated wherever he was accepted.

The Holy Spirit directed Paul to preach in Europe. Almost all the wealth of the nations in the 1900s was concentrated in Europe and North America. This is because the Bible was translated into languages spoken in Europe. The reason English-speaking countries are so financially wealthy is because John Wycliffe translated the Bible into English 800 years ago. True science and wealth grow quickly wherever the majority of the people in a nation either believe the Bible or in general terms live by biblical principles. After the crucifixion, the disciples were frightened for their lives. After they felt the nail prints in Jesus' hands, they had hope and strength. Had they never seen the resurrected Jesus, they would not have started another false religion and allowed themselves to be killed for an event that never occurred—the resurrection of Jesus Christ.

"The Revelation of Jesus Christ, which God gave unto him, to shew unto his servants things which must shortly come to pass; and he sent and signified it by his angel unto his servant John: Who bare record of the word of God, and of the testimony of Jesus Christ, and of all things that he saw. Blessed is he that readeth, and they that hear the words of this prophecy, and keep those things which are written therein: for the time is at hand. John to the seven churches which are in Asia: Grace be unto you, and peace, from him which is, and which was, and which is to come; and from the seven Spirits which are before his throne; And from Jesus Christ, who is the faithful witness, and the first begotten of the dead, and the prince of the kings of the earth. Unto him that loved us, and washed us from our sins in his own blood, And hath made us kings and priests unto God and his Father; to him be glory and dominion for ever and ever. Amen. Behold, he cometh with clouds; and every eye shall see him, and they also which pierced him: and all kindreds of the earth shall wail because of him. Even so, Amen. I am Alpha and Omega, the beginning and the ending, saith the Lord, which is, and which was, and which is to come, the Almighty" (Revelation 1:1–8).

The Apostle John is spoken to directly by Jesus Christ and is given visions of things to come. In Revelation 1:4, the seven churches of Asia are pictures of the church ages from Pentecost in the New Testament to the present. This occurred while John was imprisoned on the Isle of Patmos.

"I John, who also am your brother, and companion in tribulation, and in the kingdom and patience of Jesus Christ, was in the isle that is called Patmos, for the word of God, and for the testimony of Jesus Christ. I was in the Spirit on the Lord's day, and heard behind me a great voice, as of a trumpet, Saying, I am Alpha and Omega, the first and the last: and, What thou seest, write in a book, and send it unto the seven churches which are in Asia; unto Ephesus, and unto Smyrna, and unto Pergamos, and unto Thyatira, and unto Sardis, and unto Philadelphia, and unto Laodicea" (Revelation 1:9–11).

The Prophetic Order of the Churches

> Scholars have laid out the order of the churches as implied prophecies of this dispensation:
>
> 1. Ephesus—the apostolic age, first-century church development—Pentecost to AD 95
> 2. Smyrna—the age of persecution under the Roman government—Pentecost to AD 316
> 3. Pergamos—the church under imperial favor—AD 316 to the end of this age
> 4. Thyatira—the Dark Ages—AD 500–1500
> 5. Sardis—the age of the Reformation—AD 1500 to the end of this age
> 6. Philadelphia—the age of missionary activity beginning in the 1700s to the end of this age
> 7. Laodicea—the final stage of modernism and liberalism—1800s to the end of this age

The letters to these churches also fit this scenario. Think of the profound implications we have here! New Testament Christianity has been written into the prophecies of the book of Revelation! We know that two thousand years ago, at the onset of the dispensation of grace, Jesus knew all about us and revealed our historical heritage before each church era even came to pass.[73]

The Church of Ephesus—AD 30–95

Greeting

"Unto the angel of the church of Ephesus write; These things saith he that holdeth the seven stars in his right hand, who walketh in the midst of the seven golden candlesticks" (Revelation 2:1).

Commendation

"I know thy works, and thy labour, and thy patience, and how thou canst not bear them which are evil: and thou hast tried them which say they are apostles, and are not, and hast found them liars: And hast borne, and hast patience, and for my name's sake hast laboured, and hast not fainted" (Revelation 2:2–3).

Warning

"Nevertheless I have somewhat against thee, because thou hast left thy first love. Remember therefore from whence thou art fallen, and repent, and do the first works; or else I will come unto thee quickly, and will remove thy candlestick out of his place, except thou repent" (Revelation 2:4–5).

Praise

"But this thou hast, that thou hatest the deeds of the Nicolaitans, which I also hate" (Revelation 2:6).

Promise

"He that hath an ear, let him hear what the Spirit saith unto the churches; To him that overcometh will I give to eat of the tree of life, which is in the midst of the paradise of God" (Revelation 2:7).

The people in the Church of Ephesus had good works, endured with patience, preached against evil, and stood against false teaching. However, they lost their first love. They went through the motions. I believe that sixty-five years after the resurrection, this church got discouraged. I believe they started to understand that Jesus was not coming back in their lifetime and that persecution was ahead. God does not want us to be discouraged under any circumstances.

The Book of Revelation was given to John in approximately AD 95. The Church of Ephesus would have been encouraged after receiving this letter. All seven churches received a promise if they overcame.

---

73 J. R. Church. *Prophecy in the News*, 12–13.

Ephesus was a prominent type or example of the church in the first century. However, churches like Ephesus and all the other six churches mentioned in Revelation 2–3 existed and currently exist in this church age.

The Church at Smyrna—The Age of Persecution Under the Roman Government—AD 30–316

Greeting

"And unto the angel of the church in Smyrna write; these things saith the first and the last, which was dead, and is alive" (Revelation 2:8).

Commendation and Praise

"I know thy works, and tribulation, and poverty, (but thou art rich) and I know the blasphemy of them which say they are Jews, and are not, but are the synagogue of Satan. Fear none of those things which thou shalt suffer: behold, the devil shall cast some of you into prison, that ye may be tried; and ye shall have tribulation ten days: be thou faithful unto death, and I will give thee a crown of life" (Revelation 2:9–10).

Complaint/None—Jesus had no complaints with this church. This is the only church that Jesus did not list a complaint against. It is generally accepted that the tribulation for ten days is not a literal ten days but that this church will be severely tested, tempted, and tried in all things. This is the time period that Christians were fed to lions by the Romans.

Promise

"He that hath an ear, let him hear what the Spirit saith unto the churches; He that overcometh shall not be hurt of the second death" (Revelation 2:11).

Smyrna was a type of church prominent from AD 30–325. The church at Smyrna was financially poor but faithful to God unto death. This was the persecuted church which existed in the first three centuries after the crucifixion of Christ. However, the persecution of true Christians has been very prevalent in the past one thousand years. In the past one hundred years, it is estimated that as many Christians have been put to death for their faith as in the last two thousand years. Today, it is estimated that approximately five hundred to a thousand people are killed every day because they are Christians.

There were ten Roman emperors who persecuted the early church. Some persecuted the church more than others. Their names and dates of rule are listed below:

1. Nero, AD 67
2. Domitian, AD 81
3. Trajan, AD 108
4. Marcus Aurelius Antoninus, AD 162
5. Severus, AD 192
6. Maximus, AD 235

7. Decius, AD 249
8. Valerian, AD 257
9. Aurelian, AD 274
10. Diocletian, AD 303

The Martyrdom of the Apostles

The disciples who became the Apostles were Peter, James, John, Andrew, Philip, Thomas, Bartholomew, Matthew, James the son of Alphaeus, Simon, and Judas the brother of James. This Judas is not Judas Iscariot, but another person. Matthias was later numbered with the eleven apostles (Acts 2:26).

All but John were martyred—put to death for their faith. These men saw the miracles that Jesus performed and they saw the risen Lord Jesus. After the resurrection, Jesus showed these men in the Old Testament all the places in which He fulfilled all the prophecies and proved He was God with eternal purposes in mind.

Stephen was not an apostle but was the first martyr. Stephen was stoned to death. Peter was crucified with his head down. James was killed by the sword. John was the only apostle to die of old age. However, he was boiled in oil and lived to receive the book of Revelation on the Island of Patmos, where he was exiled rather than put to death. Andrew was tied, not nailed to a cross so his suffering would last longer before dying. Philip was pierced through the thighs and hung upside down. Thomas was pierced with a lance and killed. Bartholomew was skinned alive and crucified with his head downward. Matthew was burned at the stake. James was hit with a club to the head. Simon was crucified. Judas was tied to a cross and pierced with a javelin. Paul, according to Jerome, was beheaded the same day Peter was crucified.[74]

"Who hath believed our report? and to whom is the arm of the LORD revealed?" (Isaiah 53:1)

God revealed Himself to these men, and they believed the good report. Have you believed the good report? Are you willing to die an earthly death and not deny Christ? After salvation, the Holy Spirit will give you power to accept death rather than to deny Christ. Had these men not seen the risen Lord after the resurrection, they would not have allowed themselves to be killed for something that did not happen.

The Church at Pergamos—AD 316–present

Greeting

"And to the angel of the church in Pergamos write; These things saith he which hath the sharp sword with two edges" (Revelation 2:12).

---

74 J. R. Church. *Prophecy in the News*, 12–16.

Commendation

"I know thy works, and where thou dwellest, even where Satan's seat is: and thou holdest fast my name, and hast not denied my faith, even in those days wherein Antipas was my faithful martyr, who was slain among you, where Satan dwelleth" (Revelation 2:13).

Warning

"But I have a few things against thee, because thou hast there them that hold the doctrine of Balaam, who taught Balac to cast a stumblingblock before the children of Israel, to eat things sacrificed unto idols, and to commit fornication. So hast thou also them that hold the doctrine of the Nicolaitans, which thing I hate. Repent; or else I will come unto thee quickly, and will fight against them with the sword of my mouth" (Revelation 2:14–16).

Promise

"He that hath an ear, let him hear what the Spirit saith unto the churches; To him that overcometh will I give to eat of the hidden manna, and will give him a white stone, and in the stone a new name written, which no man knoweth saving he that receiveth it" (Revelation 2:17).

In AD 313, Constantine traveled to Italy. As he came near to Rome, about sunset, he looked toward the southern sky and saw a brightness in the shape of a cross, with an inscription which said, "In this overcome." Eusebius reported that he heard Constantine speak of this many times as being true. He said not only did Constantine see it, but his soldiers as well. That night, Constantine consulted with his men upon the meaning, and after going to sleep, claims that Christ appeared to him.

The rule of Constantine put a stop to persecutions and gave the Church peace for the next thousand years. The "Edict of Toleration" and the establishment of a Christianized Roman Empire, however, became a two-edged sword—a curse as well as a blessing for the promotion of Christianity.[75]

The letters of Pergamos and Thyatira seem to describe an era of Church history wherein the Roman government ceased its persecutions and embraced the "faith." After ministers and church leaders no longer feared persecution and death by the dreaded Roman government, they began to feed upon each other. Political maneuvering pitted one theologian against another, one church against another, and one dogma against another until Europe was plummeted into the Dark Ages.

The Ages of Pergamos and Thyatira became the most evil periods of church history, from the fourth century to this day. Thyatira depicts that era wherein the Roman Church plunged Europe into the Dark Ages. There were those in Thyatira, however,

---

75   J. R. Church. *Prophecy in the News,* 17.

who did not conform to the demands of the church hierarchy. They represent believers who started the reform movement around the time of the Crusades.[76]

"Yet I have reserved 7,000 in Israel all whose knees who have not bowed to Baal, and every mouth have not kissed it" (I Kings 19:18).

I Kings deals with Elijah, who lived around 800 BC. By that time, God stated there were only 7,000 men (this did not include women and children) in Israel who followed Him. The Dark Ages were from AD 300–1500 and paralleled the great falling away that occurred in the Old Testament. Very small numbers of people were actually Christians from AD 300–1500.

The Doctrine of Balaam

> The basic heresies cited in the letters to Pergamos and Thyatira addressed two basic problems—eating meat offered to idols and fornication. These were said to be the basic tenets in the doctrine of Balaam, the cult of the Nicolaitanes and in the teachings of Jezebel. Just how widespread this problem became is not fully known, but the injunction was the subject of a letter sent to all Gentile congregations after the first council in Jerusalem. James, the moderator of the meeting, explained the tenets of Judaism should not be forced upon Gentile Christianity, but that they abstain from meats offered to idols and from blood, and from things strangled, and from fornication.[77]

"That ye abstain from meats offered to idols, and from blood, and from things strangled, and from fornication: from which if ye keep yourselves, lye shall do well. Fare ye well" (Acts 15:29).

In the church at Pergamos, Jesus acknowledged that they were in the center of Satan's kingdom. However, this church tolerated much very serious evil. This church was a compromising church that did not know God's Word and was able to be led astray easily.

A Short History of Islam

> The descendants of Ishmael and Esau, today known as the Arabs, though mentioned scantily in the Bible as well as in Greek and Roman historical texts, played a minor role in world history until Mohammed and the Koran galvanized the Arab peoples into a fighting and conquering force. The origins of Islam, the third greatest monotheistic religion in the world, stem from Judeo-Christianity, but the Koran and Allah have very little to do with the Bible and the God of Abraham, Isaac, and Jacob.

> At the outset, Mohammed had two major groups to convert to his cause: The Judeo-Christians on the one hand and the pagans of Mecca and Medina on the other. When the Judeo-Christians rejected Mohammed and his teachings, all the emphasis was then placed on the pagans of Mecca and Medina, as well as the whole Arabian Peninsula.

---

76 J. R. Church. *Prophecy in the News*, 8.
77 J. R. Church. *Prophecy in the News*, 11–12.

The Judeo-Christian origins of Mohammed's beliefs were then put on the back burner, and the pagan Arabian origins of Islam were emphasized.[78]

According to world-renowned scholar and theologian, Dr. Robert Morey, Mohammed decided to build his new religion, Islam, on the foundations of Arabian paganism in order for it to be more palatable to the pagans who were his target audience. According to Arabian paganism, there were 360 pagan gods, one for each day of the lunar year. The greatest of these gods was Allah, originally known as alIlahi, the Moon God. This pagan Allah, the greatest in the pagan pantheon, was the war god, just as Zeus was the war god for the ancient Greeks and Romans.

In order to build his new religion, Islam, on a monotheistic basic, Mohammed abolished the other 359 lesser gods, leaving Allah as the only god. But Allah still remains a war god, and bears no resemblance to the God of Abraham, Isaac, and Jacob, which is the God of love. Allah, the moon god, the war god, is a god of the bow, the arrow, the spear, and the sword. Islam is a war religion, a warrior religion, and merciless religion in which beheading, crucifixion, and severing of arms and limbs is common practice even today.

Islam is a religion in which no "Protestant reformation" can ever be countenanced, which would allow modernization as happened in the Jewish and Christian religions. This is why the seventh century is so glorified in Islam and is the direction in which the pan-global Islamic conquest is headed. It is locked into a fossilized mindset, totally contrary to the twenty-first century. It opposes the progress and development of the renaissance and enlightenment following the dark medieval ages of Europe, and instead dreams of the distant past.

Within a hundred years of the death of Mohammed in AD 732, the Arab Moslems had succeeded in conquering North Africa and Spain, the entire Arabian Peninsula, and most of the Middle East. Christendom from that period and until Columbus discovered America was limited to a relatively tiny plot of land known as western Europe. In fact, the Islamic pincers reached even to Poitiers in France in the west and the gates of Vienna in the east. Christianity was in a very real danger of being vanquished by the Islamic hordes.

With Columbus' discovery of the New World, two new continents were opened up to Christian settlement, thus overcoming the Islamic stranglehold on Europe.

Russia also adopted Christianity in AD 995, greatly due to the Islamic invasions from the east. Therefore it was to the east that Russia turned in order to defend itself, and later to subdue its Moslem inhabitants as well as Turkish and Persian tribes, and Russia finally reached the Pacific Ocean in a "manifest destiny" quite similar to that of the Americans. Following the rise of Christian Europe came a period known as colonialism

---

78   Don McAlvany. *The McAlvany Intelligence Advisory,* 6.

in which the new European powers established footholds in the Islamic world and later carved up Africa, as well as Asia.

It was not until the advent of Communism in Soviet Russia and the period of the world wars, as well as the discovery of Petroleum, that new forces of militant Islam were unleashed, leading to the rises of renascent Islam. Today, the Communist East has been weakened (but could reemerge—especially China) and Islam considers the West as the only remaining great "Satan" whose days are numbered. The Iranian Ayatollah Janati has boldly proclaimed, "The twenty-first century will be the century of Islam."

According to Islam, there is an eternal war between the House of Peace of Islam and the House of War of the infidel non-Moslem. Islam, in its early stages, adopted a strident ideology of war between "good and evil," i.e., Islam against the infidels. All who embraced Islam were of the House of Peace—or, in Arabic, "Dar es Salaam" while all the infidels were grouped together in the "Dar el-Harb," or House of War—a war which could not end until the entire world became Moslem. Since it was impossible in so short a period to impose such a rigorous new religion on so many peoples, it was necessary to show moderation in light of the reality that perhaps the Moslem hordes were biting off more than they could chew. Therefore, a policy of compromise was established between the Moslems on the one hand and the enemies of Islam on the other hand; at least until Islam was strong enough to resume the battle of conquest.

During the early period of Islam, many Jews and Christians saw Islam as a force saving them from the harsh regimes of Orthodox Byzantium in the east and Catholicism in the west—both of which persecuted Jews and those Christians who were considered to be heretic. (A striking example of this is the conversion to Islam of the entire Bosnian nation which had been considered as a heretical form of Christianity and persecuted by the Eastern Orthodox Church.) It was decided that the Moslems would utilize these Jews and Christians to establish a firm financial and administrative organization that would allow the Moslems to consolidate power. Hundreds of years later, most of these Jews and Christians were "absorbed" by conversion into Islam.[79]

In this manner, the Moslems established themselves finally as firm majorities in each country from Morocco on the Atlantic to Indonesia on the Pacific. The infidels were divided into two categories: Jews and Christians, known as the "People of the Book." They were considered as "dhimmis"—to be protected by subjugation. The other infidels, such as Hindus, Buddhists, and other eastern sects, were to be put immediately to the sword whenever possible, because Moslems considered them pagans.

Between 1492 and 1992, Islam came under the dominion of Christian leaders with the rise of European and Russian Christendom. By 1492, the Moors were completely expelled from the Iberian peninsula (Spain and Portugal). In addition to colonizing the Americas, the two Iberian (Spain and Portugal) powers colonized the islands off

---

79 Don McAlvany. *The McAlvany Intelligence Advisory,* 7.

the west coast of Africa, the Azores and Cabo Verde, as well as numerous African and Asian areas.

In Europe, though Ottoman Turkey marched northward from Anatolia, subdued Greece, the Balkans, Hungary, Romania, and virtually conquered Vienna, Austria by the end of the 1500s, Turkey was also, now, on the retreat. After a series of wars with Russia and other European powers, Turkey was forced to withdraw from the Crimea, southern Russia, the Caucasus Mountains, Ukraine, Hungary, Romania, Bulgaria, and what are now the constituent former republics of Yugoslavia. Greece achieved its independence in 1821 and grew in size after the Balkan campaigns in the early 1900s. Except for Albania and a small piece of Europe across the Bosphorus Straits, Turkey was now almost entirely an Asiatic power. And so, the Islamic pincers from North Africa and Turkey were now retreating in defeat.

Again, Islam was forced to moderate and compromise with countries stronger than itself. More and more Islamic lands fell under European Christian dominion and administration. Missionaries were brought in and there was little Islam could do about it. Then, in the early 1900s, the world entered its modern era with the various nationalisms, world wars, and most of all, the discovery of large deposits of petroleum. Moslem leaders in Africa and Asia were suddenly influenced by western education and western power struggles, and they learned to develop the world's thirst for oil.

Since the Moslem leaders controlled the areas where the oil was located, these western powers in turn played up to the sheikhs who learned ably to play one Christian power off against the other. As the years went by, these Moslem oil sheikhs became richer and richer, and eventually took over more and more control of the oil resources until, finally, as in the case of the sheikhs of Saudi Arabia, they took over full ownership of what was rightfully theirs.

At the same time, the United Nations brought about the decolonialization of Africa and Asia, in which the European powers were forced out, leaving a power vacuum which the U.S. and USSR vied to fill. In most cases, the Moslem world was considered "Third World," i.e., neither pro-U.S. nor pro-USSR. But one thing was sure—the Moslem oil countries became very adept and skilled at manipulating the world powers to get what they wanted. Most importantly, the petrodollar and vast oil reserves made the leaders of the oil rich countries virtually omnipotent.

Now, ironically, instead of Columbus sending back gold bullion and silver to Europe to build armies and fleets, it is the Moslem "black gold," or oil, which is building the Islamic armies and fleets. It is this black gold which leads the Moslems to believe that Allah has given them the wherewithal to finally vanquish Christianity and conquer the world.

There is a new power, armed with immense oil wealth, threatening world peace and stability with its plans for establishing an all-embracing Islamic empire. And this radical Islamic movement made its biggest ever declaration of war on America and the West on September 11, 2001.[80]

Compare and Contrast Jesus and Mohammed	
Jesus	**Mohammed**
Life prophesied	No prophecy of his life
Virgin birth (heavenly Father/earthly mother)	Earthly mother and father
Sinless life	Led military campaigns
Healings and wonders	No healings or wonders
Taught love of God	Taught God aloof from the creation
Chaste life	Had eight wives
Christianity spreads as Christians put to death for belief in Jesus Christ	Islam spreads by military conquest—putting Christians, Jews, and Hindus to death
Note: I believe the people who promoted the Inquisitions and the Crusades were not born of the Spirit and were not Christians.	
Jesus directed by His Father in heaven	Mohammed received instructions while in a trance
Purpose in death and resurrection	Died suddenly
Trained disciples and apostles	No succession plan
Raised from the dead	Body still in the grave and decaying
Kingdom not of this earth	Attempting to establish an earthly kingdom
Note: A religion never rises above its leader or founder.	

Comparing the lives of Jesus Christ and Mohammed, their lives could not have been more different. The biggest difference is that Jesus was dealing with issues which occurred in eternity. He did this by blending the creator, king, and servant aspects of His life and showed us that God wants to have a personal relationship with mankind. Mohammed was a military leader and tried to establish a kingdom on earth. Jesus said His Kingdom was not of this earth. God will eventually make a new heaven and earth not made with hands.

A belief system never rises about its leader. Jesus asks for forgiveness for those who were crucifying Him. Mohammed commanded the killing of unbelievers and his severity increased as he got older. *Choose Christ.*

The Church at Thyatira—The Dark Ages—AD 500–1500

Greeting

"And unto the angel of the church in Thyatira write: These thing saith the Son of God, who hath his eyes like unto a flame of fire, and his feet are like fine brass" (Revelation 2:18).

---

80 Don McAlvany. *The McAlvany Intelligence Advisory*, 8.

Commendation

"I know thy works, and charity, and service, and faith, and thy patience, and thy works; and the last to be more than the first" (Revelation 2:19).

Complaint

"Notwithstanding I have a few things against thee, because thou sufferest that woman Jezebel, which calleth herself a prophetess, to teach and to seduce my servants to commit fornication, and to eat things sacrificed unto idols" (Revelation 2:20).

Warning

"And I gave her space to repent of her fornication; and she repented not. Behold, I will cast her into a bed, and them that commit adultery with her into great tribulation, except they repent of their deeds. And I will kill her children with death; and all the churches shall know that I am he which searcheth the reins and hearts: and I will give unto every one of you according to your works" (Revelation 2:21–23).

Promise

"But unto you I say, and unto the rest in Thyatira, as many as have not this doctrine, and which have not known the depths of Satan, as they speak; I will put upon you none other burden. But that which ye have already hold fast till I come. And he that overcometh, and keepeth my works unto the end, to him will I give power over the nations: And he shall rule them with a rod of iron; as the vessels of a potter shall they be broken to shivers: even as I received of my Father. And I will give him the morning star. He that hath an ear, let him hear what the Spirit saith unto the churches" (Revelation 2:24–29).

During the Age of Thyatira, goddess worship was introduced into the Christian religion as the virgin deity. Between the Nicolaitan priesthood and Jezebel's goddess worship, the Church was responsible for bringing on the Dark Ages—a time when the populace was kept in poverty, ignorance and superstition. The Bible was chained to the pulpit and the reading of it forbidden to the laity.

"Indulgence" for a price became a popular method of escaping the penalty of sinning. The dead could be prayed out of a concocted "purgatory" for a fee. Elaborate and expensive cathedrals were built in communities where congregations lived in stark poverty.

According to the letter, opportunity to repent was given, but the institution of the virgin deity refused. Instead, they launched a war of inquisition against those Christians whose faith was set in Christ alone. During these inquisitions of the Dark Ages, thousands of Christians were branded as heretics and tortured. Many died under the cruel antics of the Jezebel institution.[81]

Persecution of the Waldenses

Around the year 1000, a movement to return to the simplicity of the Gospel gained popularity through the preaching of the Reverend Berengarius throughout eastern France. The Reverend Peteri Bruis of Toulouse published a book entitled *Antichrist,* condemning the extra-biblical doctrines of the Roman institution and giving details about the reform movement.

By 1140, the number of converts brought increasing alarm to the pope. The pontiff wrote to several princes asking them to banish the reformers from their dominions. The Vatican began to publish books extolling the virtues of Romanism and condemning the reformers. In 1147, Reverend Henry of Toulouse preached against accepting any doctrines that could not be supported by Scripture.

Out of this movement came Reverend Peter Waldo, a native of Lyons, France, who vigorously opposed the extra-biblical doctrines of the Roman Church. His followers were known as the Waldenses. The bishop of Lyons informed Pope Alexander III, who promptly excommunicated Waldo and ordered the extermination of his followers. This war against the Waldenses introduced the infamous Inquisition.

Certain monks were authorized as inquisitors to search out and destroy the reformers. Their process was simple. An accusation was considered enough to establish guilt. No trial was needed. The accused suffered torture and execution on the word of the inquisitors.

The Reformation

Over the centuries, the reform movement continued to gain acceptance throughout Europe. In 1521, the Reverend Martin Luther, disgusted with the bigotry of the Vatican, nailed a thesis to the door of the church in Wittenburg, Germany, challenging the unscriptural practices of the Roman Church. At last, the dawn of a new era began to illuminate the Dark Ages. But the pope stepped up his persecution against the dissidents. The worst was yet to come.

In 1524, the Reverend John Clark followed the example of Martin Luther and nailed a pamphlet to the church door in Melden, France, calling the pope "the Antichrist." Clark was arrested, whipped, and branded on the forehead. Clark would not be silenced. He went to Mentz, in Lorraine, and demolished some images, for which his right hand and nose were cut off. Instead of showing pain, he began to sing Psalm 115, which forbids idolatry. His persecutors were so enraged they threw him into a fire and burned him

---

81   J. R. Church. *Prophecy in the News,* 10.

to ashes. During this time, many people in the reform movement were beaten, racked, scourged, and burned to death throughout France.[82]

The St. Bartholomew Massacre

On August 22, 1572, the Inquisition planned to carry out its most brutal massacre of Protestants. They hoped to finish the Reformation movement once and for all. The chief conspirator was none other than the king of France, who proposed a marriage between his sister and the young prince of Navarrel, the chief leader of the Protestants.

The marriage was publicly celebrated in Paris on August 18. The vows were read by the cardinal of Bourbon. They dined in great pomp and supped with the king. But on August 22, at 12:00 at night, on the eve of St. Bartholomew, the signal was given. Immediately all the houses of the Protestants were forced open at once. One of the protestant leaders, Admiral Coligny, was attached and shot in both arms. Soon after, he was slain on orders of the king.

With that signal, soldiers began a slaughter in all parts of the city. The leader of the Protestant movement was thrown out of a window into the street, where his head was cut off and sent to the pope. But that was not enough for the savage soldiers. They cut off his arms, dragged him through the streets, and hung him by his heels just outside the city.

Following his death, they slaughtered many prominent leaders of the Protestant movement. They began slaughtering the common people. So furious was their rage that they even slew Catholics whom they suspected to be not very loyal. From Paris, the destruction spread to all quarters of the realm. Within a week, over 100,000 Protestants were slaughtered. The St. Bartholomew massacre is depicted in a painting at the Vatican, with the inscription, "The Pope approves of Coligny's Death."

What started out in the days of Constantine as governmental relief for the suffering saints, eventually developed into a diabolical quest for power by the very theologians who proposed to bring utopia to the planet.

It is to this idolatrous religion that Jesus has a prophetic word. She is to be cast into "great tribulation" along with those who consort with her. Though the general view is that Thyatira diminished in the light of the Reformation, its main body of corrupt doctrine continues to this day. This Jezebel era will enter the Tribulation Period and see her end in the closing chapters of John's Revelation as Mystery Babylon, the mother of harlots, becomes the target of those very nations over whom she ruled:

"And the ten horns which thou sawest upon the beast, these shall hate the whore, and shall make her desolate and naked, and shall eat her flesh, and burn her with fire.

---

82   J. R. Church. *Prophecy in the News,* 11.

"For God hath put in their hearts to fulfil his will, and to agree, and give their kingdom unto the beast, until the words of God shall be fulfilled" (Revelation 17:16–17).

Mystery Babylon will meet the same fate as the Old Testament Jezebel. This modern institution of goddess worship will be destroyed by those very politicians who once profited by her. We are told that Jezebel was thrown out of a palace window by her bodyguards. In like manner, the kings who kept this "mother of harlots" will see to her undoing.

The savior also has a word for those generations of dedicated Christians in the reform movement:

"But unto you I say, and unto the rest in Thyatira, as many as have not this doctrine, and which have not known the depths of Satan, as they speak; I will put upon you none other burden" (Revelation 2:24).

Note that Jesus uses the same terminology used by the first Church council—"I will put upon you none other burden." After discussing the influx of Gentile converts, the church at Jerusalem decided to accept Gentile conversions without the demands of the Mosaic Law. They drafted a letter to all the churches saying:

"For it seemed good to the Holy Ghost, and to us, to lay upon you no greater burden than these necessary things;

"That ye abstain from meats offered to idols, and from blood, and from things strangled, and from fornication: from which if ye keep yourselves, ye shall do well. Fare ye well" (Acts 15:28).

Jesus tells the church of Thyatira that the dogma instituted at the Jerusalem council against fornication and eating things offered to idols was Scriptural and necessary, but that no other burden of extra-biblical doctrines should be forced upon believers. Yet, the extra-biblical doctrines developed in the Roman Church were forced upon believers. Those who did not agree were branded as heretics and slaughtered.

Pergamos and Thyatira do not paint a pretty picture. It is not pleasant to contemplate the conflicts that beset Christianity during the Dark Ages. Let us determine not to let the intolerance of the past affect us. Let us nurture a divine love for others and hold fast our faith until Christ returns.[83]

The Dark Ages are a time of expensive ornate gothic sanctuaries built with government tax money, made of black stone, surrounded by gargoyles (demons of the most hideous appearance) decorating its towers and doorways.[84]

---

83   J. R. Church. *Prophecy in the News,* 11–12.
84   J. R. Church. *Prophecy in the News,* 9.

Greeting and Complaint

"And unto the angel of the church in Sardis write; These things saith he that hath the seven Spirits of God, and the seven stars; I know thy works, that thou hast a name that thou livest, and art dead" (Revelation 3:1).

Warning

"Be watchful, and strengthen the things which remain, that are ready to die: for I have not found thy works perfect before God. Remember therefore how thou hast received and heard, and hold fast, and repent. If therefore thou shalt not watch, I will come on thee as a thief, and thou shalt not know what hour I will come upon thee" (Revelation 3:2–3).

Praise

"Thou hast a few names even in Sardis which have not defiled their garments; and they shall walk with me in white: for they are worthy" (Revelation 3:4).

Promise

"He that overcometh, the same shall be clothed in white raiment; and I will not blot out his name out of the book of life, but I will confess his name before my Father, and before his angels. He that hath an ear, let him hear what the Spirit saith unto the churches" (Revelation 3:5–6).

> Sardis becomes a type of the church of the reformation, an outgrowth of those in Thyatira who did not accept the incorporation of pagan rituals into church doctrine. The reform movement that started during the Crusades, blossomed in the 1500s with men like Martin Luther, John Calvin, Huldreich Zwingli, and John Knox. With the invention of the printing press, the Bible became available to every home. Ministers and laity alike began to return to the literal interpretation and away from the standard allegorical view of Scripture that dominated church doctrine since the days of Augustine.[85]
>
> Serious abuses also had been accepted in the Roman institution. Because the administrative structure of the church required an increasing financial budget, church positions were sold to wealthy aspirants.
>
> Critics of the church included the religious reformers John Wycliffe in England, John Huss in Bohemia, and Girolamo Savonarola in Italy. These men protested the abuses but could not stop them. During the time that the church was neglecting its spiritual leadership, a tremendous increase in religious feeling was growing among the common

---

85   J. R. Church. *Prophecy in the News,* 8.

people. A great thirst for learning developed in the 1300s and 1400s, producing the Renaissance, a secular attempt at establishing a new golden age of culture throughout Europe. Out of the Renaissance came a new appreciation for the study of Hebrew and Greek, enabling ministers to read the Bible in its original languages. Scholars began to see how the church had changed through the centuries.

The greatest influence on the reform movement was the invention of the printing press, providing Bibles and commentaries to scholars across Europe. Soon, the Bible became available to every home. It was no longer chained to pulpits, and the Roman Church could no longer keep the laity ignorant.

During the Middle Ages, the Holy Roman Emperor claimed to be the head of Europe in both secular and religious affairs. Kings ranked beneath the emperor, followed by princes, dukes, and counts. But the power of the emperor was only honorary from the beginning. The kings were actually independent. Over time, the kings became disenchanted with both the emperor and pope. Nationalism increased, and people began to look upon the pope as the political leader of a foreign country.

Also, during the Middle Ages, European cities began to increase in size, wealth, and independence. Europe's agricultural environment began to give way to manufacturing and merchandising. All of this worked against the efforts of the Roman institution to keep their practitioners enslaved to theological superstition.

Martin Luther

On October 31, 1517, Martin Luther, a monk and professor of theology, posted his Ninety-Five Theses on the door of the Castle Church in Wittenberg, Germany. The paper consisted of a series of statements that attacked the sale of indulgences (pardons from some of the penalty for sins) and other abuses of the church.

Luther believed that men could be saved only through faith in Jesus Christ. His view of religion placed man directly before God without the need for a priesthood. This view contradicted the official position of the church that salvation was obtained through both faith and works.

In January, 1521, Pope Leo X excommunicated Luther and declared him to be a heretic. Emperor Charles V ordered Luther to appear before the diet of Worms, Germany, in April, where he was ordered to recant what he had said and written. Luther replied, "Unless I am convinced by the testimony of the Scriptures or by clean reason (for I do not trust either in the pope or in councils alone, since it is well known that they have often erred and contradicted themselves), I am bound by the Scriptures I have quoted and my conscience is captive to the Word of God. I cannot and I will not retract anything, since it is neither safe nor right to go against conscience. I cannot do otherwise."

In 1530, the Lutherans presented the Augsburg Confession to the diet of Augsburg, Germany. It became the basic statements of Lutheran doctrine, and in 1555, the Holy Roman empire officially recognized the Lutheran churches.

In Switzerland, Huldreich Zwingli, a priest in Zurich, was also leading a movement for religious reform. In 1529, he met with Luther to discuss their disagreement over the interpretation of Christ's presence in the Lord's Supper. Luther regarded this as a sacrament—as a means by which God gave the people His grace. He believed in the real presence of Christ in the bread and wine. Zwingli considered the sacrament a thanksgiving to God for grace already given through the gospel. He believed the bread and wine were mere symbols of Christ's body and blood. Their quarrel led to the first major split in Protestantism.

In the 1520s, the Swiss Brethren, led by Conrad Grebel, decided that the Bible did not teach infant baptism. Their movement became known as Anabaptists (rebaptizers). They were not satisfied with Protestant efforts to reform Christianity, so they withdrew and formed their own churches. They were persecuted by both Catholic and Protestant authorities.

John Calvin helped establish Protestantism in Geneve, Switzerland, and directed efforts to convert the people of France and other countries of Western Europe. His Ecclesiastical Ordinances (1541) established the structure of a Presbyterian form of church government in which a council of elders rules each church. Calvin's followers in France were called Huguenots and came from all classes of society, including the influential noble families such as the Bourbons. They were the victims of the St. Bartholomew's Day Massacre on August 24, 1572, that was discussed previously.

In 1534, England's Henry VIII established the Reformation by an act of state. Pope Clement VII had refused to annual Henry's marriage to his first wife, Catherine of Aragon, and sanction a marriage to Anne Boleyn. Out of the controversy came the Church of England. Queen Elizabeth I (1558–1603) established a form of Protestantism that became known as Anglicanism. Englishmen who followed John Calvin were called Puritans. They opposed Anglicanism because it was Episcopal (governed by bishops) and preferred the Presbyterian form of church government.

In Scotland, John Knox introduced Calvin's teachings and Presbyterian system. In 1560, the Scots made Protestantism their state religion. England forced Ireland to adopt Protestantism as the state religion, but the Irish people remained loyal Catholics. The resulting conflict remains a serious problem to this day.

These brave ministers took hold of a Europe steeped in the Dark Ages and brought about one of the greatest religious revivals in history. Their views may vary, but their efforts opened the door for the gospel to be carried around the world. Indeed, these were overcomers:

"He what overcometh, the same shall be clothed in white raiment; and I will not blot out his name out of the book of life, but I will confess his name before my Father, and before his angels.

"He that hath an ear, let him hear what the Spirit saith unto the churches" (Revelation 3:5–6).

The message to Sardis finds its fulfillment in the Reformation. The Christianity of the Dark Ages had a name, but no life. The gospel was diluted with various pagan rituals, the sale of indulgences, the unscriptural teaching of purgatory, etc. Those who pulled away from the Roman institution were not perfect men, but they were overcomers.

They refused to defile their garments with the heresies that had crept into the Roman Church. We can rejoice in their testimony and the promise that they shall walk with Christ and be presented to the Father and the holy angels.

The church of Sardis symbolized the reformation era. During this period of history the church was reformed but not revived. Some essential doctrines were reclaimed, such as the truth that people can be justified with God only by faith. But these changes did not shake loose rituals and human traditions of the medieval church. Legalism set in but few tasted the power of Christian living.[86]

The Church at Philadelphia—Beginning the Age of Missionary Activity—AD 1700–the end of this age

Greeting and Praise

"And to the angel of the church in Philadelphia write; These things saith he that is holy, he that is true, he that hath the key of David, he that openeth, and no man shutteth; and shutteh, and no man openeth; I know thy works: behold, I have set before thee an open door, and no man can shut it: for thou hast a little strength, and hast kept my word, and hast not denied my name. Behold, I will make them of the synagogue of Satan, which say they are Jews, and are not, but do lie; behold, I will make them to come and worship before thy feet, and to know that I have loved thee" (Revelation 3:7–9).

The Age of the Philadelphia Church represents the age of great revivals and missionary activity—the very era in which we live. It is the age to which the door of evangelism was opened about three centuries ago with the Great Awakening of 1727. The resulting era of modern missions grew out of those great Protestant revivals and their return to a literal interpretation of the Bible. The name Philadelphia comes from a Greek term meaning "brotherly love," and represents an inner joy and friendliness that has characterized this era.

The resulting era of modern missions, with William Carey (India—1793), David Livingstone (Africa—1840), and Hudson Taylor (China—1853), missionaries were

---

86   J. R. Church. *Prophecy in the News,* 11–12.

welcomed in far-flung countries. Emerging societies wanted England's best in theology, education, and medicine. William Carey is called, "the father of modern missions." By the dawn of the 1900s, England's missionary societies were sponsoring over 10,000 missionaries. In this century, the United States took up the mantle and helped to sponsor missionaries on an unprecedented scale.

Like a creeping cancer, socialism is gaining the attention of greedy political leaders. Unlike the gospel, socialism is diametrically opposed to the development of the human spirit, but most self-serving politicians do not understand its long-term destructive results.[87]

The Great Awakening

Following the years of the Reformation, cold, lifeless formalism settled over the Protestant movement. It was an era when men seemed to be content to simply confess a creed. However, God began to move in a mighty way.

Cold Protestant churches in Europe and England began to experience the warmth of revival. God raised up fiery evangelists to stir the hearts of men to experience a Philadelphian love not seen since the first century. Great revivals grew out of a love for the truth of the Word of God. In those days Bibles were being printed and distributed all over Europe and America. The common man could obtain a copy of God's Word and read it for himself.

Beginning in 1727, a new phenomenon shook the theological world. It started in Germany in the Moravian community. Nikolas Count Ludwig von Zinzendorm started a twenty-four-hour-a-day prayer meeting that resulted in the historical Great Awakening. Over the next sixty-five years the Moravians sent out 300 missionaries and greatly influenced the Christians in England and America.

In 1739, the English evangelist George Whitefield preached a series of revivals in Boston, New York, and Philadelphia. During the period of the Great Awakening, nine Bible colleges were established in America. Church membership exploded. Wild frontier towns were tamed with the gospel. The missionary movement of that period brought men like David Brainerd to preach among the Indians.

In England, George Whitefield and John Wesley were having phenomenal results. Whitefield preached in virtually every village in England, Scotland and Wales, crossing the Atlantic seven times to hold revivals in America, and preaching some 18,000 sermons. In 1739, John Wesley preached an open-air revival at Bristol and witnessed the beginning of a phenomenal spiritual reaction among the people that has continued to this day—the era of mass evangelism.

---

87   J. R. Church. *Prophecy in the News*, 14.

Over a period of sixty-five years, Wesley traveled a quarter of a million miles on horseback, preached 40,000 sermons, wrote 233 books, and with his brother, Charles, published 9,000 hymns. His ministry produced 750 preachers in England, 350 in America, 76,986 Methodists in England, and 57,621 in America.

The Great Awakening of 1727 was the beginning of the period of great revivals that affected every nation in the world to this very day—truly the Age of Philadelphia.[88]

William Carey was responsible for organizing the first of these missionary societies and earned the title of "the father of modern missions." As a young man, Carey learned how to cope with poverty. He became a shoemaker at eighteen and suffered financial reversal before he was twenty. However, by 1792, Carey has convinced his colleagues to support his proposal for a missionary society. William Carey became the first missionary, and though the following years would be filled with hardship, his vision caught on and soon, other missionary societies were sending out the gospel around the world.

Upon arriving in India, William Carey formed a team of men to translate the Bible into thirty-four Asian languages. They compiled dictionaries of Sanskit, Marathi, Punjabi, and Telegu. They formed a Bible college, started churches, and established nineteen mission stations.

They opened 100 rural schools and encouraged the education of girls. Carey started the Horticultural Society of India; served as a professor at Fort William College, Calcutta; printed the first Indian weekly newspaper, *The Friend of India;* and introduced the concept of a savings bank to assist poor families. His vision for foreign lands inspired tens of thousands to give themselves for the spread of the gospel.

Among the many missionaries that sprang out of the Great Awakening was Hudson Taylor. He was born in Yorkshire, England in 1832, and came to know the Lord after reading a Christian tract. Soon after, he felt God's call to be a missionary in China and began to study medicine in order to prepare himself for what was to be his life's work. Hudson Taylor was able to complete his medical studies, revise a Chinese New Testament, and organize the China Inland Mission. Twenty-two new recruits accompanied him back to China in 1866.

Then the suffering increased. Marie died in childbirth. His daughter died from water on the brain. His second wife died of cancer. Through all of this, Hudson Taylor clung to the biblical promise. "My grace is sufficient for thee: for my strength is made perfect in weakness." His mission to reach the heart of China continued. By 1895 the China Inland Mission had 641 missionaries and 462 Chinese helpers at 260 mission stations. During the Boxer Rebellion of 1900, fifty-six of these missionaries were martyred and hundreds of Chinese Christians were killed. But that did not stop the work of the mission. In the years following, the number of missionaries quadrupled. Because of

---

88   J. R. Church. *Prophecy in the News*, 16.

men like Hudson Taylor, the gospel continued to flourish after the communist takeover of the country.[89]

Promise

"Because thou hast kept the word of my patience, I also will keep thee from the hour of temptation, which shall come upon all the world, to try them that dwell upon the earth. Behold, I come quickly: hold that fast which thou hast, that no man take thy crown. Him that overcometh will I make a pillar in the Temple of my God, and he shall go no more out: and I will write upon him the name of my God, and the name of the city of my God, which is new Jerusalem, which cometh down out of heaven from my God: and I will write upon him my new name. He that hath an ear, let him hear what the Spirit saith unto the churches" (Revelation 3:10–13).

> In Revelation 3:11, Jesus said, "Behold, I come quickly." There can be no doubt that this promise of Christ's return is given in the era of great revivals and missionary effort—the age in which we live now. Christ assures us that He is coming very soon— "quickly." Most Philadelphians are convinced that Jesus is coming soon. It seems to be a part of our spiritual insight.[90]

The Philadelphia Church was and is the evangelistic church. The Great Awakening was a major revival in North America before the Revolutionary War. The great worldwide evangelical movements were from AD 30–300 and then from the 1700s until now. Wycliffe Bible Translators are in the process of translating the Bible into over a thousand languages. Cameron Townsend started Wycliffe Bible Translators in about 1920. The Philadelphia Church had little strength. However, God is doing a great work, and God opens and shuts doors. When God opens doors, this type of church walks through them.

Mormonism—AD 1830

Mormonism is also known as the Church of Latter-Day Saints. This religion was founded by Joseph Smith in 1830. They have a different Jesus than historical Christianity. They believe Jesus and Satan are spirit brothers. It is a false religion that believes Jesus and Satan presented a plan to God concerning mankind and that Jesus' plan was accepted and Satan's plan was rejected.

Jehovah's Witnesses—late 1880s

The Jehovah's Witness religion was founded by William Russell in the late 1800s. They have a different Jesus than historical Christianity in that they believe Jesus was the archangel Michael. They do not believe in the resurrection of Jesus Christ. They believe in the spiritual resurrection of Jesus Christ, but not a flesh-and-bone resurrection of Jesus Christ.

---

89   J. R. Church. *Prophecy in the News,* 17.
90   J. R. Church. *Prophecy in the News,* 18.

Greeting

"And unto the angel of the church of the Laodiceans write: These things saith the Amen, the faithful and true witness, the beginning of the creation of God" (Revelation 3:14).

Complaint

"I know thy works, that thou art neither cold nor hot: I would thou wert cold or hot" (Revelation 3:15).

Warning

"So then because thou art lukewarm, and neither cold nor hot, I will spue thee out of my mouth. Because thou sayest, I am rich, and increased with goods, and have need of nothing; and knowest not that thou art wretched, and miserable, and poor, and blind, and naked: I counsel thee to buy of me gold tried in the fire, that thou mayest be rich; and white raiment, that thou mayest be clothed, and that the shame of thy nakedness do not appear; and anoint thine eyes with eyesalve, that thou mayest see" (Revelation 3:16–18).

Promise

"As many as I love, I rebuke and chasten: be zealous therefore, and repent. Behold, I stand at the door, and knock: if any man hear my voice, and open the door, I will come in to him, and will sup with him, and he with me. To him that overcometh will I grant to sit with me in my throne, even as I also overcame, and am set down with my Father in his throne. He that hath an ear, let him hear what the Spirit saith unto the churches" (Revelation 3:19–22).

> Laodicea was characterized by being "lukewarm," with the warning that Christ would "spue" them out of His mouth. Historically speaking, it appears that the Savior kept His promise. The description of the church that was "neither hot nor cold" alludes to a basic insincerity on the part of that congregation. Had the church simply been "cold" we could say that they had no pretension to being religious and were honest enough to admit their unbelief and disband. The word "hot" would represent the opposite—a warm and zealous love for serving God. The fact that they were "neither hot nor cold" reveals a dishonesty or hypocrisy on their part. They claimed to be faithful while undermining the faith of others. The Savior had a right to expect either an open and honest opposition or warm-hearted love, but found only an indifference to Him and His cause. He found a church where love was professed but did not exist; where vows had been assumed but not fulfilled. There is an essential meanness in such a character trait.[91]

---

91 J. R. Church. *Prophecy in the News,* 14–15.

A Laodicean never sees himself in need of salvation. He does not consider himself in the pitiful position of a "sinner." He may even be a member of the church and is therefore "safe." He will resist all efforts to convert him because he feels that he does not need to be. Anyone who doubts his sincerity is meddlesome and judgmental. No one has a right to assume that he is insincere. Consequently, there are more converts among the outcasts of society than there are among the so-called "upper class."

Laodicea has become synonymous with liberal theology, commonly called Modernism. The movement began in the early 1700s, taking root in Europe during the "Age of Reason."

German theologians were the most notorious in their use of rationalistic techniques in dealing with the text of the Scriptures. They worked under the assumption that all evidence must be regarded as suspect until proven valid. Two areas of the Bible were particularly targeted—miracles and prophecies. Both were rejected as impossible in the course of human experience.

Another influence upon Modernism was evolutionary philosophy espoused by the British naturalist, Charles Darwin (1809–1882). After returning from a science expedition around the world (1831–1836) aboard the H. M. S. Beagle, Darwin concluded that his collection of plants and animals proved that all life evolved over millions of years rather than being designed and created by God.

As his theories gained attention and acceptance, liberal theologians were all too quick to radically alter their thoughts on the Genesis account of creation and the history of Israel. The modernists failed to examine the validity of the evolutionary theory as a basis for historical and literary biblical studies. They had rather believe a lie.[92]

I believe the total rejection of creationism by Germany is the reason that Germany stated World War I and World War II.

A man can only be forgiven if he feels the need to be. Conviction usually comes in moments of despair and wealth tends to induce a false sense of security—to allay one's conviction—to dull one's spiritual perception of eternal prospects. A wealthy person has no concept of the wretchedness of his soul. He is oblivious to the fact that he is spiritually poor and blind to eternal truths.

They may have read the Scriptures, but had no understanding of God's overall plan for the future of the human race. Frankly, they refused to believe the prophetic aspects of God's Word.[93]

---

92 J. R. Church. *Prophecy in the News,* 15.
93 J. R. Church. *Prophecy in the News,* 15–16.

During the twentieth century, Modernism affected most mainline denominations by infiltrating their colleges and seminaries. There is hardly a church that has been spared from some form of its insidious system of disbelief. The very foundational principles of biblical authority have been undermined. The two biblical themes liberal theologians have focused on for their attacks are "miracles" and "prophecy." All in all, liberal theology teaches that man does not really need God, but can solve the problems that beset mankind on its own.[94]

Finally, our Savior has a promise for the overcomer in Laodicea:

"To him that overcometh will I grant to sit with me in my throne, even as I also overcame, and am set down with my Father in his throne" (Revelation 3:21).

This promise indicates that the church age is ending and the long-awaited kingdom is about to appear. Note that, beginning with Ephesus, the Savior takes us on a journey through six thousand years of human history.

In the promise of Ephesus, Christ takes us back to the Garden of Eden and allows the overcomer to "eat of the tree of life" (Revelation 2:7), a reference to the beginning of history.

In the promise to Smyrna, Christ takes us back to the sin of Adam and the awful consequences of sin. It also shows us God's great purpose in His plan of the ages—mainly, to redeem the overcomer from the "second death" (Revelation 2:11).

In the promise to Pergamos, Christ takes us back to the days of the Exodus and feeds the overcomer with heavenly provisions—the "hidden manna" (Revelation 2:17). He also provides the overcomer with a "white stone" and a "new name," symbols of the Rock that cared for the chosen people—Jehovah's new wife in the wilderness.

In the promise to Thyatira, Christ takes us back to Joshua and David—to the establishment of the kingdom in the Promised Land. This is a foreview that Israel and the church will be given the kingdom—"power over the nations" (Revelation 2:26)—at the end of the church age. Christ will return in triumph at the Battle of Armageddon as depicted in the description, "he shall rule them with a rod of iron; as the vessels of a potter shall they be broken to shivers" (Revelation 2:27). The "morning star" (Revelation 2:28) refers to Christ, who is the fulfillment of every detail in the prophecies of the Bible. All of this is promised to the overcomer.

In the promise to Sardis, Christ takes us back to Calvary and the establishment of the Abrahamic Covenant—a covenant of grace offering eternal life. The overcomer is promised "white raiment" and a place in "the book of life" (Revelation 3:5).

---

94   J. R. Church. *Prophecy in the News*, 18.

In the promise to Philadelphia, Christ takes us to the end of the church age, just as He did in the letter to Laodicea, and refers to the "Temple of my God," to the ineffable and the heretofore unknowable "name of my God," and to the "city of my God" (Revelation 3:12), which is the New Jerusalem.

The promise to the Church of Laodicea: "To him that overcometh will I grant to sit with me in my throne, even as I also overcame, and am set down with My Father in His throne (Revelation 3:21). This promise indicates that the church age is ending and the long-awaited kingdom is about to appear.

All of these promises to overcomers in every church age extend beyond the seven thousand years of history into eternity. All that is here is temporal. Our ultimate promise is that we shall live with Christ throughout the cycles of eternity—that we are blessed beyond measure for having trusted in Him, who loves us.[95]

The Fruits of the Church Age

- Hospitals, which essentially began during the Middle Ages
- Universities, which also began during the Middle Ages. In addition, most of the world's greatest universities were started by Christians for Christian purposes.
- Literacy and education of the masses.
- Representative government, particularly as it has been seen in the American experiment.
- The separation of political powers.
- Civil liberties.
- The abolition of slavery, both in antiquity and in modern times.
- Modern science.
- The discovery of the New World by Columbus.
- Benevolence and charity; the Good Samaritan ethic.
- Higher standards of justice.
- The elevation of the common man.
- The high regard for human life.
- The civilizing of many barbarian and primitive cultures.
- The codifying and setting to writing of many of the world's languages.
- The greater development of art and music. The inspiration for the greatest works of art.
- The countless changed lives transformed from liabilities into assets to society because of the gospel.
- The eternal salvation of countless souls![96]

The fruits of the true Christian church are unchallenged. Wherever true Christianity was embraced and established, true science and humanity flourished. Wherever non-biblical religions have been established, poverty and ignorance flourished. For a nation to prosper, its peoples must believe the Ten Commandments.

---

95   J. R. Church. *Prophecy in the News,* 18.
96   D. James Kennedy. *What If Jesus Had Never Been Born?* 3.

The Institution of Slavery

The terrible institution of slavery existed in the four southern states at the time of the Revolutionary War in 1776. It continued and expanded until the time of the Civil War in 1861 to 1865. Over six hundred thousand Americans died in the Civil War, and America is the only nation ever to fight a civil war to end the institution of slavery.

It was Christians who first pushed for the end of slavery in the USA as well as in Great Britain. Christians understood that all mankind was created in the image of God. No nation has ever fought a civil war to end slavery. Slavery continues to this day in many non-Christian nations.

What man meant for evil—bringing slaves to North America—God meant for good. No matter our shade or color, all of mankind is technically different shades of the same color. We should all take advantage of the blessing of being a citizen of the USA.

I strive to be a slave for Christ. A slave has no rights. As a Christian, I do not have the right to be a racist. Again, all of us going back to Noah and further back to Adam are all related.

The Christian Foundation of the United States of America and the Effects of Non-Christian Beliefs on the USA

The Supreme Court ruled in 1799: "By our form of government, the Christian religion is the established religion; and all sects and denominations of Christians are placed upon the same equal footing" *(Runkel v. Winemiller, 1799)*.[97]

James Madison stated, "We have staked the whole future of American civilization, not upon the power of government, far from it. We have staked the future … upon the capacity of each and all of us to govern ourselves, to sustain ourselves, according to the Ten Commandments of God."

Madison did not believe viewing the Ten Commandments was a violation of the Constitution; in fact, he believed that obeying them was its very basis![98]

John Adams stated, "Our Constitution was made only for a moral and religious people. It is wholly inadequate to the government of any other."[99]

John Quincy Adams stated, "The highest glory of the American Revolution was this: it connected, in one indissoluble bond the principles of civil government with the principles of Christianity."[100]

Patrick Henry stated, "It cannot be emphasized too strongly or too often that this great nation was founded, not by religionists, but by Christians; not on religions, but on the gospel of Jesus Christ!"[101]

---

97 David Barton. *The Myth of Separation by David Barton,* 151.
98 David Barton. *The Myth of Separation,* 155.
99 David Barton. *The Myth of Separation,* 146.
100 David Barton. *The Myth of Separation,* 125.
101 David Barton. *The Myth of Separation,* 25.

John Jay, First Chief Justice of the United States Supreme Court stated, "Providence has given to our people the choice of their rulers, and it is the duty … of our Christian nation to select and prefer Christians for their rulers."[102]

"No free government now exists in the world unless where Christianity is acknowledged, and is the religion of the country...Its foundations are broad and strong, and deep … it is the purest system of morality, and only stable support of all human laws" (Pennsylvania Supreme Court, 1824).[103]

Thomas Jefferson declared, "And can the liberties of a nation be thought secure when we have removed their only firm basis, a conviction in the minds of the people that these liberties are of the gift of God? That they are not to be violated but with His wrath? Indeed, I tremble for my country when I reflect that God is just: that His justice cannot sleep forever."[104]

Abraham Lincoln asserted that schools are the future, "The philosophy of the school room in one generation will be the philosophy of the government in the next."[105]

> Martin Luther expressed, "I am much afraid that schools will prove to be the great gates of hell unless they diligently labor in explaining the Holy Scriptures, engraving them in the hearts of youth. I advise no one to place his child where the scriptures do not reign paramount. Every institution in which men are not increasingly occupied with the Word of God must become corrupt."[106]
>
> "Atheism may be a religion under the establishment clause" *(Malnak v. Yogi*, 1977).
>
> "Secular humanism may be a religion for purposes of First Amendment" *(Grove v. Mead School District*, 1985).[107]

The question is not whether religion is in the schools, but rather whose religion is in the public school systems. The religion of the state is whatever religion is being taught to the children. The religion being taught in America's school systems is a combination of atheism, secular humanism, evolution, and new age religions. Children in essence are being taught that Christianity is a false belief system. Evolution is taught as a fact. There may be a God, but God is not personal. Man and governments decide what is right through trial and error. Many times children are taught to worship the creation rather than the creator. Our school systems and TV send so many mixed signals it is no wonder our nation's youth are in trouble.

Since the Supreme Court's rulings and the teaching of evolution, the rates of unwed mothers, violent crime, sexually transmitted diseases, and divorce have all skyrocketed. SAT scores have gone down because we have taught children there is no purpose in life. Our purpose in life is to love God with all

---

102 David Barton. *The Myth of Separation*, 35.
103 David Barton. *The Myth of Separation*, 251.
104 David Barton. *The Myth of Separation*, 176.
105 David Barton. *The Myth of Separation*, 264.
106 David Barton. *The Myth of Separation*, 264.
107 David Barton. *The Myth of Separation*, 182.

our heart, mind, soul, and strength and to love fellow man as ourselves. We have in essence told the children there is no personal God and to pursue money, sex, drugs, and alcohol—but to never smoke cigarettes!

The last fifty years of our nation's history have been very difficult. Fifty years ago, two-thirds of Americans believed in moral absolutes. Presently about one-third of Americans believe in moral absolutes. I define moral absolutes as believing God created everything from nothing abruptly. Because of God's power, He gets to determine what is good and what is evil—and thus, the Ten Commandments are relevant for today, because God wrote them in stone. Our educational standards have deteriorated in the same period of time.

In a sermon by Dr. Glen Schultz at Houston's First Baptist Church in September, 2001, Schultz stated the following:

> In the 1950s, our youth lost their innocence.
> In the 1960s, our youth lost their respect for authority.
> In the 1970s, our youth lost their understanding of what true love is.
> In the 1980s, our youth lost their hope for the future.
> In the 1990s, our youth lost their belief in absolute truth.

In essence, I believe that because of the teaching of evolution in our nation, the youth do not see any purpose to life. Many teenagers don't even understand that they have a soul. In the 1950s, youth lost their innocence in knowing and seeing more evil at a younger and younger age. In the 1960s, they lost their respect for authority because of the Supreme Court's decision to ban school prayer and because of the Vietnam War. In the 1970s, they lost their capacity to know the difference between the love of husband and wife and knew free sex outside marriage. The Supreme Court also told us in essence that the unborn were blobs of tissue not created in the image of God, because there is no God. In the 1980s, the youth lost their hope in the future, and suicide rates went up as the culture of death moved into music. In the 1990s, many of the youth believed that since they do not know the truth, no one can know the truth. Many people even question the right of people to state that they know the truth.

Summary

"Jesus saith unto him, I am the way, the truth, and the life: no man cometh unto the Father but by me" (John 14:6).

This sums up the New Testament. The only way to heaven is through the finished work of Jesus Christ which was performed on the cross.

Signs of the Second Coming of Jesus Christ

God wants us to:

- Understand that He declared the end at the beginning of time
- Prepare for the future
- Not get mad at Him as times get tougher
- Stay close to Him and obey His voice
- Not believe false teachers
- Endure to the end with victory
- Always have hope and faith
- Have joy and peace even in difficult times

The Battle is for Souls

God is already victorious and will show His wisdom, justice, love, grace, and power to all His created beings through the events leading to the resurrection of the saints and the second coming of Jesus Christ.

Those involved in the battle can be classified in one of three ways:

Faithful	*Still in Doubt*	*Losers*
Seraphim	Unfaithful mankind but	Satan (Lucifer)
Cherubim	still open to the gospel	Fallen angels
Archangels	of Jesus Christ	Antichrist
Angels		All those who do now and will
Saints—redeemed mankind		forever reject the grace of God

A person will either live by faith in God or will choose rebellion against God by rejecting Jesus Christ. You have this choice and no other choice—faith in God or rebellion against God.

God judges individuals and nations and will use the following to get one's attention:

Wars	Financial prosperity	Famine
Sickness	Financial loss	Drought
Earthquakes	Disease	Compassionate Christians
Disasters of all types	Floods	Fear of death and hell

I became a Christian after studying biblical prophecy. I had difficulty believing some portions of the Old Testament. However, I came to the conclusion that if the Bible predicted the restoration of the State of Israel prior to the second coming of Jesus Christ, then the Bible was a reliable book concerning history, prophecy, and how we should conduct our lives. After studying the Bible for seventeen years, I am more convinced of this fact than when I first became a Christian.

Biblical Christianity explains history and predicts the future at the rate of 100 percent accuracy. God created intelligent beings with a free will to rebel against Him or to love and believe Him. God does not intend to allow evil to exist forever. The second coming of Jesus Christ is an event to bring the creation one step closer to the elimination of death, evil, destruction, and rebellion. The events of the second coming will help to ensure no further rebellions in the future. The second coming of Jesus Christ will show the futility of fighting against God and God's Word, the Bible.

One way God proves He is God is through the creation of the dimension of time. There is one time which is comprised of the past, present, and future. God proves He created time through Bible prophecy. All other belief systems are either based upon philosophy, unbelief, or rebellion. Islam, Hinduism, and Buddhism are all philosophical. Mormonism and Jehovah's Witnesses are full of false prophecies. Secular humanism and atheism are religions based upon the thought process that there is no design, order, or purpose in the universe. Over the years, humanism and atheism have less appeal because there is no promise of an afterlife, which runs contrary to what God has written in your soul. God has written eternity in your soul. Because of this, there is a rise in the popularity of new age religions. New age religions are based upon the occult and the old lie that man is God or can be equal to God.

Literally thousands of verses in the Bible deal with the event of the second coming of Jesus Christ. It is estimated that for every one verse that predicts the first coming of Jesus Christ, there are ten verses which tell us about the second coming. Listed below are some major signs of the second coming of Jesus Christ.

Major Signs of the Second Coming of Jesus Christ:

The Introduction and Proliferation of Nuclear Weapons and Man's Ability to End Mankind
The Increase in Knowledge and Understanding in Science and of the Bible
The Rebirth of the State of Israel
The Increase in Earthquakes, Famine, Disease, Deception, Wars, Rumors of Wars, Abortion, and Cloning
The Gospel Preached to the World and the Dramatic Rise in False Religions
The State of Humanity
Jerusalem Surrounded by its Enemies

The Empires of the World and the Alignment of the Nations
The Abomination of Desolation Prophesied by the Prophet Daniel
One World Economy and Debt

The Introduction and Proliferation of Nuclear Weapons and Man's Ability to End Mankind

Jesus stated in Matthew 24:21–22 in approximately AD 32, "For then shall be great tribulation, such as was not since the beginning of the world to this time, no, nor even shall be. And except those days be shortened there should be no flesh saved: but for the elect's sake those days shall be shortened."

Jesus stated that without the intervention of God to stop us from destroying each other, the people of planet earth would in fact kill each other until none were left. This would have been impossible prior to the introduction of nuclear weapons. We have the capability to destroy life on this planet many times over again. This capability was not achieved until the 1970s with the introduction of the arms race in nuclear weapons.

"The burden of Damascus. Behold, Damascus is taken away from being a city, and it shall be a ruinous heap" (Isaiah 17:1).

The Bible prophesies the destruction of Damascus, located in present-day Syria. Damascus is the oldest continuous city that has never been destroyed by war. When Damascus is destroyed, a major Bible prophecy will be fulfilled. If you are alive and see the destruction of Damascus, know that the resurrection of the saints and the second coming of Jesus Christ is a hand. If you are not saved, time is short to call upon the Lord Jesus Christ to be saved.

"The earth also is defiled under the inhabitants thereof; because they have transgressed the laws, changed the ordinance, broken the everlasting covenant. Therefore hath the curse devoured the earth, and they that dwell therein are desolate: therefore the inhabitants of the earth are burned, and few men left" (Isaiah 24:5–6, 20).

"And I looked, and behold a pale horse: and his name that sat on him was Death, and Hell followed with him. And power was given unto them over the fourth part of the earth, to kill with sword, and with hunger, and with death, and with the beasts of the earth" (Revelation 6:8).

"By these three was the third part of men killed, by the fire, and by the smoke, and by the brimstone, which issued out of their mouths" (Revelation 9:18).

In the future, I believe there will be nuclear wars and more terrorist attacks. These verses sound like nuclear war.

"Thou wilt keep him in perfect peace, whose mind is stayed on thee: because he trusteth in thee" (Isaiah 26:3).

The last seventeen books of the Old Testament are full of chapters of the judgment of God. However, every few pages God will put verses such as Isaiah 26:3 at the end of a discourse of destruction. These verses are for our encouragement, and we are not to fear the future.

The Increase in Knowledge and Understanding in Science and of the Bible

"And at that time shall Michael stand up, the great prince which standeth for the children of thy people: and there shall be a time of trouble, such as never was since there was a nation even to that same time: and at that time thy people shall be delivered, every one that shall be found written in the book. And many of them that sleep in the dust of the earth shall awake, some to everlasting life, and some to shame and everlasting contempt. And they that be wise shall shine as the brightness of the firmament; and they that turn many to righteousness as the stars for ever and ever. But thou, O Daniel, shut up the words, and seal the book, even to the time of the end: many shall run to and fro, and knowledge shall be increased …. And I heard, but I understood not: then said I, O my Lord, what shall be the end of these things? And he said, Go thy way, Daniel: for the words are closed up and sealed till the time of the end. Many shall be purified, and made white, and tried; but the wicked shall do wickedly: and none of the wicked shall understand; but the wise shall understand" (Daniel 12:1–4, 8–10).

Since the beginning of time man rode on horses, donkeys, and camels. The last 100 years has seen the advent of automobiles, planes, and trains. We have all seen the graphs of the increase in knowledge, with knowledge doubling every two to five years depending upon who you listen to or believe. Knowledge and understanding of the Bible has been increasing in the same manner. Bible verses that were difficult to understand 400 years ago are easily understood today. Wise believers will lead others to the God of the Bible. Many prophecies in the Bible could not be understood until the last days in which we are living.

"The secret things belong unto the LORD our God: but those things which are revealed belong unto us and to our children for ever, that we may do all the words of this law" (Deuteronomy 29:29).

The secret things also include recent scientific advances in computers, medicine, space travel, etc. God reveals the secret things in His timing.

The Rebirth of the State of Israel

Dispersion and Regathering of Israel—Deuteronomy 28:62–68—Moses—1350 BC

"And ye shall be left few in number, whereas ye were as the stars of heaven for multitude; because thou wouldest not obey the voice of the LORD thy God. And it shall come to pass, that as the LORD rejoiced over you to do you good, and to multiply you; so the LORD will rejoice over you to destroy you, and to bring you to nought; and ye shall be plucked from off the land whither thou goest to possess it. And the LORD shall scatter thee among all people, from the one end of the earth even unto the other; and there thou shalt serve other gods, which neither thou nor thy fathers have known, even wood and stone. And among these nations shalt thou find no ease, neither shall the sole of thy foot have rest: but the LORD shall give thee there a trembling heart, and failing of eyes, and sorrow of mind: And thy life shall hang in doubt before thee; and thou shalt fear day and night, and shalt have none assurance of thy life: In the morning thou shalt say, Would God it were even! and at even thou shalt say, Would God it were morning! for the fear of thine heart wherewith thou shalt fear, and for the sight of thine eyes which thou shalt see. And the LORD shall bring thee into Egypt again with ships, by the way whereof I spake unto thee, Thou shalt see it no more again: and there ye shall be sold unto your enemies for bondmen and bondwomen, and no man shall buy you" (Deuteronomy 28:62–68).

God warned Israel that if they stopped obeying His Word and laws that He would destroy the nation of Israel and that the Jews would be scattered to the end of the earth. Furthermore, God said the Jews would be in constant fear for their lives, night and day. This is exactly what has happened. Israel rejected Jesus as the Messiah, which was foreordained by God—which brings the riches of salvation to the Gentiles.

Deuteronomy 30:1–9—Moses—1350 BC

"And it shall come to pass, when all these things are come upon thee, the blessing and the curse, which I have set before thee, and thou shalt call them to mind among all the nations, whither the LORD thy God hath driven thee, And shalt return unto the LORD thy God, and shalt obey his voice according to all that I command thee this day, thou and thy children, with all thine heart, and with all thy soul; That then the LORD thy God will turn thy captivity, and have compassion upon thee, and will return and gather thee from all the nations, whither the LORD thy God hath scattered thee. If any of thine be driven out unto the outmost parts of heaven, from thence will the LORD thy God gather thee, and from thence will he fetch thee: And the LORD thy God will bring thee into the land which thy fathers possessed, and thou shalt possess it; and he will do thee good, and multiple thee above thy fathers. And the LORD thy God will circumcise thine heart, and the heart of thy seed, to love the LORD thy God will all thine heart, and with all thy soul, that thou mayest live. And the LORD thy God will put all these curses upon thine enemies, and on them that hate thee, which persecuted thee. And thou shalt return and obey the voice of the LORD, and do all his commandments which I command thee this day. And the LORD thy God will make thee plenteous in every work of thine hand, in the fruit of thy body, and in the fruit of thy cattle, and in the fruit of thy land, for good: for the LORD will again rejoice over thee for good, as he rejoiced over thy fathers" (Deuteronomy 30:1–9).

In Deuteronomy 30:3, God states that the Jews would return from all the nations of the earth. The State of Israel was reestablished as a nation in 1948. God states that those who believe Him and His promises have a circumcised heart. In other words, a believer will have a new heart.

Jeremiah 16:14–15—600 BC

"Therefore, behold, the days come, saith the LORD, that it shall no more be said, The LORD liveth, that brought up the children of Israel out of the land of Egypt; But, The LORD liveth, that brought up the children of Israel from the land of the north, and from all the lands whither he had driven them: and I will bring them again into their land and I gave unto their fathers" (Deuteronomy 30:1–9).

In this verse, God is speaking about Himself. God states that the regathering of the Jewish people in the 1900s is literally a bigger miracle than was the parting of the Red Sea.

Jeremiah 23:3–8—600 BC

"And I will gather the remnant of my flock out of all countries whither I have driven them, and will bring them again to their folds; and they shall be fruitful and increase. And I will set up shepherds over them which shall feed them: and they shall fear no more, nor be dismayed, neither shall they be lacking, saith the LORD. Behold, the days come, saith the LORD, that I will raise unto David a righteous Branch, and a King shall reign and prosper, and shall execute judgment and justice in the earth. In his days Judah shall be saved, and Israel shall dwell safely: and this is his name whereby he shall be called, THE LORD OUR RIGHTEOUSNESS. Therefore, behold, the days come, saith the LORD, that they shall no more say, The LORD liveth, which brought up the children of Israel out of the land of Egypt; But, The LORD liveth, which brought up and which led the seed of the house of Israel out of the north country, and from all countries whither I had driven them; and they shall dwell in their own land" (Jeremiah 23:3–8).

Jeremiah 30:3—600 BC

"For, lo, the days come, saith the LORD, that I will bring again the captivity of my people Israel and Judah, saith the LORD: and I will cause them to return to the land that I gave to their fathers, and they shall possess it" (Jeremiah 30:3).

Isaiah 10:22—725 BC

"For though thy people Israel be as the sand of the sea, yet a remnant of them shall return: the consumption decreed shall overflow with righteousness" (Isaiah 10:22).

Isaiah 11:10–15—725 BC

"And in that day there shall be a root of Jesse, which shall stand for an ensign of the people; to it shall the Gentiles seek: and his rest shall be glorious. And it shall come to pass in that day, that the Lord shall set his hand again the second time to recover the remnant of his people, which shall be left, from Assyria, and from Egypt, and from Pathros, and from Cush, and from Elam, and from Shinar, and from Hamath, and from the islands of the sea. And he shall set up an ensign for the nations, and shall assemble the outcasts of Israel, and gather together the dispersed of Judah from the four corners of the earth. The envy also of Ephraim shall depart, and the adversaries of Judah shall be cut off: Ephraim shall not envy Judah, and Judah shall not vex Ephraim. But they shall fly upon the shoulders of the Philistines toward the west; they shall spoil them of the east together: they shall lay their hand upon Edom and Moab; and the children of Ammon shall obey them. And the LORD shall utterly destroy the tongue of the Egyptian sea; and with his mighty wind shall he shake his hand over the river, and shall smite it in the seven streams, and make men go over dryshod. And there shall be an highway for the remnant of his people, which shall be left, from Assyria; like as it was to Israel in the day that he came up out of the land of Egypt" (Isaiah 11:10–15).

In Isaiah and Jeremiah, God states that *He will restore the State of Israel a second time.* The first restoration of Israel was around 500 BC with the return of the Jews from Babylon, which was known as the Babylonian captivity. The second restoration of Israel occurred with the 1948 reestablishment of the State of Israel and Jews returning from the four corners of the earth.

Isaiah 43:5–6—725 BC

"Fear not: for I am with thee: I will bring thy seed from the east, and gather thee from the west: I will say to the north, Give up; and to the south, Keep not back: bring my sons from far, and my daughters from the ends of the earth" (Isaiah 43:5–6).

These verses state the relative ease for the Jews to return from North and South America, Europe, and Asia. Isaiah 43:6 implies the difficulty of returning from the North and the South. Great diplomatic efforts were expended to get the release of the Jews from the former Soviet Union (North) during the 1980s and 1990s as well as from Ethiopia in the South.

Isaiah 54:7–10—725 BC

"For a small moment have I forsaken thee; but with great mercies will I gather thee. In a little wrath I hid my face from thee for a moment; but with everlasting kindness will I have mercy on thee, saith the LORD thy Redeemer. For this is as the waters of Noah unto me: for as I have sworn that the waters of Noah should no more go over the earth; so have I sworn that I would not be wroth with thee, nor rebuke thee. For the mountains shall depart, and the hills be removed; but my kindness shall not depart from thee, neither shall the covenant of my peace be removed, saith the LORD that hath mercy on thee" (Deuteronomy 30:1–9).

God considers a few thousand years as a moment compared to eternity.

Romans 11:1–3—AD 60

"I say then, Hath God cast away his people? God forbid. For I also am an Israelite, of the seed of Abraham, of the tribe of Benjamin. God hath not cast away his people which he foreknew. Wot ye not what the scripture saith of Elias? how he maketh intercession to God against Israel, saying, Lord, they have killed thy prophets, and digged down thine altars; and I am left alone, and they seek my life" (Romans 11:1–3).

The Apostle Paul tells us under the guidance of the Holy Spirit that God would not cast away Israel forever.

"Now learn a parable of the fig tree; When his branch is yet tender, and putteth forth leaves, ye know that summer is nigh: So likewise ye, when he shall see all these things, know that it is near, even at the doors. Verily I say unto you, This generation shall not pass, till all these things be fulfilled. Heaven and earth shall pass away, but my words shall not pass away" (Matthew 24:32–35).

This verse is interpreted by many prophecy teachers as the generation that sees the reestablishment of the State of Israel will also see the second coming of Jesus Christ. The fig tree is a picture and type of the State of Israel. Israel was a state when the feasts of Passover, Firstfruits, and Pentecost were fulfilled with the death, burial, and resurrection of Jesus Christ and the start of the church age. Some of the fall feasts will be fulfilled in the second coming of Jesus Christ, which I believe will only occur with the reestablishment of the State of Israel.

The Increase in Earthquakes, Famine, Disease, Deception, Wars, Rumors of Wars, Abortion, and Cloning.

Jesus spoke in the first person in all of Matthew 24.

"And Jesus went out, and departed from the Temple: and his disciples came to him for to shew him the buildings of the Temple. And Jesus said unto them, See ye not all these things? verily I say unto you, There shall not be left here one stone upon another, that shall not be thrown down. And as he sat upon the mount of Olives, the disciples came unto him privately, saying, Tell us, when shall these things be? and what shall be the sign of thy coming, and of the end of the world? And Jesus answered and said unto them, Take heed that no man deceive you. For many shall come in my name, saying, I am Christ; and shall deceive many. And ye shall hear of wars and rumors of wars: see that ye be not troubled: for all these things must come to pass, but the end is not yet. For nation shall rise against nation, and kingdom against kingdom: and there shall be famines, and pestilences, and earthquakes, in divers places. All these are the beginning of sorrows. Then shall they deliver you up to be afflicted, and shall kill you: and ye shall be hated of all nations for my name's sake. And then shall many be offended, and shall betray one another, and shall hate one another. And many false prophets shall rise, and shall deceive many. And because iniquity shall abound, the love of many shall wax cold. But he that shall endure unto the end, the same shall be saved. And this gospel of the kingdom shall be preached in all the world for a witness unto all nations; and then shall the end come" (Matthew 24:1–14).

"Then if any man shall say unto you, Lo, here is Christ, or there; believe it not. For there shall arise false Christs, and false prophets, and shall shew great signs and wonders; insomuch that, if it were possible, they shall deceive the very elect" (Matthew 24:23–24).

"For as in the days that were before the flood they were eating and drinking, marrying and giving in marriage, until the day that Noe entered into the ark, And knew not until the flood came, and took them all away; so shall also the coming of the Son of man be" (Matthew 24:38–39).

It is estimated that during the 1900s, close to 200 million people were killed due to wars, massacres, murders, and government-made famines. This could be a low estimate.

- Eighteen million people were killed in World War I, which was started by secular humanists in Germany.
- Twenty million Russians were killed and/or starved to death by Lenin and Stalin, both of whom were atheists.
- Fifty million people were killed in World War II. Hitler's religious beliefs were a combination of deism, atheism, secular humanism, evolution, eastern religions, and the occult. Hitler believed in reincarnation. Japan is primarily a Buddhist country.
- Thirty to sixty million Chinese were killed by Mao Tse Tung over many decades. Mao was an atheist.

There are over thirty countries either at war or close to war. Just recently, the United States declared war on international terrorism. The entire Middle East is either at war or could easily be thrown into war. The following is a list of nations that are at war or have major internal and external disputes.

The entire Middle East

Haiti	Columbia	Peru
Ecuador	Northern Ireland	Sierre Leone
Liberia	Zaire	Angola
Burundi	Rwanda	Tanzania
Algeria	Bosnia	Kosovo
Chechnya	Azerbaijan	Krsygstan
Kashmir	Sir Lanka	Indonesia
India/Pakistan	Burma	
East Timor	China/Taiwan	
North Korea/South Korea		

"He that leadeth into captivity shall go into captivity: he that killeth with the sword must be killed with the sword. Here is the patience and the faith of the saints" (Revelation 13:10).

Violence is a cottage industry in the world. Small arms, knives, and mines are in all nations except those that are under sheer tyranny. In nations under sheer tyranny, the people do not tend to kill each other; however, their governments tend to kill them in great numbers. "He (Nimrod) also gradually changed the government into tyranny. Nimrod saw no other way of turning men from the fear of God, but to bring them into constant dependency upon his power."[108] This statement was written about 1900 years ago by the historian Josephus. It is the most interesting non-biblical quote I have ever read. Nimrod was the leader of Babylon in the times of the Tower of Babel and the confusion of the languages around 4100 years ago. Most leaders in government use tyranny so that their fellow countrymen will fear them more than they fear God (i.e. Hitler, Stalin, etc.). All leaders that act like this have the spirit of death and the spirit of antichrist on them.

"And he said,`What hast thou done? The voice of thy brother's blood crieth unto me from the ground`" (Genesis 4:10).

Hundreds of millions of babies have been aborted in the last 100 years. In the spirit, their deaths cry out for justice and bring a spirit of death and violence to nations that justify and allow abortion.

"Ye shall keep my statutes. Thou shalt not let thy cattle gender with a diverse kind: thou shalt not sow thy field with mingled seed: neither shall a garment mingled of linen and woollen come upon thee" (Leviticus 19:19).

---

108 William Whiston. *The Works of Josephus Translated* (Hendrickson Publishers) 35.

Cloning and mixing of seed for forbidden by God. I believe this verse does not just deal with the mixing of linen and wool but also of science going to places where God says to stay out. I don't believe God will allow mankind of mix mankind and animal hybridization for long. God warns against redesigning DNA chains in mankind, animals, and plants. Man can not improve upon a DNA chain that God originally designed.

The Gospel Preached to the World and the Dramatic Rise of False Religions

Matthew 28:18–20—AD 32—Jesus Spoke This after His Resurrection

"And Jesus came and spake unto them, saying,`All power is given unto me in heaven and in earth. Go ye therefore, and teach all nations, baptizing them in the name of the Father, and of the Son, and of the Holy Ghost: Teaching them to observe all things whatsoever I have commanded you: and, lo, I am with you alway, even unto the end of the world. Amen`" (Matthew 28:18–20).

There are over 6,700 languages in the world. A very large percentage of the world's population speaks either English, Mandarin, Spanish, Farsi, Portuguese, German, Japanese, Russian, French, or Hindi; this accounts for approximately 70 percent of the people on earth.

Over 300 language groups have an adequate Bible. Another 800 language groups have an adequate New Testament. Over a thousand more language groups have at least one book in the Bible. Over the last hundred years, particularly since the work of Wycliffe Bible Translators began approximately eighty years ago, results have grown exponentially. There are close to five thousand people around the world who are in full-time service to the translating of the Bible. About 300 million out of 6 billion people have no portion of the Bible written in their mother tongue.

"If ye continue in the faith grounded and settled, and be not moved away from the hope of the gospel, which ye have heard, and which was preached to every creature which is under heaven; whereof I Paul am made a minister" (Colossians 1:23).

The gospel was preached to the world in the first century and is continuing today.

The State of Humanity

II Timothy 3:1–7—AD 60

"This know also, that in the last days perilous times shall come. For men shall be lovers of their own selves, covetous, boasters, proud, blasphemers, disobedient to parents, unthankful, unholy, Without natural affection, trucebreakers, false accusers, incontinent, fierce, despisers of those that are good, Traitors, heady, highminded, lovers of pleasures more than lovers of god; Having a form of godliness, but denying the power thereof: from such turn away. For of this sort are they which creep into houses, and lead captive silly women laden with sins, led away with divers lust, Ever learning, and never able to come to the knowledge of the truth" (II Timothy 3:1–7).

Blasphemers are persons who are against God. The fight to keep God out of the minds of our children over the past fifty years has been unmerciful. Isaiah 3:12 states, "As for my people, children are their oppressors, and women rule over them." Our nation has moved beyond disobedient children to a nation with many school districts and their employees and parents being afraid of the children they are supposed to be teaching.

A major example of a person without natural affection would be a woman having a child and throwing the child into the trash after giving birth. II Timothy 3:4 mentions traitors. I believe that a number of traitors to the United States of America will ultimately play a major part in the weakening of the United States—starting with the Rosenbergs, who helped the Soviet Union gain the atomic bomb to the present. For relatively small amounts of money and because of hatred of God and His people, many US citizens have given to nations that desire to destroy our way of life the technology to do just that.

Jerusalem Surrounded by Its Enemies

Genesis 14:18–20—1900 BC—The City of Jerusalem

"And Melchizedek king of *Salem* brought forth bread and wine: and he was the priest of the most high God. And he blessed him, and said, Blessed be Abram of the most high God, possessor of heaven and earth: And blessed be the most high God, which hath delivered thine enemies into thy hand. And he gave him tithes of all" (Genesis 14:18–20).

Salem mentioned here is now Jerusalem.

Genesis 22:2—1850 BC—Abraham Willing to Offer Isaac as a Sacrifice

"And he said, Take now thy son, thine only son Isaac, whom thou lovest, and get thee into the land of *Moriah*; and offer him there for a burnt offering upon one of the mountains which I will tell thee of" (Genesis 22:2).

Mt. Moriah is in Jerusalem and is the location where Abraham was to sacrifice Isaac but was stopped by God.

II Samuel 24:24–25—1000 BC—David Purchases the Threshingfloor

"And the king said unto Araunah, Nay; but I will surely buy it of thee at a price: neither will I offer burnt offerings unto the LORD my God of that which doth cost me nothing. So David bought the threshingfloor and the oxen for fifty shekels of silver. And David built there an altar unto the LORD, and offered burnt offerings and peace offerings. So the LORD was intreated for the land, and the plague was stayed from Israel" (II Samuel 24:24–25).

This threshingfloor is the temple mount area in Jerusalem. This is the last time that this land was purchased. It has changed hands by war many, many times, but David was the last person to purchase it.

I Kings 8:10–13—950 BC—The Temple Filled with the Glory of God

"And it came to pass, when the priests were come out of the holy place, that the could filled the house of the LORD, So that the priests could not stand to minister because of the cloud: for the glory of the LORD had filled the house of the LORD. Then spake Solomon, The LORD said that he would dwell in the thick darkness. I have surely built thee an hour to dwell in, a settled place for thee to abide in for ever" (I Kings 8:10–13).

This is Solomon's temple in Jerusalem as it was completed and dedicated. The Holy Spirit was so heavy in the temple that the priests had to leave the temple.

Matthew 27:33–35—AD 30

"And when they were come unto a place called Golgotha, that is to say, a place of a skull, They gave him vinegar to drink mingled with gall: and when he had tasted thereof, he would not drink. And they crucified him, and parted his garments, casting lots: that it might be fulfilled which was spoken by the prophet, They parted my garments among them, and upon my vesture did they cast lots" (Matthew 27:33–35).

Jesus was crucified just outside the walls of Jerusalem.

Ezekiel 48:15—The Profane Place

"And the five thousand, that are left in the breadth over against the five and twenty thousand, shall be a profane place for the city, for dwelling, and for suburbs: and the city shall be in the midst thereof" (Ezekiel 48:15).

I believe the profane place is the Muslim Dome of the Rock in Jerusalem, which was prophesied by Ezekiel in ~757 BC and was fulfilled around AD 685.

Revelation 15:7–8—The Temple in Heaven in the Near Future

"And one of the four beasts gave unto the seven angels seven golden vials full of the wrath of God, who liveth for ever and ever. And the Temple was filled with smoke from the glory of God, and from his power; and no man was able to enter into the Temple, till the seven plagues of the seven angels were fulfilled" (Revelation 15:7–8).

This temple is in heaven and is to be fulfilled in the near future. The same smoke (cloud) mentioned in I Kings 8:10 above is the Holy Spirit here in Revelation 15:8.

Revelation 21:9–10, 22–23—The New Jerusalem from Heaven

"And there came unto me one of the seven angels which had the seven vials full of the seven last plagues, and talked with me, saying, Come hither, I will shew thee the bride, the Lamb's wife. And he carried me away in the spirit to a great and high mountain, and shewed me that great city, the holy Jerusalem, descending out of heaven from God… And I saw no Temple therein: for the Lord God Almighty and the Lamb are the Temple of it. And the city had no need of the sun, neither of the moon, to shine in it: for the glory of God did lighten it, and the Lamb is the light thereof" (Revelation 21:9–10, 22–23).

This is the New Jerusalem which will never be destroyed. Death and hell will be thrown into the lake of fire, but the saints of God will live in the presence of God in heaven forever.

"At destruction and famine thou shalt laugh: neither shalt thou be afraid of the beasts of the earth" (Job 5:22).

As we see destruction on the earth, God tell us not to fear but to laugh. If a nuclear missile comes you way, catch it with your teeth with great confidence.

"The burden of the word of the LORD for Israel, saith the LORD, which stretcheth forth the heavens and layeth the foundation of the earth, and formeth the spirit of man within him. Behold, I will make Jerusalem a cup of trembling unto all the people round about, when they shall be in the siege both against Judah and against Jerusalem. And in that day will I make Jerusalem a burdensome stone for all people: all that burden themselves with it shall be cut in pieces, though all the people of the earth be gathered together against it. In that day, saith the LORD, I will smite every horse with astonishment, and his rider with madness: and I will open mine eyes upon the house of Judah, and will smite every horse of the people with blindness … In that day shall the LORD defend the inhabitants of Jerusalem; and he that is feeble among them at that day shall be as David; and the house of David shall be as God, as the angel of the LORD before them. And it shall come to pass in that day, that I will seek to destroy all the nations that come against Jerusalem. And I will pour upon the house of David, and upon the inhabitants of Jerusalem, the spirit of grace and of supplications: and they shall look upon me whom they have pierced, and they shall mourn for his only son, and shall be in bitterness for him, as one that is in bitterness for his firstborn" (Zechariah 12:1–4, 8–10).

Three major points for the verses above:

1. Jerusalem will be a cup of trembling and a burdensome stone to the world.
2. All the nations that burden themselves with Jerusalem will be cut to pieces.
3. All the people of the earth will gather against Jerusalem.

These verses are like reading the daily newspaper. Great concern and upheaval surround Jerusalem. The United Nations deals with the state of Jerusalem constantly. Jerusalem is a burden, because no one can come up with answers that will be accepted by all those who burden themselves with Jerusalem. The nations which burden themselves with Jerusalem are burdened with war and terrorism. This is exactly what the Bible said would happen. Just a few hundred years ago, Jerusalem was an insignificant city that had been overrun nineteen times in four thousand years.

Nations and Peoples to be Judged

All nations that burden themselves with Jerusalem, all false prophets, Ammon, the islands of the sea, Meschech, Tubal, Persia, Libya, Syria, Egypt, Assyria, Ethiopia, Tyre, Ephraim, Jerusalem, Gomer,

Gog, Zion, Symrna, Edom, Babylon, Damascus, Philistia, Moab, and the kings of the East will be judged harshly.

God will also judge unfaithful Israel and idolatry. The purpose of judgment is to bring repentance by faith before seeing God face-to-face at the judgment seat of Christ. God will forgive all who turn to His Son, Jesus Christ.

God will, in Zechariah 12:9 eventually destroy all nations which come against Jerusalem. In Zechariah 12:10, God states that prior to and during the second coming of Jesus Christ, Israel will look upon whom they have pierced. Zechariah was written approximately 550 years prior to the crucifixion of Christ. Zechariah 12:10 is one of the few verses in the Old Testament which is a prophecy of the first and second comings of Jesus Christ in the same sentence.

The Empires of the World and the Alignment of the Nations

"God hath spoken once; twice have I heard this; that power belongeth unto God" (Psalm 62:11).

"For God speaketh once, yea twice, yet man perceiveth it not" (Job 33:14).

Solomon stated there is nothing new under the sun, which means that history repeats itself. When God speaks twice, this also means that history repeats itself.

"David said moreover, The LORD that delivered me out of the paw of the lion, and out of the paw of the bear, he will deliver me out of the hand of this Philistine. And Saul said unto David, Go, and the LORD be with thee" (I Samuel 17:37).

David killed a Lion, then he killed a bear, and eventually, David killed Goliath. With the murder of six million Jews in WWII, many Jews sought security by recreating the State of Israel. England attempted to prevent Israel from becoming a nation; however, Israel became a nation after the intervention of the United States on the behalf of the Jews in 1947–1948. Many Christians and Jews who believe the promises of God believe God has control over all history. History is *his story*, which is God's story. We believe that God was not surprised and in fact ordained Israel to be reestablished as another proof of the existence of God. God created the dimension of time and all that occurs within time.

Bible prophecy proves the existence of God through thousands of Bible prophecies fulfilled exactly on time and perfectly. England chose not to bless the Jewish people and has declined significantly as a world power since 1948. Israel will be used by God to bring down the bear (Islam and/or Russia) in the future, and eventually the Antichrist, who is a type of Goliath. The Bible says that Goliath was six cubits and a span tall and has a spear weighing 600 shekels of iron. Goliath had a lot of sixes associated with Him, as does the Antichrist, whose number is 666. I believe that is what the Bible means when it states that God speaks twice or three times and that man does not perceive it.

"In the first year of Belshazzar king of Babylon Daniel had a dream and visions of his head upon his bed: then he wrote the dream, and told the sum of the matters. Daniel spake and said, I saw in my vision by night, and, behold, the four winds of the heaven strove upon the great sea. And four great beasts came up from the sea, diverse one from another. The first was like a lion, and had eagle's wings: I beheld till the wings thereof were plucked, and it was lifted up from the earth, and made stand upon the feet as a man, and a man's heart was given to it. And behold another beast, a second, like to a bear, and it raised up itself on one side, and it had three ribs in the mouth of it between the teeth of it: and they said thus unto it, Arise, devour much flesh. After this I beheld, and lo another, like a leopard, which had upon the back of it four wings of a fowl; the beast had also four heads; and dominion was given to it. After this I saw in the night visions, and behold a fourth beast, dreadful and terrible, and strong exceedingly; and it had great iron teeth: it devoured and brake in pieces, and stamped the residue with the feet of it: and it was diverse from all the beasts that were before it; and it had ten horns" (Daniel 7:1–7).

First beast	=	Lion	=	Great Britain
		Eagle's wings	=	USA
Second beast	=	Bear	=	Islamic nations surrounding Israel and/or Russia
Third beast	=	Leopard	=	Germany and European Union
Fourth beast	=	Exceeding beast	=	World government broken into ten regions

Daniel 7:3 describes four beasts—all diverse from the other. The first beast was like a lion and had eagle's wings, stood on its feet as a man, and was given a man's heart. The national symbol of England is a lion, and the national symbol for the USA is the American bald eagle. The eagle's wings are plucked off. I believe the Bible teaches that the USA will not be the world's sole super power in the future. The lion will be given a man's heart; I believe this indicates that a Christian revival will occur in Great Britain in the years ahead.

I believe the eagle's wings being plucked off has two meanings. One I believe to be the Revolutionary War of 1776 when the USA separated itself from England. Currently the USA and England see eye-to-eye on the threat of Iraq. In the years ahead, I believe there will be sufficient problems that the USA and England part ways.

When the king of the jungle (lion/England) and the king of the air (eagle/USA) have joined forces, they have always defeated the bloodthirsty animal (leopard/Germany). The lion kills only when hungry. The leopard kills when full or hungry and is more dangerous. I don't believe that England or the USA would have successfully won WWI and WWII without joining forces.

"That in blessing I will bless thee, and in multiplying I will multiply thy seed as the stars of the heaven, and as the sand which is upon the sea shore; and thy seed shall possess the gate of his enemies" (Genesis 22:17).

These gates of the seas include the Suez Canal, the Panama Canal, the Cape of Good Hope, the Rock of Gibraltar, Singapore, Hong Kong, and the Falkland Islands. During World War II, England and the United States possessed all the major canals and waterways. Currently nations that are not allies of Britain and the United States are in control of all of these waterways.

The second beast mentioned is a bear, and I believe this beast is symbolized by Russia and/or the Islamic countries surrounding Israel. A bear moves relatively slowly compared to lions, eagles, and leopards and devours flesh brutally. Islam has been at war since Mohammed founded the religion 1400 years ago. There are approximately 190 nations in the world, of which sixty are predominately Islamic. Most of the major hot spots in the world involve these Islamic nations, except for the conflicts involving China/Taiwan and North/South Korea.

God told Abraham in approximately 1920 BC that Ishmael would multiply exceedingly and would be a great nation. God further stated that Ishmael's descendants would be like a wild man (Genesis 16:12), with his hand against every man, and every man against his hand. Mohammed was a descendent of Ishmael. The Islamic nations will stop fighting each other long enough to attempt to destroy Israel. I would not be surprised if this occurred after the events mentioned in Isaiah 17:1–3, which describes the destruction of Damascus and portions of Israel that were given to the tribe of Israel named Ephraim.

Even though it looks like Israel will be pushed into the sea in the years ahead, they will never totally be destroyed, and eventually one-third of Israel will call upon the Lord Jesus Christ in faith.

The bear is also a symbol of Russia. The bear devours much flesh. The former Soviet Union and now Russia has killed tens of millions of people in the last century and has financed wars around the world. I believe Russia will eventually be caught up in wars in the Middle East and possibly in wars against the USA—and both will be weakened substantially.

"And the word of the LORD came unto me, saying, Son of man, set thy face against Gog, the land of Magog, the chief prince of Meshech and Tubal, and prophesy against him. And say, Thus saith the Lord GOD; Behold, I am against thee, O Gog, the chief prince of Meshech and Tubal: And I will turn thee back, and put hooks into thy jaws, and I will bring thee forth, and all thine army, horses and horsemen, all of them clothed with all sorts of armour, even a great company with bucklers and shields, all of them handling swords: Persia, Ethiopia, and Libya with them; all of them with shield and helmet: Gomer, and all his bands; the house of Togarmah of the north quarters, and all his bands: and many people with thee. Be thou prepared, and prepare for thyself, thou, and all thy company that are assembled unto thee, and be thou a guard unto them. After many days thou shalt be visited: in the latter years thou shalt come into the land that is brought back from the sword, and is gathered out of many people, against the mountains of Israel, which have been always waste: but it is brought forth out of the nations, and they shall dwell safely all of them" (Ezekiel 38:1–8).

Nations that will attack Israel and send terrorists into the world:

Ancient Nations	Possible Modern Nations	Direction of Attack
Gog, Land of Magog	Ashkenaz Scythians	From the North
Meschech and Tubal	Northern Asia Minor	From the North
Persia	Iran and portions of Iraq	From the West
Ethiopia	Ethiopia	From the South
Libya	Libya	From the South

| Gomar | Southern Greece and/or Northern Turkey/Germany | From the North and West |
| Togarmah | Uzbekistan, Kazakstan Tajikistan, portions of Turkey, Kyrgyzstan | From the North and East |

The third beast is a leopard. This leopard had four wings and four heads. I believe Germany is symbolized by the leopard.

Four Heads	*Four Wings*
Charlemagne Franco/German	1st Reich—AD 800
Bismarck	2nd Reich—AD 1864–1871
Hitler	3rd Reich—AD 1933–1945
Antichrist	4th Reich—Future Event

The fourth beast, I believe, is the New World Order from which the Antichrist will emerge. The fourth beast in Daniel 7:7 is dreadful, terrible, strong, exceeding, has great iron teeth that devour and destroy, and has *ten horns*.

"And I stood upon the sand of the sea, and saw a beast rise up out of the sea, having seven heads and ten horns, and upon his horns ten crowns, and upon his heads the name of blasphemy. And the beast which I saw was like unto a leopard, and his feet were as the feet of a bear, and his mouth as the mouth of a lion: and the dragon gave him his power, and his seat, and great authority" (Revelation 13:1–2).

I believe the seven heads mentioned here are the seven continents. I believe the seven continents will be divided into ten regional authorities. This will be under a one-world government.

The ten horns will most likely be broken down as follows:

1. North America
2. South America
3. Western Europe and Israel
4. Russia
5. Middle East and Northern Africa, Pakistan (except Israel)
6. Sub-Sahara Africa
7. India to the Philippines
8. China and North Korea
9. Japan and South Korea
10. Australia / New Zealand and Antarctica

The above is an excerpt from the Club of Rome model for World Government published 1973. I believe the Antichrist will come out of Europe—but possibly the USA.

"And there are seven kings; five are fallen, and one is, and the other is not yet come' and when he cometh, he must continue a short space. And the beast that was, and is not, even he is the eighth, and is of the seven, and goeth into perdition. And the ten horns which thou sawest are ten kings, which have received no kingdom as yet; but receive power as kinds one hour with the beast. These have one mind, and shall give their power and strength unto the beast" (Revelation 17:10–13).

There are seven kings. I believe these represent the seven empires that have greatly affected the history of Israel.

		Approximate Dates	
1.	Egypt	2400–725 BC	Abraham, Isaac, Jacob
2.	Assyria	900–600 BC	Overthrows Northern Ten Tribes of Israel
3.	Babylonian (Lion)	575–505 BC	Overruns Jerusalem
4.	Medo-Persian (Bear)	530–325 BC	Gentile Rule
5.	Greece (Leopard)	325–75 BC	Alexander the Great
			Greek Empire Broken into Four Dynasties
6.	Rome (Exceeding Beast)	75 BC–present	
		75 BC–AD 300	Roman Ceasars
		AD 300–present	Catholic Church (part that is not saved)
7.	Germany—Nazi	AD 1933–1945	Adolf Hitler—Nazi Germany
8.	Antichrist	Future Events	European Union and/or a
	The 8th is with the 7th		World Government

The Abomination of Desolation Prophesied by the Prophet Daniel

In Matthew 24:3, days before the crucifixion of Jesus, His disciples asked Jesus, "What will be the sign of your coming and the end of the age?"

However, Jesus said in Matthew 24:15, "Therefore when you see the Abomination of Desolation, spoken by Daniel the Prophet, standing in the holy place." Matthew 24:21 says, "For then shall be great tribulation, such as was not since the beginning of the world to this time, no, nor ever shall be."

"And he shall confirm the covenant with many for one week: and in the midst of the week he shall cause the sacrifice and the oblation to cease, and for the overspreading of abominations he shall make it desolate, even until the consummation, and that determined shall be poured upon the desolate" (Daniel 9:27).

"When ye therefore shall see the abomination of desolation, spoken of by Daniel the prophet, stand in the holy place" (Matthew 24:15).

"Now we beseech you, brethren, by the coming of our Lord Jesus Christ, and by our gathering together unto him, That ye be not soon shaken in mind, or be troubled, neither by spirit, nor by word, nor by letter as from us, as that the day of Christ is at hand. Let no man deceive you by any means: for that day shall not come, except there come a falling away first, and that man of sin be revealed, the son of perdition; Who opposeth and exalteth himself above all that is called God, or that is worshipped; so that he as God sitteth in the Temple of God, shewing himself that he is God" (II Thessalonians 2:1–4).

The Abomination of Desolation has historically been considered an event involving the Antichrist. This event would occur after a third Jewish temple would begin to be built in Jerusalem. The Abomination of Desolation is an event that occurs when a world leader professes to be God.

The Jews are preparing for a last-days temple. At the present time, preparations are being made to rebuild the temple on the Temple Mount in Jerusalem. In this temple, the Jews anticipate the presence of God. Christians believe God dwells in temples not made by hands, which is the true church. The Islamic Mosque of Omar is either on or in close proximity to where the temple will be built; I believe it is on it. This is the same place where Abraham was to offer Isaac but was stopped by an angel when Abraham showed he believed God's promise. Isaac was a picture of Christ.

"But I will settle him in mine house and in my kingdom for ever: and his throne shall be established for evermore" (I Chronicles 17:14).

The Jewish people believe this verse and others mean they must rebuild the temple. To not do so would profane God.

"And I will shake all nations, and the desire of all nations shall come: and I will fill this house with glory, saith the LORD of hosts. The silver is mine, and the gold is mine, saith the LORD of hosts" (Haggai 2:7–8).

There are currently many Jewish groups involved in the preparation and construction of this temple. This would include the Temple Mount Faithful. Practicing Jews believe that when the Messiah comes, He will end wars. These practicing Jews believe Israel will be the light of God to all nations, and all nations will be blessed by the State of Israel through the Jewish people.

Christians believe the Jews will build the temple, but that the Antichrist, who will deceive the nations, will proclaim himself to be God—but in fact will be the embodiment of Lucifer, the devil, and Satan. Great tribulation will fill the world. Many of the practicing Jews believe that God brought them back into the land of Israel. Christians agree with this assessment. Practicing Jews believe that if they possess the land of Israel and do not rebuild the temple, they would be in rebellion to God. Jewish leadership believes building the temple will bring the Messiah.

John 5:39–47—Jesus Sstated that the Jews would not Receive Him but would Receive Another

"Search the scriptures; for in them ye think ye have eternal life: and they are they which testify of me. *And ye will not come to me, that ye might have life.* I receive not honour from men. But I know you, that ye have not the love of God in you. *I am come in my Father's name, and ye receive me not: if another shall come in his own name, him ye will receive.* How can ye believe, which receive honour one of another, and seek not the honour that cometh from god only? Do not think that I will accuse you to the Father: there is one that accuseth you, even Moses, in whom ye trust. For had ye believed Moses, ye would have believed me: for he wrote of me. But if ye believe not his writing, how shall ye believe my words?" (John 5:39–47).

Many people in Israel and in the world will believe that the Antichrist is the Messiah. Some people will not believe that the Antichrist is the true Messiah, and the government of the Antichrist will fall apart in a short period of time—anywhere from 3.5 years or less from when he comes upon the scene.

Most of Israel is secular. Most of the driving force for the re-establishment of Israel came from secular Jews. This is not to say that religious Jews have little or no power in Israel.

In the temple, there are requirements for vessels and various other implements to perform animal sacrifices. This includes the training of people to perform these activities. All of this is occurring as we now live. I believe for the temple to be rebuilt, the Jews will need to have total control of the Temple Mount in Jerusalem. In all likelihood, for this to occur, there will be a major war in the Middle East. This war could be the war mentioned in Ezekiel 38–39.

A Comparison of Jesus Christ to the Antichrist

Jesus Christ	*Antichrist*
Christ came from heaven (John 6:38)	*The Antichrist will come from hell (Revelation 11:7)*
Christ came in His Father's name (John 5:43)	*The Antichrist will come in his own name (John 5:43)*
Christ humbled Himself (Philippeans 2:8)	*The Antichrist will exalt himself (II Thessalonians 2:4)*
Christ was despised and afflicted (Isaiah 53:3)	*The Antichrist will be admired and lauded (Revelation 12:3–4)*
Christ came to do His Father's will (John 6:38)	*The Antichrist will come to do his own will (Daniel 11:36)*
Christ came to save (Luke 19:10)	*The Antichrist will come to destroy (Daniel 8:24)*
Christ is the Good Shepherd (John 10)	*The Antichrist will be the Evil Shepherd (Zechariah 11:16–67)*
Christ is the Truth (John 14:6)	*The Antichrist will be "the lie" (II Thessalonians 2:11)*

Christ is the Mystery of Godliness, God manifested in the flesh (I Timothy 3:16)	The Antichrist will be "The Mystery of Iniquity" Satan manifested in the flesh (II Thessalonians 2:7–9), the living son of Satan[110]

The Battle of Armageddon and the Second Coming of Jesus Christ

"And at the time of the end shall be king of the south push at him: and the king of the north shall come against him like a whirlwind, with chariots, and with horsemen, and with many ships; and he shall enter into the countries, and shall overflow and pass over. He shall enter also into the glorious land, and many countries shall be overthrown: but these shall escape out of his hand, even Edom, and Moab, and the chief of the children of Ammon. He shall stretch forth his hand also upon the countries: and the land of Egypt shall not escape. But he shall have power over the treasures of gold and of silver, and over all the precious things of Egypt: and the Libyans and the Ethiopians shall be at his steps. But tidings out of the east and out of the north shall trouble him: therefore he shall go forth with great fury to destroy, and utterly to make away many. And he shall plant the tabernacle of his palace between the seas in the glorious holy mountain; yet he shall come to his end, and none shall help him" (Daniel 11:40–45).

Push at Him	=	The Antichrist
King of the South	=	Muslim Nations
King of the North	=	Russia
Glorious Land	=	Israel
Edom, Moab, Ammon	=	Jordan
Egypt and Libya	=	North Africa
Ethiopia	=	Black Africa
East	=	China, possibly other Asian Islamic Asian nations[110]

"And the sixth angel poured out his vial upon the great river Euphrates; and the water thereof was dried up, that the way of the kings of the east might be prepared. And I saw three unclean spirits like frogs come out of the mouth of the dragon, and out of the mouth of the beast, and out of the mouth of the false prophet. For they are the spirits of devils, working miracles, which go forth unto the kings of the earth and of the whole world, to gather them to the battle of that great day of God Almighty. Behold, I come as a thief. Blessed is he what watcheth, and keepeth his garments, lest he walk naked, and they see his shame. And he gathered them together into a place called in the Hebrew tongue Armageddon" (Revelation 16:12–16).

I believe the King of the East mentioned in Daniel 11:44 is the same King of the East mentioned in Revelation 16:12. Armageddon is a physical, literal place located in Northern Israel. As we speak, the focus of the world is on Israel.

---

109 John Hagee. *The Beginning of the End* (Thomas Nelson Publishers) 136.
110 Hal Lindsey. *The Everlasting Hatred: The Roots of Jihad*, 240.

Lucifer—the devil, known as Satan—is successful in convincing the people of the world to come to war over Israel. Revelation 9:16 specifically states that a 200 million-man army will march toward Israel in the last day. When the Apostle John wrote Revelation, it is estimated that there were only 200 million people on the earth. Twenty years ago, mainland China boasted it could put together a 200 million-man army itself.

"For our conversation is in heaven; for whence also we look for the Saviour, the Lord Jesus Christ: Who shall change our vile body, that it may be fashioned like unto his glorious body, according to the working whereby he is able even to subdue all things unto himself" (Philippians 3:21–22).

"Now this I say, brethren, that flesh and blood cannot inherit the kingdom of God; neither doth corruption inherit incorruption. Behold, I shew you a mystery; We shall not all sleep, but we shall all be changed, In a moment, in the twinkling of an eye, at the last trump: for the trumpet shall sound, and the dead shall be raised incorruptible, and we shall be changed. For this corruptible must put on incorruption, and this mortal [must] put on immortality" (I Corinthians 15:50–53).

"But I would not have you to be ignorant, brethren, concerning them which are asleep, that ye sorrow not, even as others which have no hope. For if we believe that Jesus died and rose again, even so them also which sleep in Jesus will God bring with him" (I Thessalonians 4:13–14).

These above verses deal with the resurrection of the saints, which is frequently called the rapture.

"And I saw heaven opened, and behold a white horse; and he that sat upon him was called Faithful and True, and in righteousness he doth judge and make war. His eyes were as a flame of fire, and on his head were many crowns; and he had a name written, that no man knew, but he himself. And he was clothed with a vesture dipped in blood: and his name is called The Word of God. And the armies [which were] in heaven followed him upon white horses, clothed in fine linen, white and clean. And out of his mouth goeth a sharp sword, that with it he should smite the nations: and he shall rule them with a rod of iron: and he treadeth the winepress of the fierceness and wrath of Almighty God. And he hath on his vesture and on his thigh a name written, KING OF KINGS, AND LORD OF LORDS …. And the beast was taken, and with him the false prophet that wrought miracles before him, with which he deceived them that had received the mark of the beast, and them that worshiped his image. These both were cast alive into a lake of fire burning with brimstone. And the remnant were slain with the sword of him that sat upon the horse, which sword proceeded out of his mouth: and all the fowls were filled with their flesh" (Revelation 19:11–16, 20–21).

These verses describe the visible second coming of Jesus Christ at the Battle of Armageddon. When we speak of the second coming of Jesus Christ, we are not speaking about a person being born of a woman in the recent past. What Christians are describing is the same person, Jesus Christ, who God raised from the dead in AD 30–32. He will return at the Battle of Armageddon to prevent mankind from destroying itself.

"Go to now, ye rich men, weep and howl for your miseries that shall come upon you. Your riches are corrupted, and your garments are motheaten. Your gold and silver is cankered; and the rust of them shall be a witness against you, and shall eat your flesh as it were fire. Ye have heaped treasure together for the last day. Behold, the hire of the labourers who have reaped down your fields, which is of you kept back by fraud, crieth: and the cries of them which have reaped are entered into the ears of the Lord of sabaoth. Ye have lived in pleasure on the earth, and been wanton; ye have nourished your hearts, as in a day of slaughter. Ye have condemned and killed the just; and he doth not resist you. Be patient therefore, brethren, unto the coming of the Lord. Behold, the husbandman waiteth for the precious fruit of the earth, and hath long patience for it, until he receive the early and latter rain. Be ye also patient; stablish your hearts: for the coming of the Lord draweth nigh" (James 5:1–8).

In the United States of America, our old economy is in trouble. The old economy includes the industrial production of such items as cars, steel, paper, clothing, shoes, and a multitude of other items which used to be manufactured in the United States. The new economy, which includes the dot.com companies, has not produced the jobs many people thought it would.

There is a strong reliance on foreign investments and a massive problem of global overcapacity of manufacturing. This causes price wars and currency fluctuations. Americans get cheap products from overseas while foreign workers are paid a few dollars a day for their labor and thus cannot afford to purchase products from the USA.

This has helped to cause an explosion in personal, corporate, and government debt around the world. The Achilles heel of the US financial system is debt. Government, corporate, and private debt in 1991 was $14.5 trillion and rose to $28 trillion by the year 2000. The USA has a $400 billion annual trade deficit, which has been increasing substantially every year as we are more dependent on foreign oil than ever. Financial derivative investments are financial time bombs.

In 2000–2001, close to $5 trillion was lost by investors in the United States stock markets—and the rest of the world has experienced even worse results. Furthermore, our inmate population is at about 2 million prisoners in the United States alone.

Corporate bankruptcies are rising, and at the same time, corporate sales and earnings are falling. Personal bankruptcies are rising quickly, and almost 10 million Americans went bankrupt in the 1990s.

We are living in an age in which nineteen plane hijackers can hijack four planes in one day and cause a ripple effect, destroying $250 billion of wealth in a matter of a few months. Argentina went bankrupt, owning other countries $130 billion. America and Japan are the two biggest economies in the world, accounting for 46 percent of the world's gross national product. Japan is in its twelfth year of recession, with little hope of recovery in sight.

The population in the United States of America is aging, which will bring about a rise in medical costs as well as costs for the Social Security program. AIDS, as well as other sexually transmitted diseases, will take their toll on world economies. Another major time bomb is the depletion of fresh water supplies around the world.

Over two-thirds of the world's population lives in very poor countries, and the debt situation in these countries is even worse. Any country that was poverty-stricken in the year 1900 was still poverty-stricken in the year 2000, with the exception of a few countries with small populations living on top of billions of barrels of oil. Only those nations that have had the Bible translated into their mother tongue for many centuries have experienced financial prosperity.

Many people in the United States complain about immigration. I believe because the United States is doing an inadequate job of taking the gospel to foreign countries, God is bringing immigrants to the United States so we can tell them the good news of Jesus Christ.

Summary of Second Coming Events

To briefly summarize future events, I will speculate using general terms. With the advent of the nuclear age, we now have the ability to destroy the planet. God will not let this happen. God will eventually stop us from destroying ourselves. In 1948, Israel became a state, which is one of the most prophesied events in the Bible. Second coming events come alive with the reestablishment of Israel. When the term "Armageddon" arises, most people don't understand that Armageddon is a physical, literal location in Northern Israel.

The Bible says Jerusalem will be surrounded by its enemies. The United Nations came into being shortly after World War II, as did the State of Israel. Of the 172 Security Council resolutions passed before 1990, ninety-seven were directed against Israel. Of the 690 general assembly resolutions voted before 1990, 429 were directed against Israel. The biggest major dispute in the world is the status of Jerusalem. The Jews declare it as their capital, and the Muslims want it. Others want to make it a universal city.

There is a major rise in the interest in the hereafter around the world. Few people in the world believe in the annihilation of the soul after death. There has been a dramatic rise in false religions as well as tremendous gains in taking the gospel of Jesus Christ to the world.

Christians are being killed for the faith in unbelievable numbers. Violence fills the earth as the population increases. There are over 6 billion people on the Earth. The net worth of a small number of billionaires is estimated to be equivalent to the net worth of the 3 billion poorest people in the world. Many of these 3 billion poorest people are saved and are thus richer than Bill Gates (if he is not saved).

Two-thirds of the world's population is functionally illiterate (4 billion people). One-third of the world's population is under fifteen years old, with the vast majority of these people being raised in extreme poverty and under false religions.

The Bible directly or indirectly mentions many nations. Frequently nations are mentioned with the use of alliteration and symbols through animals such as the lion, eagles, wings, bears, leopards, and exceeding fierce beasts.

Lion = Great Britain
Eagle's Wings = USA
Bear = Russia and/or Islamic Nations
Leopard = Germany
Exceeding Beasts = New World Order

David is a picture of Israel when the State of Israel was established. David (Israel) killed a lion, then a bear, and then Goliath. Israel became a state in 1948. Prior to this, England had control of the area in the Middle East which now includes Israel. At this time ,England was still a major colonial power. In the future, Israel will defeat the Muslims and/or the Russian bear in a war which will I believe also neutralize the USA. Lastly, David—who killed Goliath—is also a type of Christ, and Goliath is a picture of the Antichrist. God will use Israel to bring down the Antichrist.

Just prior to the second coming of Jesus Christ, the kings of the east—which is communist China—will be drawn to destruction at the battle of Armageddon. The Lord Jesus Christ Himself will throw Satan and all his followers into the bottomless pit for a period of time which is frequently called the millennium.

At the end of the millennium, the devil will be released for a little while. The devil, believe it or not, will deceive the nations again. The nations again will come against Jerusalem, and God will devour these nations. This shows the total depravity of an unregenerated mankind.

The Millennium

Micah 4:3—Swords Beat into Plowshares

"And he shall judge among many people, and rebuke strong nations afar off; and they shall beat their swords into plowshares, and their spears into pruninghooks: nation shall not lift up a sword against nation, neither shall they learn war any more" (Micah 4:3).

Isaiah 11:6–7—The Change in the Nature of Animals

"The wolf also shall dwell with the lamb, and the leopard shall lie down with the kid; and the calf and the young lion and the fatling together; and a little child shall lead them. And the cow and the bear shall feed; their young ones shall lie down together: and the lion shall eat straw like the ox" (Isaiah 11:6–7).

Revelation 20:1–3—Satan Bound for 1,000 years

"And I saw an angel come down from heaven, having the key of the bottomless pit and a great chain in his hand. And he laid hold on the dragon, that old serpent, which is the Devil, and Satan, and bound him a thousand years, And cast him into the bottomless pit, and shut him up, and set a seal upon him, that he should deceive the nations no more, till the thousand years should be fulfilled: and after that he must be loosed a little season" (Revelation 20:1–3).

Revelation 20:7–10—Satan Released and Deceives the Nations Again

"And when the thousand years are expired, Satan shall be loosed out of his prison, And shall go out to deceive the nations which are in the four quarters of the earth, Gog and Magog, to gather them together to battle: the number of whom is as the sand of the sea. And they went up on the breadth of the earth, and compassed the camp of the saints about, and the beloved city: and fire came down from God out of heaven, and devoured them. And the devil that deceived them was cast into the lake of fire and brimstone, where the beast and the false prophets are, and shall be tormented day and night for ever and ever" (Revelation 20:7–10).

During the millennium, the powers of hell will be bound and will not be allowed to tempt the minds of mankind. Great prosperity will occur with extended lifetimes; enhanced technology and deep wisdom of God will be made known and seen in ways still hidden to saints today.

The war machines will be silent and the predatory nature of animals will cease. However, the purpose of the millennium is to show the depravity of mankind. Revelation 20:7–9 tells us that those who come against the camp of the saints will be as the sand of the sea. That means almost all of mankind will have fallen away from God and the Son of God, Jesus Christ, by the end of the millennium.

I believe this will be fulfilled at the last of the seven feasts of the Lord—Tabernacles—in which the Jews would make a booth or covering (camp of the saints).

"Enter ye in at the strait gate: for wide is the gate, and broad is the way, that leadeth to destruction, and many there be which go in thereat: Because strait is the gate, and narrow is the way, which leadeth unto life, and few there be that find it" (Matthew 7:13–14).

Most people throughout all the ages will reject Jesus as Lord and Savior—or they will be the offspring of people who rejected or killed the apostles, prophets, and missionaries. Please don't be one of these people. Remember, Jesus said, "Except a man be born again, he cannot see the kingdom of God."

Well, I have worked hard for many years in the preparation and the writing of this book. I have written it for my loved ones, friends, co-workers, and customers to help point all to the salvation of their souls through the finished work of Jesus Christ on the cross. Thank you for reading my book. Hopefully this has helped you to better understand the Bible.

Summary

1. Jesus Christ of Nazareth was God in the flesh. He left eternity, was born of a virgin, became a man, and is the gate—the way, the truth, and the life. Only through Him is the way to eternal life (John 14:6; Isaiah 7:14).

2. You understand in your soul that you have an eternal soul and spirit (Ecclesiastes 3:11).

3. By looking at the creation, all mankind understands that they are created beings (Romans 1:19–23).

4. God has given all men light in their souls to believe the truth as mentioned in these first three points (John 1:9).

5. God was before the beginning and has an eternal purpose for mankind (Genesis 1:1).

6. God is Spirit, and those who worship God must worship Him in spirit and in truth. God is love. It is impossible to love God, whom you cannot see, when you do not love your fellow man, whom you do see (John 4:16, 20, 23–24).

7. God created free-will beings, including seraphim, cherubim, archangels, and angels, whose beginning was in eternity past (Isaiah 6:2; Ezekiel 10:5; Jude 1:9; Hebrews 1:5; Job 38:7).

8. In eternity past, some free-will beings desired to be equal with God. Their leader's name was Lucifer, and this desire started all the misery that has occurred in the heavens and the earth. Rebellion entered into eternity, which brings war and strife (Isaiah 14:12–17).

9. Created, free-will beings only have the free will to choose between options which God gives them. You have the choice of heaven or hell, not heaven, hell, or someplace else (Revelation 20:6, 15).

10. God gives created, free-will beings guidelines for acceptable behavior and unacceptable behavior. Created beings with a free will can be in God's perfect will, acceptable will, or good will or be in rebellion against God (Romans 12:1–2).

11. Jesus Christ was crucified before the creation of the world. God is always on plan A (I Peter 1:20).

12. God created the time, matter, space, and dimension (which mankind lives in) to put down the rebellion of free-will, created beings that were created in eternity past (Genesis 3:15).

13. God's plan was through the person of Jesus Christ, the Son of God, that God would show all created beings with a free will that dwell in heaven the manifold wisdom of God (Ephesians 3:10).

14. Jesus was 100 percent God and 100 percent man, and He entered into the creation as a man. God is able to demonstrate His attributes through fallen mankind by entering into the creation as God in the flesh. It would be impossible to show many attributes of God any other way (John 1:14).

15. Attributes that Jesus Christ showed mankind include forgiveness, love, joy, peace, loyalty, faithfulness, humbleness, long-suffering, patience, meekness, and self-control that otherwise could not be understood to the fullest unless God did it Himself (Galatians 5:22–23).

16. The genealogies in the Bible are true, and Adam and Eve are real, historical persons who were created abruptly approximately six thousand years ago (Luke 3:23–38).

17. God told Adam and Eve that they could eat of every tree but of the tree in the middle of the Garden of Eden. This was the tree of the knowledge of good and evil. Satan tempted Eve, and Adam and Eve both ate of the tree of the knowledge of good and evil. These events would lead to the eventual total judgment and downfall of Satan and those who believe his voice (Genesis 2:17).

18. All of mankind and civilizations have occurred as a result of Adam and Eve. Mankind did not evolve from non-living elements and monkeys. The sole purpose of evolution is to do away with being responsible to a personal God. Noah's flood and the Tower of Babel were historical events (Genesis 1:21; Genesis 6–9; Genesis 11:1–9).

19. The Bible has a scarlet cord of symbolism of Jesus Christ in the Old Testament that includes many types and shadows of Jesus Christ displayed in mankind.

20. There are seven major Jewish feasts of the Lord. They include the Feast of Passover, Feast of Unleavened Bread, Feast of Firstfruits, Feast of Pentecost, Feast of Rosh Hashanah, Feast of Yom Kippur, and the Feast of Tabernacles. Jesus Christ has or will fulfill types and shadows of all of these feasts in His first and second comings (Exodus 12–20; Numbers 10; Leviticus 23:26–34).

21. The Ten Commandments listed in Exodus 20 are very important. Any person who has a god other than the God of the Bible as their true and living god will eventually spend eternity in the lake of fire. Dishonoring one's parents, murder, and sexual relations outside marriage are pardonable offenses with very serious consequences. However, having a false god is not a pardonable offense (Exodus 20).

22. Jesus showed His power and authority over the creation by miraculous healings and controlling natural acts such as blowing winds and high seas by just speaking to them (Matthew 12:15–21; Matthew 8:23–27).

23. Jesus frequently healed people and forgave them their sins. After healing and forgiving people, He frequently said, "Go and sin no more." Jesus did not say, "Go and try your best" (John 8:11).

24. Jesus taught in parables that lost people would not understand, and He frequently taught about the kingdom of God or the kingdom of heaven. He taught in such a way that those searching for truth would find it and that those not searching for truth would not find it or understand it (Matthew 13:3–23).

25. Jesus fulfilled over 300 prophecies in the Old Testament of the coming of the Messiah and the Savior of the world. At that time, many Jews were looking for a conquering lion to defeat the Romans—but instead, they received a suffering lamb. Today those who do not believe in the resurrection of Jesus Christ believe that Jesus was a good and wise man but do not believe the thousands of Bible verses that deal with the second coming of Christ. See the Old Testament section of this book.

26. In approximately 3900 BC, the first murder on the earth occurred when Cain killed Abel. The blood of Abel cried out from the ground for justice. Our desire from God must be mercy, not justice (Genesis 4:8–10).

27. The last seven statements Jesus said while He was on the cross are all very important. Jesus' first words as He was being nailed to the cross were, "Father, forgive them; they know not what they do." This shows the forgiving nature of God and has been an example for the church to stop the cycle of violence (Luke 23:34; Acts 7).

28. Salvation is agreeing with God that Jesus Christ was God in the flesh, led a sinless life, and was the Passover lamb who was crucified for our sins. Jesus was buried and raised from the dead on the third day by God (Romans 10:9–10).

29. Jesus said, "You must be born again to see the kingdom of God" (John 3:3).

30. At the time of verbal confession of sin and belief that Jesus was God in the flesh, the Holy Spirit of God will enter into the new believer in Christ, which is the time at which your soul will be saved. God's Holy Spirit will direct your soul and spirit in the ways of God (Ezekiel 36:26–27).

31. The four gospels of Jesus Christ are the books of Matthew, Mark, Luke, and John. The remainder of the New Testament is used for doctrine, godly living, and prophecy concerning the church age and the second coming of Jesus Christ.

32. I suggest that all people purchase a Bible with brief chapter explanations—especially a red-letter Bible, which is a Bible wherein the words of Jesus are in red ink.

33. The resurrection of Jesus abolished death and brought life and immortality to all those who believe the gospel (I Timothy 1:10).

34. Prayer is talking to God. A saved person can go to the throne of grace and pray and talk to God directly in the spirit (Hebrews 4:16).

35. God hears the prayers of lost people, but there is not a personal relationship with God without Jesus Christ. Without the indwelling of God's Holy Spirit, there is no hope (John 1:12).

36. God proves Himself as the creator of time, matter, and space in Bible prophecy and specifically the second coming of Jesus Christ. In knowing and directing events in the future, God proves He created the dimension of time. Past, present, and future are as one time to God, and He lives in the past, present, and future equally (Isaiah 46:10).

37. Major prophecies of the second coming of Jesus Christ include exponential increases in knowledge and the ability of mankind to kill all of mankind with nuclear weapons. Another major prophesied event includes the reestablishment of the State of Israel as Jews came back to Israel from the four corners of the earth (Matthew 24:22; Jeremiah 16:14–15).

38. Other signs of the times include natural disasters, diseases, famine, the rise of false religions, and the gospel being preached to the ends of the earth. The earth is filled with violence, and the state of humanity is sliding downwards (Matthew 24; II Timothy 3:1–9).

39. Jerusalem is the center of worldwide conflict, and various empires of the world are in place and/or are getting into the place that the Bible predicts will bring on the battle of Armageddon (Zechariah 12:1–10).

40. The world economies are riddled with debt, and the peoples of the world have high needs and expectations of their governments.

41. At some time in the future, the USA's influence and power in the world will diminish. In the near future, either Europe or a United Nations entity primarily controlled by European countries will be the leading world power and have authority up to and possibly including world government (Daniel 7:1–14).

42. The resurrection of the saints—frequently called the rapture—and the second coming of Jesus Christ are in the near future. Our bodies, while on the earth, are bodies of flesh, bone, and blood. Our bodies in heaven after the resurrection will be like Jesus' resurrected body, which was a body of flesh and bone without blood (Philippians 4:20–21; I Thessalonians 4:13–18; I Corinthians 15:50–53).

43. Satan and his demons will be taken from the atmosphere and will be placed in hell. After one thousand years, they will be released to deceive the inhabitants of the earth for a short season. After deceiving the nations one last time, Satan and all unbelievers will be put into the lake of fire (Revelation 20:7–10, 15).

44. The first heavens and the first earth will pass away, and believers will live in a new heaven and a new earth (Revelation 21:1).

45. Hell and the lake of fire are eternal, as are the location of the souls of unbelievers. In heaven and in the lake of fire, a person has their five senses, which include sight, taste, hearing, touch, and smell. There will be no hope in hell (Luke 16:19–31).

46. No mind can comprehend the glories and riches of eternity for the saved souls of mankind (I Corinthians 2:9).